THE CHARTERED INSTITUTE OF MARKETING

D1581044

Chartered Postgraduate Diploma in Marketing

SUPPORT TEXT

Emerging Themes

Valid for assessments up to September 2013

The Chartered
Institute of Marketing

BPP
LEARNING MEDIA

First edition October 2012

ISBN 9781 4453 9149 6

e-ISBN 9781 4453 7622 6

British Library Cataloguing-in-Publication Data
A catalogue record for this book
is available from the British Library

Published by

BPP Learning Media Ltd
Aldine House, Aldine Place
142-144 Uxbridge Road
London W12 8AA

www.bpp.com/learningmedia

Printed in the United Kingdom by Polestar Wheatons

Hennock Road
Marsh Barton Industrial Estate
Exeter, Devon
EX2 8RP

Your learning materials, published by BPP Learning
Media Ltd, are printed on paper obtained from
traceable sustainable sources.

All our rights reserved. No part of this publication may be
reproduced, stored in a retrieval system or transmitted, in
any form or by any means, electronic, mechanical,
photocopying, recording or otherwise, without the prior
written permission of BPP Learning Media Ltd.

The contents of this book are intended as a guide and not
professional advice. Although every effort has been made to
ensure that the contents of this book are correct at the time
of going to press, BPP Learning Media makes no warranty
that the information in this book is accurate or complete and
accept no liability for any loss or damage suffered by any
person acting or refraining from acting as a result of the
material in this book.

We are grateful to The Chartered Institute of Marketing for
permission to reproduce in this text the unit syllabus.

Lead authors: Michelle Gledhill
                 Alex Janes

©
BPP Learning Media Ltd
2012

A note about copyright

Dear Customer

What does the little © mean and why does it matter?

Your market-leading BPP books, course materials and
e-learning materials do not write and update themselves.
People write them: on their own behalf or as employees of an
organisation that invests in this activity. Copyright law protects
their livelihoods. It does so by creating rights over the use of
the content.

Breach of copyright is a form of theft – as well as being a
criminal offence in some jurisdictions, it is potentially a serious
breach of professional ethics.

With current technology, things might seem a bit hazy but,
basically, without the express permission of BPP Learning
Media:

- Photocopying our materials is a breach of copyright

- Scanning, ripcasting or conversion of our digital materials
  into different file formats, uploading them to facebook or
  e-mailing them to your friends is a breach of copyright

You can, of course, sell your books, in the form in which you
have bought them – once you have finished with them. (Is this
fair to your fellow students? We update for a reason.) Please
note the e-products are sold on a single user licence basis: we
do not supply 'unlock' codes to people who have bought them
second-hand.

And what about outside the UK? BPP Learning Media strives
to make our materials available at prices students can afford
by local printing arrangements, pricing policies and
partnerships which are clearly listed on our website. A tiny
minority ignore this and indulge in criminal activity by illegally
photocopying our material or supporting organisations that do.
If they act illegally and unethically in one area, can you really
trust them?

Contents

The Chartered
Institute of Marketing

1 Studying for The Chartered Institute of Marketing (CIM) qualifications

There are a few key points to remember as you study for your CIM qualification:

(a) You are studying for a **professional** qualification. This means that you are required to use professional language and adopt a business approach in your work

(b) You are expected to show that you have 'read widely'. Make sure that you read the quality press (and don't skip the business pages), *Marketing*, *The Marketer*, *Research* and *Marketing Week* avidly.

(c) Become aware of the marketing initiatives you come across on a daily basis, for example, when you go shopping look around and think about why the store layout is as it is; consider the messages, channel choice and timings of ads when you are watching TV. It is surprising how much you will learn just by taking an interest in the marketing world around you.

(d) Get to know the way CIM write its exam papers and assignments. It uses a specific approach (the Magic Formula) which is to ensure a consistent approach when designing assessment materials. Make sure you are fully aware of this as it will help you interpret what the examiner is looking for (a full description of the Magic Formula appears later).

(e) Learn how to use Harvard referencing. This is explained in detail in our CIM Chartered Postgraduate Diploma Assessment Workbook.

(f) Ensure that you read very carefully all assessment details sent to you from CIM. There are strict deadlines to meet, as well as paperwork to complete for any assignment or project you do. You also need to make sure you have your CIM membership card with you at the exam. Failing to meet any assessment entry deadlines or completing written work on time will mean that you will have to wait for the next round of assessment dates and will need to pay the relevant assessment fees again.

2 The Chartered Postgraduate Diploma Syllabus

The Chartered Postgraduate Diploma in Marketing is aimed at Brand Managers, Strategic Marketing Managers, Business Development Managers and middle to senior Marketing Managers. If you are a graduate, you will be expected to have covered a minimum of half your credits in marketing subjects. You are therefore expected at this level of the qualification to demonstrate the ability to manage marketing resources and contribute to business decisions from a marketing perspective and pass the diagnostic entry test to level 7.

The aim of the qualification is to provide the knowledge and skills for you to develop an 'ability to do' in relation to strategic marketing planning and leading its implementation. CIM qualifications concentrate on applied marketing within real work-places.

The complete Chartered Postgraduate qualification is split into two stages. Stage 1 comprises four units. Stage 2 is a work-based project that should enable those who pass it, with the relevant experience and continuing professional development, to become Chartered Marketers.

The Stage 1 qualification contains four units:

- Unit 1 Emerging Themes
- Unit 2 Analysis and Decision
- Unit 3 Marketing Leadership and Planning
- Unit 4 Managing Corporate Reputation

The syllabus, as provided by CIM, can be found below with reference to our coverage within this Study Support Text.

Unit characteristics – Emerging Themes

You should be able to critically evaluate the impact of a range of new and emerging themes on marketing, business organisations and the changing marketing environment. In addition, this unit will also help you to build and refine the skills necessary to anticipate and adapt to future changes. In undertaking a critical evaluation of the key themes, you should be able to take a strategic perspective of the impact of these themes at a sectoral or industry level, as well as upon the organisation you work for, or another one you know well.

By the end of the unit, you should be able to critically assess and evaluate the significance of various emerging themes, to demonstrate an ability to recognise the strategic importance of key themes, and to consider how best to take them into account when developing and implementing marketing strategies. Finally, by the end of the unit you will have established strategies and mechanisms for anticipating future trends and emerging themes.

Note the syllabus includes the themes, but the actual content (examples below in brackets) will be updated annually to reflect the one, two or three most influential recent developments.

Potential macro-environmental emerging themes

- Political (eg devolution, network governance)
- Economic (eg credit crunch)
- Social (eg changing demographics, migration, health and obesity)
- Technological (eg emerging technologies and their impact on business, social networking, 3D printing)
- Environmental (eg climate change)

Potential meso-environmental emerging themes

- Marketing's new ground (eg societal/social and green marketing, digital marketing)
- Changing consumers (eg customer power, ethical consumption)
- Changing nature of competition and supply chains (eg collaboration and competition)

Potential micro-environmental themes

- Contemporary business strategies (eg business sustainability and the triple bottom line)
- The marketing professional (eg intelligence gathering, creative and flexible thinking)

Overarching learning outcomes

By the end of the unit, you should be able to:

- critically evaluate a range of key emerging macro-environmental themes and make a critical assessment of their significance for a specific sector or industry

- propose strategic marketing responses to the key emerging themes judged to have the greatest potential impact on a specific sector. Responses should reflect contemporary marketing practice (ie marketing's new ground) and demonstrate creativity.

 The Chartered Institute of Marketing

SECTION 1 – Macro and meso emerging themes (weighting 50%)

		Covered in chapter(s)
1.1	Critically evaluate macro-environmental emerging themes and assess/forecast their potential impact upon one specific sector or industry: ■ Changes in political governance systems and political focus ■ Contemporary economic opportunities/challenges ■ Social change (at local and global levels) ■ Emerging technologies ■ Environmental challenges ■ Methods of forecasting/predicting change	1, 3, 4
1.2	Critically evaluate meso-environmental themes and assess/forecast their potential impact upon a specific sector or industry: ■ Changes in consumer behaviour ■ Changes in nature/structure of competition ■ Changes in nature/structure of supply chains	5, 6, 7

SECTION 2 – Meso and micro emerging themes (weighting 50%)

		Covered in chapter(s)
2.1	Judge the importance of a range of emerging themes to a particular organisation: ■ Scenario planning ■ Impact/risk assessment	2
2.2	Develop contemporary strategic marketing and business responses to a prioritised emerging theme: ■ Marketing's 'new ground' ■ Contemporary business strategies	8, 9
2.3	Propose methods by which marketing professionals can anticipate and adapt to change: ■ Sources of data and intelligence ■ Developing intellectual skills and creativity ■ New forms of networking	2, 10

3 Assessment

The unit covered by this Study Support Text (Unit 1 **Emerging Themes**) is assessed by way of a work-based assignment with three specific components, each with an obligatory word-count. You are to undertake critical research into a chosen emerging theme, as the basis for the discussion paper, following the instructions of the assignment brief. You should present in tabular form a summary and evaluation of the sources used for your research. Second, you are required to produce a discussion paper that demonstrates a critical awareness and an in-depth understanding of the relevant theme and its impact on the sector or industry.

Finally, you will need to write an industry blog and prepare a posting that introduces the key points covered in your discussion paper.

Finally, you are required to produce a summary of your discussion paper in a specified format. This could be for either an internal or external audience.

4 The Magic Formula

The Magic Formula is a tool used by CIM to help both examiners write exam and assignment questions, and you, to more easily interpret what you are being asked to write about. It is useful for helping you to check that you are using an appropriate balance between theory and practice for your particular level of qualification.

Contrary to the title, there is nothing mystical about the Magic Formula and simply by knowing it (or even mentioning it in an assessment) will not automatically secure a pass. What it does do, however, is to help you to check that you are presenting your answers in an appropriate format, including enough marketing theory and applying it to a real marketing context or issue.

The Magic Formula for the Chartered Postgraduate Diploma in Marketing is shown below:

Figure A   The Magic Formula for the Chartered Postgraduate Diploma in Marketing

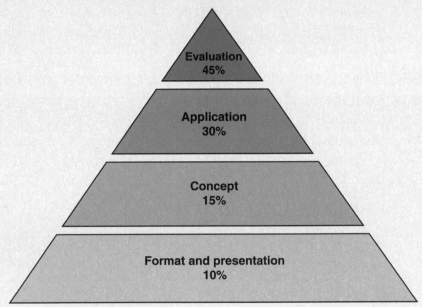

You can see from the pyramid that for the Chartered Postgraduate Diploma marks are awarded in the following proportions:

- **Presentation and format – 10%**

  You are expected to present your work professionally which means that assignments and projects should **always** be typed. Even in an exam situation attention should be paid to making your work look as visually appealing as possible. CIM will also stipulate the format that you should present your work in. The assessment formats you will be given will be varied and can include things like reports to write, slides to prepare, press releases, discussion documents, briefing papers, agendas and newsletters.

- **Concept – 15%**

  Concept refers to your ability to state, recall and describe marketing theory.

- **Application – 30%**

  Application-based marks are given for your ability to apply marketing theories to real life marketing situations. For example, a question may ask you to discuss the definition of marketing and how it is applied within your own organisation. Here you are not only using the definition but are applying it in order to consider the market orientation of the company.

The Chartered Institute of Marketing

- **Evaluation – 45%**

  Evaluation is the ability to asses the value or worth of something, sometimes through careful consideration of related advantages and disadvantages, or weighing up of alternatives. Results from your evaluation should enable you to discuss the importance of an issue using evidence to justify your opinions.

  For example, if you were asked to evaluate whether or not your organisation adopts a marketing approach you should provide reasons and specific examples of why you think it might take this approach, as well as considering why it may not take this approach, before coming to a final conclusion.

5 A guide to the features of the Study Support Text

Each of the chapter features (see below) will help you to break down the content into manageable chunks and ensure that you are developing the skills required for a professional qualification.

Chapter feature	Relevance and how you should use it
Introduction	Shows why topics need to be studied and is a route guide through the chapter
Syllabus reference	Outlines the syllabus learning outcomes covered in the chapter
Chapter topic list	Study the list, each numbered topic denotes a numbered section in the chapter
Key term	Highlights the core vocabulary you need to learn
Activity	An application-based activity for you to complete
The Real World	A short case study to illustrate marketing practice
Exam tip/Assessment tip	Key advice based on the assessment
Chapter roundups	Use this to review what you have learnt
Further reading	Further reading will give you a wider perspective on the subjects you're covering

6 Additional resources

To help you pass Stage 1 of the Chartered Postgraduate Diploma in Marketing we have created a complete study package. The **Chartered Postgraduate Diploma Assessment Workbook** covers three units of the Chartered Postgraduate Diploma level: Analysis and Decision, Marketing Leadership and Planning and Managing Corporate Reputation. Practice questions and answers and tips on tackling assignments are included to help you succeed in your assessments. The **Emerging Themes Study Support Text** is a support text written by CIM's Emerging Themes Examiner and is designed to guide you through the Emerging Themes unit. It includes guidance on researching themes for different sectors, illustrative examples, publication protocols and best practice on how to present your assessment.

Our A6 set of spiral bound **Passcards** are handy revision cards and are ideal to reinforce key topics for the assessment.

7 Your personal Study Plan

Preparing a Study Plan (and sticking to it) is one of the key elements to learning success.

Think about the number of hours you should dedicate to your studies. Guided learning hours will include time spent in lesson, working on fully prepared distance learning materials, formal workshops and work set by your tutor. We also know that to be successful, students should spend **approximately three times** the amount of time spent working through guided learning conducting self study. This means that for the entire qualification with four units you should spend time working in a tutor guided manner and approximately three times that completing recommended reading, working on assignments, and revising for exams. This Study Support Text will help you to organise this portion of self study time.

Now think about the exact amount of time you have (don't forget you will still need some leisure time!) and complete the following tables to help you keep to a schedule.

	Date	Duration in weeks
Course start		
Course finish		Total weeks of course:
Assignment received:	Submission date:	Total weeks to complete:

Content chapter coverage plan

Chapter	To be completed by	Revised?
Emerging themes in context		
Identifying trends		
Macro-environment, political, ethical and economic factors		
Emerging themes in organisations' environment		
Consumer behaviour insights		
Competition		
Supply chain insights		
Strategic thinking		
Changing the scope of the organisation and its operations		
Emerging themes within organisations		

The Chartered
Institute of Marketing

CHAPTER 1

Emerging themes in context

Introduction

This chapter will enable you to review what you've learnt in earlier CIM studies about the nature and importance of the external environment.

A strategic approach to marketing is built on the organisation being outward looking rather than just internally focused. That external view of the world starts with clarity about the sector in which it operates and how it is changing. Macro level forces drive the fortunes of sectors and organisations – they are the catalysts for strategic wear-out for businesses, which fail to identify and respond robustly to changes. These changes impact on the market environment in which organisations operate. The healthy eating trends encourage consumers to be more selective and discerning about their food choices and new technology may introduce new types of competitor or customer solutions.

It is the changing environment and emerging themes, which make the task of marketing both challenging and dynamic. A solution that had competitive advantage yesterday may have a short life span if the customer's needs and priorities change.

The syllabus for this Unit is not topic specific; it will evolve in real time to reflect the emerging themes in your sector and industry. You should find it highly relevant to your current role. It will also help you build the attitude and skills needed to be aware of future emerging themes.

Topic list

PEST and STEEPLE revisited	1
Change and the planning gap	2
The business reality	3
An emerging theme	4

1.1	Critically evaluate macro-environmental emerging themes and assess/forecast their potential impact upon one specific sector or industry:
	■ Changes in political governance systems and political focus
	■ Contemporary economic opportunities/challenges
	■ Social change (at local and global levels)
	■ Emerging technologies
	■ Environmental challenges
	■ Methods of forecasting/predicting change

▶ **Assessment tip**

Throughout this module, you will be directed to different sources of information for research and further reading. Take time as you do this to do two things:

1   Check the source in terms of its relevance to your sector – keep a list of useful sources and websites. It will save you time later.

2   Think about the articles that you are reading – pay attention to style and tone, accuracy, source, bias so that you are able to evaluate them.

1 PEST and STEEPLE revisited

▶ **Key term**

Environmental scanning can be defined as 'the study and interpretation of the political, economic, social and technological events and trends which influence a business, an industry or even a total market'. The factors which need to be considered for environmental scanning are events, trends, issues and expectations of the different interest groups.

Business does not operate within a vacuum. A solid understanding of the external environment by environmental scanning (as you should already know) is vital for the marketer.

1.1 PEST and STEEPLE

Industry and sectors operate in a dynamic and ever changing external environment. This external environment consists of a number of forces that cannot be directly changed by the organisations (individually or collectively) within the sector, but which impact directly and indirectly on the sector and the organisations within it.

You are likely to be familiar with these forces from earlier CIM studies. Often referred to by the mnemonics PEST or STEEPLE they are outlined in Table 1.1, below.

The Chartered Institute of Marketing

Table 1.1   PEST / STEEPLE forces

PEST	STEEPLE
Political and Legal	Social, cultural and demographic
Economic	Technological
Social, cultural and demographic	Economic and demographic
Technological and environmental	Environmental
	Political
	Legal
	Ethical

The external environment drives the fortunes of the sectors and organisation, generating both opportunities that can be exploited (or missed) and threats that can be anticipated (or addressed head on).

External environments are continuously evolving but the pace of change has accelerated as environments become more dynamic and uncertain. In the past, environments changed slowly, new technology took years to be commercialised, social and cultural changes were all more predictable in a population that was less connected and mobile. When change is slow organisations have plenty of time to react to it – forecasting is less of a requirement.

Today, the external environment changes rapidly, sometimes unexpectedly. The credit crunch demonstrates only too clearly how swift and significant change can be. An interconnected global economy suffered the aftershocks of the sub-prime problems in the USA almost simultaneously. The repercussions of these economic aftershocks are still being felt in the Eurozone with significant implications in Ireland, Italy, Greece and Spain.

1.2 Degrees of environmental complexity

Not all organisations face similar environments and they differ in their form and complexity. One of the main problems that organisations face is the degree of uncertainty and this can be classified as stable or dynamic and simple or complex.

In simple/static conditions the environment is relatively straightforward to understand and is not undergoing significant change. In situations of relatively low complexity, it may be possible to identify some predictors of environmental influences by looking at past trends. However, this type of low-level complexity is more of a theoretical extreme as markets and industries face increasingly high levels of uncertainty.

In dynamic conditions, managers need to consider future environments and the degree of uncertainty increases. Organisations may employ structured ways of making sense of the future such as scenario planning or they may rely on more active sensing of environmental changes through ideas lens.

Organisations in complex situations face an environment, which is both difficult to predict and scan. They may also face dynamic conditions and therefore face a combination of uncertainly and complexity. With more sophisticated technology this condition of greatest uncertainty and complexity is more prevalent. (Johnson & Scholes, 2002)

▶ Key term

A **scenario** is a detailed and plausible view of how the environment of an organisation might develop in the future based on groupings of key environmental influences and drivers of change about which there is a high level of uncertainty. Scenario planning can be used to develop long-range contingency plans, for example the oil industry where there is a need to make predictions for up to 20 years. But scenario planning also has merit for organisations with much shorter time horizons. It encourages organisations to consider alternative views of the future. Scenarios have three key elements:

– building the scenarios around the key drivers

– development of strategic contingency plans

– for each scenario developed monitoring the environment to assess the impacts and adjusting strategies and plans accordingly.

THE REAL WORLD

Spain's unprecedented double-dip recession will last for at least a further 18 months and poses a threat to the rest of Europe, the IMF has stated. Predicting a lost decade of growth for the Eurozone's fourth biggest economy, the Washington-based fund said the outlook was 'very difficult' and the fresh austerity measures announced by the government of the prime minister, Mariano Rajoy, would have 'a significant impact on growth'.

In its annual Article 4 health check, the IMF predicted it would take until 2017 for national output to return to its 2007 level, before the global financial crisis hit.

Figures released by the country's national statistics institute revealed that the second quarter, traditionally a time when employment picks up for the tourism season, saw joblessness rise to 24.6% as 53,000 more people joined dole queues. That broke a record set during Spain's last major recession 18 years ago.

More than 5.7 million Spaniards are unemployed.

The under-25s are suffering most, with 53% of jobseekers unable to find work.

(Elliott, L. *et al*, 2012)

You can see just from this small example that an environmental change can impact on performance at country as well as company level, but that change may not be felt equally by all industries or firms within a sector. The focus of this unit is at sector or industry level rather than organisation level. However, we shall look at both to demonstrate the importance of awareness and vigilance in market analysis. For example:

THE REAL WORLD

The world monetary crisis, combined with the Arab Spring, in countries with high levels of tourism from Western Europe and a succession of natural disasters, from flooding in Thailand to the Japanese tsunami, made 2011 a difficult year for the global travel industry. However, the economic recession has created opportunities. A survey, of more than 1,000 UK adults, conducted by BDRC Continental in 2012, suggested the UK is rated marginally higher than western Europe and the Mediterranean as a likely holiday destination for Britons. The survey found 70% of families plan a holiday of seven or more nights in the UK this year, up from 59% in 2011.

Similarly, within sectors not everyone is impacted equally – in the UK retail sector '*value*' brands such as Primark and Pound Shop have expanded and grown while Pizza Express has benefited from increased eating at home (compared with other pizza restaurants who do not have any '*at home*' supermarket stocked products like Pizza Express).

The Chartered Institute of Marketing

Within a sector those organisations and managers who are aware of their external environment, understand its significance, are alert to emerging trends and themes and are most likely to be able to respond to both threats and opportunities generated by a changing business landscape.

This first unit of your Chartered Postgraduate Diploma is intended to provide you with the knowledge and tools to ensure:

- your planning and marketing activities are based on a realistic assessment of the future environment
- you have tools and skills to help you forecast
- you can take a lead in helping your sector and organisation prepare for future changes
- you are able to be flexible in response to unexpected changes – taking a more **emergent** approach to business planning.

But, of course, it is not just economic change that drives the fortunes of sectors or organisations. Identifying the macro trends is one thing but the emerging themes are the result of how these changes are acted on by customers, suppliers and competitors. Failing to keep up with changes and emerging themes is the real cause of failure. So, for example, the credit crunch is encouraging a pattern of '**thrift**' amongst customers. Avoiding waste and value purchasing are strong emerging themes, which may outlive the current economic downturn and need to be reflected in marketing activities and even new business models.

Management guru Gary Hamel says that businesses today are more likely to fail because they become irrelevant, not because they are inefficient. They lose touch with changing customer needs or fail to respond to new competitors who enter the market with new business models. Hamel's (2000) quote from his book *Leading the Revolution* is more graphic but encapsulates the danger of failing to keep abreast of those emerging trends:

'In today's business environment those who live by the sword shall be shot by those who don't'.

ACTIVITY 1.1

Access *The Forces of Change* /the driver and trends primer produced by Business in the Community (2011):

http://www.bitc.org.uk/resources/publications/visioning_the_future.html

1 Evaluate the changes identified in the primer and according to most significant global impact.
2 Identify which of the trends identified are affecting your industry.
3 Select one of the trends and assess the impacts on your industry.

1.4 Identifying and selecting an emerging theme

Once you have defined and scoped your market you can start to identify the external STEEPLE factors that are impacting upon it.

The key here is to be as thorough and specific as possible.

So, rather than just talk about '**economy**' it may be the availability of consumer credit that correlates directly to levels of demand. There may be a number of changes that, in turn, could affect the availability of credit.

Similarly, you might have '**employment levels**' as an economic factor, but the true factor may be employment levels amongst 18 to 25 year olds.

Remember also that you are looking always for emerging trends and themes. You may not always be able to be specific about what the '**change**' will be but you may be more certain there **will** *be* a change. For example, a trend for increased legislation in an area, technology breakthroughs or greater policing of internet sites are highly likely to change although we may not know exactly what the change will be.

▶ **Assessment tip**

Conduct a detailed STEEPLE analysis of the industry that you work in. Use a variety of sources to identify the key trends and reference these in the STEEPLE analysis. Once you have identified the trends, consider their relevance and importance by listing both the negative and positive impacts.

Table 1.2 STEEPLE analysis of the industry you work in

Factor	Positive impacts	Negative impacts
Economic		
Social		
Political		
Legal		
Environmental		
Technological		
Ethical		

Once you have conducted the STEEPLE analysis rank the factors in order of long-term impact on your industry.

1.4.1 Example: drivers of obesity in children

Environmental changes influence demand and supply. You are, therefore, looking for factors that directly influence customers and competitors. You can break the process down into two steps, step one involves identifying **drivers** and step two identifying **key trends**.

To illustrate this we can look at the health and obesity issues for children.

First, look at the changes coming together that have created the problem. These could be seen to be the emerging themes leading to problems of health and obesity in children.

The Chartered
Institute of Marketing

Figure 1.1   Drivers of obesity in children

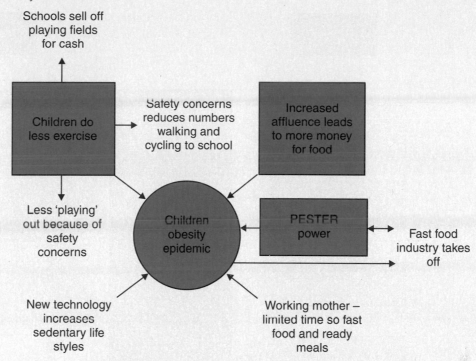

You can see that a number of changes happened, all of which could be seen to contribute to the emerging theme of childhood obesity.

These contributing factors range from changes in school funding and governance that allowed school playing fields to be sold, through to unnecessary fears about child safety that encouraged families to drive kids to school (aided by the greater affluence and the two-car family).

New products and services, from games to fast food, encouraged less activity and more calories. At the same time children's power grew. At home, 'pester power' and at school the 'choice' in school dinners led to the 'chicken twizzler' (spiral strips of processed meat) condemned by UK celebrity chef Jamie Oliver for its awful nutritional profile.

So, if you were a children's clothes manufacturer, or a marketer working in the fast food sector, how easy would increasing waistlines of children have been to forecast?

Perhaps more importantly, now child obesity is on the agenda, how is it likely to change things going forward? What will be the sector responses and the impact on marketers and marketing?

Access the following report on CIM's website for further reading:
http://www.cim.co.uk/files/mktingtochildren.pdf

1.4.2 Force field analysis

Kurt Lewin's (1943) force fields analysis is a tool more normally associated with helping understand and implement change.

We are using it here to help us turn an overview of the 'emerging theme' and factors driving it into more specific analysis that could help us to evaluate the likelihood of change happening and, therefore, how seriously the sector needs to consider it.

Figure 1.2   Force fields analysis for obesity in children

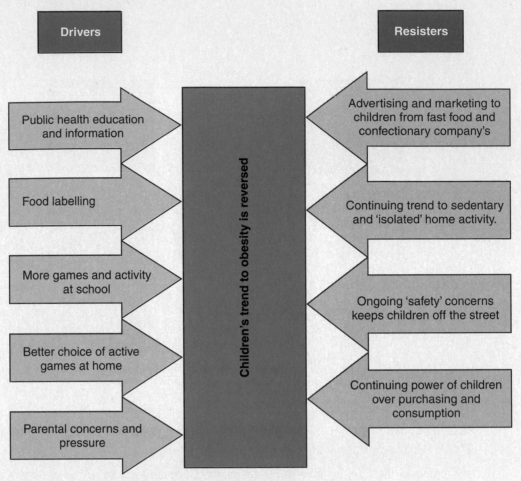

1.5 Strategic wear-out

▶ **Key term**

Strategic wear-out occurs when an organisation does not adequately assess changes in its external operating environment and thus continues with the same strategy and approach.

Failure to respond to the changing environment leads to business failure (strategic wear-out). In fast moving environments, there is a real danger of **strategic wear-out**. This occurs when a strategy that has worked well for an organisation ceases to be effective. If the organisation fails to notice the changes in the market conditions, becomes complacent and 'sticks to its knitting' it will find business performance falls. The speed of its demise depends on the speed with which its market is changing. For example, Nokia was slow to enter the smartphone market and posted losses of 1.41bn euros in the first half of 2012 and continues to lose market share to Samsung and Apple. (BBC, 2012)

There are many instances where products have been replaced. A few recent examples include:

- Digital cameras reduced the need for film development
- Music downloads are forecast to overtake CD sales in USA in 2012
- Movies on demand mean fewer trips to the DVD rental shop

The changing fortunes of different sectors can be traced to macro-environmental changes that have impacted upon them.

The Chartered
Institute of Marketing

Prahalad and Hamel (1996) highlight the challenges of environmental change, which they point out is creating a growing disconnection between what customers want (driven by changing lifestyles, attitudes and behaviours) and what companies think they want (driven too often by what they can make).

Figure 1.3   A growing disconnect in the exchange process

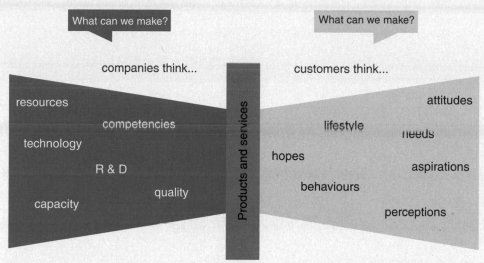

Improved communications and information amplifies any disconnect

(Adapted from Prahalad and Hamel, 1996)

According to Prahalad and Hamel (1996) this disconnect is magnified by improved information and communication for customers. Social networks, internet searches and reviews from other users have all contributed to changes in the balance of power in the marketplace and the creation of buyer markets.

ACTIVITY 1.2

Note: Changing buyer power is an example of an emerging theme highlighted in the syllabus for this unit. Evaluate how buyer power has changed in your sector or industry over recent years and identify what have been the catalysts of this change.

So business takes place in an ever changing environment and recent years have seen the pace of change quicken – new technology, economic collapse, legal and social changes can all be cited as examples of the speed of change. Effective managers, therefore, have to set up systems to ensure they are alert to emerging changes in their sector and then they should have the foresight to prepare for them at the organisational level.

2 Change and the planning gap

2.1 But, why are these changes so important?

It is the changes in the external environment that generate threats. They can reduce demand, raise costs or erode margins and so determine the bottom line of your planning gap. The planning gap is a forecast of what profits you might expect going forward if you were to **do nothing different** – in other words if you were to keep offering the same products to the same customers despite the changing environment.

This is, of course, a future forecast of the financial impact of changes in your sector – the result of your awareness of those emerging themes and their potential implications for performance if you fail to respond. Clearly, complacency amongst management is not a recipe for success.

THE REAL WORLD

Woolworths, a UK high street retail chain, selling book, CDs, clothing and confectionary, did not fail simply because of the impact of the credit crunch. It had already become **irrelevant** to its customers – people were no longer sure why they should go to Woolworths. The credit crunch simply speeded up the inevitable result of catastrophic strategic wear-out. Woolworths had continued to offer the same products to the same customers despite the changing customer and competitor landscape.

▶ **Key term**

Gap analysis identifies gaps between the optimised allocation and integration of the inputs (resources), and the current allocation level. This reveals areas that can be improved. Gap analysis involves determining, documenting, and approving the variance between business requirements and current capabilities. Such analysis can be performed at the strategic or operational level of an organisation.

Figure 1.4 following, represents what is known as the planning gap. The graph shows the difference between the value of market opportunities compared with a worsening market condition within a relatively stable business environment.

Figure 1.4   The planning gap

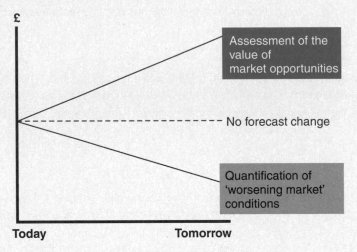

Luckily, the changing environment brings with it opportunities as well, providing managers with options to counter the potential downward push from environmental threats. So, the top line of the planning gap is a realistic forecast of the potential value of those positive environmental changes were the business to take advantage of them by responding with new product and marketing strategies.

The planning gap shapes the scope of your **rational** planning. Where you are now, where might you go, and what will happen if you do nothing different. You can see how much business needs to be retained and how challenging your acquisition strategies need to be to take advantage of the emerging opportunities.

The Chartered Institute of Marketing

Figure 1.5   Gap analysis

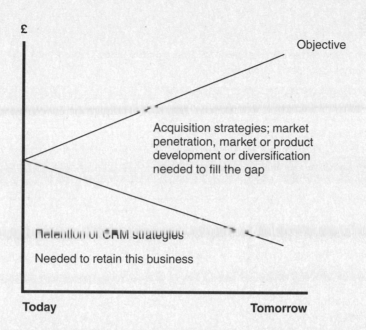

£

Objective

Acquisition strategies; market
penetration, market or product
development or diversification
needed to fill the gap

Retention or CRM strategies

Needed to retain this business

Today   **Tomorrow**

2.2 Where do the opportunities come from?

On its own, a change in the environment does not translate into new business. Revenue is generated by selling goods and services to customers – a combination of products and markets. The Ansoff Matrix (Table 1.3) captures the four strategic options open to an organisation that wants to grow the top line of its business, ie boost revenues.

Table 1.3   The Ansoff matrix

	Existing products	New products
Existing markets	Market penetration	Product development
New markets	Market development	Diversification

These strategic opportunities arise from those changes in the environment and how you, your customers and competitors, respond to them. So, for example, a faster pace of life and concerns about work-life balance generate opportunities for time-saving solutions. Examples include prepared meals and ingredients pre-weighed and combined to make home cooked meals easier and quicker.

Even threats in the external environment can be converted into product/market opportunities. Recession may be reducing demand for your premium priced products but it may open up the opportunity for an economy range. For example, the M&S response of a 'dine in for £10 for 2' offer to attract thrifty shoppers, looking for an alternative to an expensive meal out, which has now been widely copied by other UK food retailers.

In this way, external changes in the environment can impact on your expected revenues and margins (positively or negatively) and they can be the catalyst for new business in the form of new customer segments, greater average spend or new products and solutions.

Have a look at the changes in the external environment suggested below. How would you expect them to impact on the organisations in the sectors identified? Evaluate

The UK higher education sector has undergone changes in the funding mechanism and visa regulations which have resulted in a decline in student numbers	
Continued climate change will result in longer, warmer summers in the UK – how might this affect ice cream manufacturers?	
The newspaper industry recognises that more people are getting their news online	
A revolutionary scheme involving battery swapping has increased ownership of electric cars by 30%.	
There is evidence that more people are using comparison websites before purchasing insurance products – how might that impact on motor insurance providers?	
Credit is difficult to get for core SME customers – what are the implications for software suppliers?	
There is evidence that more competitors within a sector are collaborating to gain greater economies of scale	
The credit crunch has boosted the 'stay at home' holiday industry – what are the implications for UK theme parks and entertainment providers?	

2.3 Summarising the underlying challenge

The reason for the emphasis CIM is placing on emerging themes in this qualification becomes clear when you review just how significant those underlying changes are.

Figure 1.6 Key drivers of underlying change

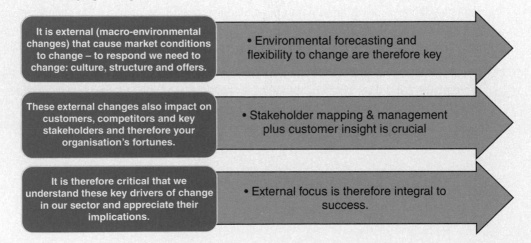

The Chartered Institute of Marketing

3 The business reality

When you consider the significance of environmental change on performance you might expect forecasting and awareness of emerging themes to be high on management's agenda and the focus of much effort and energy. The business reality is often very different:

- Many organisations produce their business plans without any apparent consideration of the external environment in which they are operating.

- If external factors are considered, they are too often assessed in terms of today's state. This is clearly unhelpful when you consider that we are trying to plan for business tomorrow. In other words, it is not the current rate of inflation or customers' attitudes to fast food that matter, it is what we try to forecast these will be in one, two or five years. It is the emerging themes and changes that matter to business fortunes because these are the early indicators of change.

- Forecasting environmental change and future impact is hard and an art not a science. However, a rational and well thought through, robust approach can be used.

- Few organisations dedicate staff to the monitoring of the environment or take steps to identify and monitor emerging themes. At best, the external environment is reviewed superficially as part of the annual planning process and one element of the SWOT analysis.

In truth, environmental auditing, or scanning, is a fundamental responsibility of management. Its business plan is needed to steer the organisation through this changing environment over the next three to five years.

Failure to audit the environment fully is equivalent to navigating a ship with eyes closed and is likely to result in the business running aground or crashing into something.

ACTIVITY 1.4

Take the business pages from a broadsheet paper or a business magazine like *The Economist* or *Management Today*.

Review each of the articles and identify how many of them relate directly or indirectly to a change in the external/macro environment.

Analyse the nature of that change and any implications for the sector you are working in.

How useful was the article in assisting you to evaluate the changes?

3.1 What is an emerging theme?

▶ **Key term**

Contemporary issues and **emerging themes** are terms used by CIM to highlight the most potent forces currently influencing sectors of the economy and, in turn, business practices and marketing strategy. Emerging themes exist where there is some indication of a future change but it is not yet an established factor. The earlier you can accurately identify and factor in such future influences, the more effective your strategy is likely to be.

By definition, it is not possible for CIM to be specific about what this year's emerging themes will be – they will change. Two years ago, the credit crunch was unlikely to have been on the agenda. Today, you might consider the emerging theme to be deflation and the impact that might have on the economy and your markets.

Amongst the potential emerging themes highlighted in the syllabus are:

Table 1.4   Potential emerging themes

Political	Protest and democracy
Economic	Credit crunch
Social	Changing demographics, migration, social networking and communication health and obesity
Technology	Emerging advancements like nanotechnology and 3D printing
Environmental	Climate change
Marketing's new ground	Social, green and digital marketing
Changing consumers	Customer power and ethical consumption
Changing nature of competition and supply chains	Collaboration, disintermediation and competition
Contemporary business strategies	Business sustainability and the triple bottom line
The impact on the marketing professional	Intelligence gathering, creative, and flexible thinking

3.2 How things have changed

By taking something of a long view, we can see how the changing external environment has affected business and the role and activity of marketers.

From a seller's market

Until 1954, the UK still had rationing, demand exceeded supply and customer choice and the role for marketing were both very limited. Organisations could improve profit if they improved their output so the focus was internal on improving efficiency.

...to a buyer's market

Over time macro-environmental change shifted the balance of power:

- Technology reduced barriers to entry in some sectors, for example, in creative industries while in others it increased capacity.

- Political changes created a growing single market in Europe and opened up trade with China, both bringing new competitors as well as new customers.

- Regulatory changes reduced entry barriers, for example, building societies were allowed to compete with banks.

- A steady proliferation of media gave customers access to new sources of information.

As these changes took place, so the market conditions changed and supply gradually matched and, then exceeded, demand. The result was a steady change in buyer power creating a theme that has been in evidence for some time!

The role of marketing began to develop, initially as a sales support role with a focus on promotion and communication, to more recently (in light of strong buyer markets) becoming the organisation's architect of competitive advantage. How firms do business and use marketing has changed significantly.

This new strategic role requires marketers to deliver customer insight to the business in ways that help the company decide what benefits will deliver a 'valued offer' to the targeted segments.

The changing dynamics can be seen in Figure 1.7 below. Proliferation of product and media since the 1950s led to this switch from seller's to buyer's market, with the customer now in the driving seat.

The Chartered Institute of Marketing

Figure 1.7 Changing market dynamics

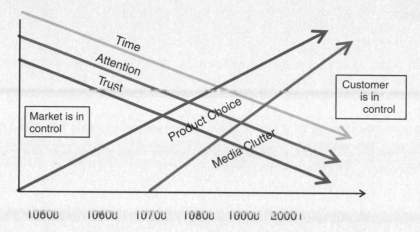

....and the impact of recession

The credit crunch and recession have not reversed the buyer's market. On the contrary, reduction in demand magnifies the excess of supply over demand. Not all players will survive so the emphasis is on trying to ensure your organisation is truly market-oriented. Companies who have perhaps paid only lip service to customer-led decision-making are working very hard to establish a meaningful strategic role for marketing in today's tough economic climate.

3.3 A broader stakeholder agenda

> ▶ **Key term**
>
> **An emerging theme – competition for attention**
>
> To date, marketers have had to compete for a **share of wallet** and income was a key segmentation variable. Marketers recognised the increased customer choice made possible by a buyer's market and this has been facilitated by comparison sites such as *www.compare themarket.com* which allow customers to easily compare prices and service offer The proliferation of media we are enjoying today will have significant implications for marketers as it will influence how, when and where marketers communicate with customers. Permission to communicate with customers cannot be assumed – **their time and attention** will be scarce commodities that we will need to compete for, so **relevance** will become increasingly critical.

While many organisations are still coming to grips with the reality of a market orientation there is plenty of evidence of what today's emerging trends around **corporate social responsibility (CSR)** as detailed in section 4, below, will mean to business and the role of marketers.

'A number of emerging trends are driving this agenda, from climate change to waste, demands for better corporate governance and concerns about society. For companies, there is a need to expand their agendas to include the needs of employees, the community and the general public. This is referred to as societal marketing or human orientation.

Organisations have to assess their costs and value-added in terms of economic, social and environmental impact. Reporting on the **triple bottom line** (**TBL**) and making decisions about whether CSR initiatives should be simply a matter for compliance, the matching of industry best practice, or be used as a differentiator.

The phrase 'The triple bottom line' was first coined in 1994 by John Elkington, the founder of a British consultancy called SustainAbility. His argument was that companies should be preparing three different (and quite separate) bottom lines. **The first** is the traditional measure of corporate profit–the 'bottom line' of the profit and loss account. **The second** is the bottom line of a company's **'people account'** – a measure in some shape or form of how socially responsible an organisation has been throughout its operations. **The third** is the bottom line of the company's **'planet account'** – a measure of how environmentally responsible it has been. The triple bottom line (TBL) thus consists of three Ps: profit, people and planet. It aims to measure the financial, social and environmental performance of the corporation over a period of time. Only a company that produces a TBL is taking account of the full cost involved in doing business. ' (The Economist, 2009)

Access the following article:

Blayney, S. M. (2011) The good, the bad and the indifferent: marketing and the triple bottom line, *Social Business*, Vol. 1 (2), pp173-187.

Questions

1   Using the triple bottom line model, evaluate to what extent your organisation is adopting the principles and the effect this is having on your organisation.

2   Outline any criticisms of triple bottom line principles.

THE REAL WORLD

Unilever Sustainable Living Plan

In November 2010, the Unilever Sustainable Living Plan was launched. Unilever publicly committed to a ten-year journey towards sustainable growth, with around 60 specific targets embedding this new thinking into its business. What makes the Unilever Sustainable Living Plan different is that it applies right across the value chain. Unilever is taking responsibility, not just for its own direct operations, but for its suppliers, distributors and – crucially – for how consumers use brands like Dove, Knorr, Lipton, Lifebuoy and Pureit.

The plan's objectives are that, by 2020 Unilever will:

- help more than one billion people improve their health and well-being
- halve the environmental footprint of the making and use of Unilever products
- source 100% of its agricultural raw materials in a sustainable fashion

For more information about Unilever's Sustainable Living Plan and its stakeholder engagement see
https://www.unilever.com/sustainable-living

---

4 An emerging theme

▶ **Key term**

Corporate social responsibility (CSR) is a form of corporate self-regulation integrated into a business model. CSR policy functions as a built-in, self-regulating mechanism whereby a business monitors and ensures its active compliance with the spirit of the law, ethical standards, and international norms. The goal of CSR is to embrace responsibility for the company's actions and encourage a positive impact through its activities on the environment, consumers, employees, communities, stakeholders and all other members of the public sphere who may also be considered as stakeholders.

There is a growing sense of distrust among consumers towards corporations. Consumers have been exposed to some critical events recently that have led them to question our social and commercial institutions as well as brands in general.

The Chartered
Institute of Marketing

4.1 Corporate social responsibility

THE REAL WORLD

The banking sector and high-risk investment strategies are universally blamed for causing the recession in the Eurozone and USA. However, despite this, UK banks have failed to improve their corporate reputations and there have been more cases which have resulted in a growing mistrust of banks:

Libor, the London inter-bank lending rate, is considered to be one of the most crucial interest rates in finance. It underpins trillions of pounds worth of loans and financial contracts. In June 2012, Barclays was fined £290m, after some of its derivatives traders were found to have attempted to rig this key rate and public confidence in banks was again affected.

UK banks have been widely criticised by both customers and shareholders for excessive salaries and bonuses.

The Personal Protection Insurance (PPI) misselling scandal, where banks have been forced to compensate customers has provoked further unrest. The total amount in compensation for customers is forecast to reach 8 billion GBP.

A United States Senate committee found that HSBC had allowed £9 billion in suspect transactions from countries such as Mexico and Russia. Many are suspected to have involved money-laundering, and HSBC has admitted failing to monitor the transactions properly.

In June 2012, the failure on the software update at RBS, which also owns NatWest and Ulster Bank, meant that a significant number of customers were unable to have money transferred into, or out of, their accounts. The banks now face the possibility of reimbursing millions of customers who have incurred extra costs because of the computer problem. Customer trust is at an all-time low and the impact of the reputational damage is immense.

ACTIVITY 1.6

From carefree to careful

Is there any evidence of this trend in your sector?

What are/would/could be the implication of this trend for your organisation?

Plan A because there is no Plan B

Marks and Spencer is one of the UK's leading retailers, with over 21 million people visiting its stores each week. It offers clothing and home products, as well as foods, sourced from around 2,000 suppliers globally. It employs over 78,000 people in the UK and abroad, and has over 700 UK stores, plus an expanding international business.

Overall, its clothing and homeware sales account for 49% of business. The other 51% of business is in food, where it sells fresh produce and groceries, partly-prepared meals and ready meals.

The company is known for its green credentials as a result of its five-year eco plan, Plan A, in which it aimed to become carbon neutral and send no waste to landfill by 2012. (M&S, 2012)

In 2001 M&S announced it was only going to sell free-range eggs as part of a wider commitment to animal welfare. The operational implications of what could seem like a tactical decision, in reality, were huge. Four thousand products were affected and hundreds of suppliers had to make changes in order to become compliant.

The change was promoted with TV ads featuring the live free-range hens in shopping trolleys. Measuring the impact of this initiative was harder. It was believed to contribute to M&S regaining the lead over Waitrose as the 'quality' food provider that year.

M&S also introduced a £200m investment and a '100 point eco plan' to become a carbon-neutral retailer, within five years.

There are five key areas where M&S believes it can tackle the biggest challenges facing it as a retailer:

1   Climate change
2   Waste
3   Sustainable raw materials
4   Health
5   Being a fair partner

Plan A, 2011

The past six months has seen the launch of two major, new, Plan A customer initiatives. The third and most successful was the 'One Day Wardrobe Clearout', followed by 34,000 M&S customers getting involved in the Big Butterfly Count 2011.

In June, M&S launched Forever Fish – a major campaign to help customers and their children learn more about fish, clean our British beaches and protect marine life.

Funded by the profits from the 5p carrier bag charge at M&S Food halls, M&S will set-up and run a 'school of Fish' over the next three years to encourage as many of their 21 million customers and 78,000 employees as possible to help the Marine Conservation Society (MCS) clean British beaches. M&S will invest over £1 million in WWF projects to help manage better UK fish stocks and protect the world's oceans. This is intended to help customers to make healthy and more sustainable choices, by promoting more high quality, sustainably-sourced fish and introducing lesser known and more plentiful species such as Dab and Flounder.

In July, M&S announced a new partnership with UNICEF to transform the lives of the world's poorest children. M&S is asking customers not to take hangers home, when they buy clothes, in which case it will donate 50p for every £1 saved from hanger recycling to UNICEF, the world's leading children's organisation. The aim is to raise at least £1.9million over the next three years to fund a critical new project in two locations within the Mymensingh and Dhaka regions of Bangladesh, providing all the basics that children need for a better future, such as clean water, education and healthcare. (M&S, 2011)

Visit the M&S Plan A site at http://www.plana.marksandspencer.com/

Assess for yourself the scale of the CSR strategy and the implications it has for the business.

How is the emerging CSR agenda affecting your sector? What are the opportunities and threats it might generate?

CSR driven opportunities	CSR driven threats

- The macro environment is constantly changing. Changes are increasingly rapid. Those changes drive the fortunes of sectors and organisations – generating opportunities and threats.

- Those who fail to respond proactively miss the window of opportunity and are likely to experience the irrelevancy of strategic wear-out

- PEST/STEEPLE

- The impact on credit crunch for overseas holidays v UK holidays

- The example of health and fitness concerns

- Emerging themes from the credit crunch – thrifty shoppers

- The planning gap

- How threats drive the bottom-line and opportunities the top-line objective

- The danger of strategic wear-out and Gary Hamel's caution about the dangers of irrelevancy

- Throughout this chapter you have been applying the learning to your own sector

FURTHER READING

Accenture (2012) Latest thinking. http://www.accenture.com/us-en/research/Pages/index.aspx

Useful for up to date insights and publications into a range of sectors.

Anon (2011) Future high streets. Business in the Community,
http://www.bitc.org.uk/resources/publications/future_high_streets.html

Anon (2011) Leave those kids alone – responsible marketing to children. CIM White Paper,
http://www.cim.co.uk/files/mktingtochildren.pdf

Anon (2012) Consumers and the Economic Outlook Quarterly Update, February 2012.

Digital Trends UK, Mintel.

Anon (2012) Euro in Crisis. Financial Times, http://www.ft.com/indepth/euro-in-crisis [Accessed on 25 October 2012].

Anon (2012) Frugal innovation by social entrepreneurs in India, March 2012. Business in the Community,
http://www.bitc.org.uk/resources/publications/serco_institute.html

Anon (2012) The future of manufacturing. World Economic Forum, http://www.weforum.org/reports/future-manufacturing

Hume, M. and Mills, M. (2011) Building the sustainable iMuseum: is the virtual museum leaving our museums virtually empty? *International Journal of Nonprofit & Voluntary Sector Marketing*. August, Vol16(3), pp275-289.

Marketing Magazine

Marketing Week

McKinsey & Company, http://www.mckinsey.com/

Useful for up-to-date insights and publications into a range of sectors

The Chartered Institute of Marketing

Reyneke, M. *et al* (2012) Managing brands in times of economic downturn: How do luxury brands fare? *Journal of Brand Management.* April, Vol 19(6), pp457-466.

REFERENCES

Anon (2009) Triple bottom line. The Economist, http://www.economist.com/node/14301663 [Accessed on 3 October 2012]

CIM (2011) Leave those kids alone – responsible marketing to children. CIM White Paper, http://www.cim.co.uk/files/mktingtochildren.pdf

Anon (2011) Visioning the future. Business in the community, http://www.bitc.org.uk/resources/publications/visioning_the_future.html [Accessed 25 October 2012]

Anon (2012) Sustainable living. Unilever, http://www.unilever.com/sustainable-living/ [Accessed 25 October 2012]

Ansoff, I. (1957) Strategies for diversification. *Harvard Business Review*, Vol35 Issue 5,Sep-Oct, pp113-124.

Blayney, S. M. (2011) The good, the bad and the indifferent: marketing and the triple bottom line. *Social Business*, Vol1(2), pp173-187.

Elliott, L. (2012) Angela Merkel and François Hollande pledge to safeguard embattled euro. The Guardian, http://www.guardian.co.uk/business/2012/jul/27/debt-crisis-emu [Accessed on 25 October 2012]

Hamel, G. (2000) *Leading the Revolution*. Harvard, Harvard Business School Press.

Howell, J. (2012) Nokia set to announce more losses. BBC, http://www.bbc.co.uk/news/business-18900413 [Accessed on 25 October 2012]

Johnson, G. and Scholes, K. (2002) *Exploring Corporate Strategy*. Harlow, Prentice Hall.

Lewin K. (1943) Defining the "Field at a Given Time". *Psychological Review.* 50: 292-310. Republished in *Resolving Social Conflicts & Field Theory in Social Science.* Washington, D.C., American Psychological Association, 1997.

Prahalad, C.K. and Hamel, G. (1996) *Competing for the Future*. Harvard, Harvard Business School Press.

The activities included in this chapter are included to stimulate discussion and debate in relation to emerging themes and therefore hopefully assist you in selecting the ones you will use, considering the impacts from both a global and industry perspective. As such there are no definitive answers.

Activity 1.1

Review *The forces of change*/the driver and trends primer produced by Business in the Community. The document will help you identify areas of change specifically relevant to your organisation and stimulate you to think about the likely impact these will have.

Discussion points

1   How will these changes impact on your business model?

2   How will this balance shift affect your markets, operations and supply chains?

3   How will your business compete with new entrants?

4   Who will be your employees and customers of the future and where will they be?

5   How will you compete for global talent?

6   How will you effectively compete when the 'expertise advantage' of northern economies has disappeared?

Activity 1.2

Discussion points

1   Identify the key buyers/customers for your products and services. How much do they contribute in terms of sales revenue, profit, corporate reputation?

2   How have your buyers/customers changed? Are they more international, do they spend more or less than five years ago?

3   How, in B2B markets, have your relationships developed with your top buyers? Are they more adversarial, or are you working in a more partnership approach?

4   How, in B2C markets, has the customer's behaviour affected your marketing strategy? For example, are banks having less of a traditional high street presence, due to technology and developments in online banking?

Activity 1.3

For each of the suggested scenarios, consider the following discussion points.

1   What are the potential opportunities in terms of new markets, customers, product/service development, brand extensions?

2   Consider the threats, current marketing strategy, competitive nature of the industry, business models.

Activity 1.4

Your analysis will depend on whether you pick an industry-specific example such as Retail Renaissance (19 May 2012) in *The Economist* which highlighted potential impacts in the banking sector, or a more general article such as *The Vanishing North* a special report by *The Economist* (June 16 2012) which looks at how global warming is affecting trade, energy and the environment which has wider implications.

Activity 1.5

Discussion points

1   Does your industry measure financial, social and environmental measures? If not, why not? With so much emphasis on CSR, and global environmental concerns should cost and profit still reign supreme?

2   Only when companies measure their social and environmental impact will we have socially and environmentally responsible organisations. Discuss.

3   Is the TBL a realistic model or an ideal?

4   Can organisations set comparable measures to measure profit, social and environmental impacts?

Activity 1.6

Discussion points

1   How significant is customer trust in your industry?

2   Highlight the key factors that impact on customer trust in your industry. For example, service/product delivery, availability of alternatives, brand equity.

Activity 1.7

Discussion points

1   Evaluate how Plan A has impacted on Marks and Spencer's marketing strategy and corporate reputation.

2   Compare your analysis with a similar high street retailer of your choice eg, Asda Walmart, John Lewis/Waitrose. What are the similarities and differences?

3   Assess the ROI for Marks and Spencer.

4   Is CSR being adopted in your industry/sector? Give examples of projects/initiatives and compare these with those of other students in your class.

5   Is it a major objective or implemented at a more tactical level? Justify your explanation.

The Chartered Institute of Marketing

CHAPTER 2

Identifying trends

Introduction

In this chapter, we look at the essential task of auditing your marketing environment. This is one of the cornerstones of marketing, and you will have covered it in previous levels of the Institute's qualification. We cannot emphasise enough the importance of clear, consistent and methodical analysis.

The chapter begins by considering which industry or market should be scanned. This is not quite as simple as it initially sounds as, increasingly, organisations span several industries and many markets. In order to identify emerging trends, it is vital that focus is clear and sufficiently broad so that relevant opportunities and threats are not overlooked.

The second section moves on to look at macro-environmental factors. We examine information that should be collected and how to apply some of the most commonly used tools in the final sections.

Topic list

Which industry or market are we scanning?   (1)

Conducting a deeper analysis of macro-environmental factors   (2)

Collecting environmental information   (3)

Trend analysis and adding key uncertainties to the mix   (4)

Making sense of the changes – mitigating risks and scenario planning   (5)

2.1	Judge the importance of a range of emerging themes to a particular organisation:
	■ Scenario planning ■ Impact/risk assessment
2.3	Propose methods by which marketing professionals can anticipate and adapt to change:
	■ Sources of data and intelligence ■ Developing intellectual skills and creativity ■ New forms of networking

1 Which industry or market are we scanning?

> ▶ **Key terms**
>
> **Industry**
>
> For the purposes of this text, an **industry** is defined as 'a group of firms producing products that are close substitutes for each other' (Porter, 1980). An industry or sector is distinct from a market in that it is principally characterised by the attributes of the producers rather than those of customers. Industries can serve many different groups of customers or markets.
>
> **Market**
>
> A **market** is an aggregate of people who have needs for a product or a service and who have the ability, willingness and authority to purchase such products. We are dealing with people, but the market is usually expressed in Volume and Value

The problem with analysis undertaken by many organisations is not the methods they use but the context and focus of their work. For even a modest SME, there are often activities that span several markets and product or solution areas. Any analysis completed at the organisational level will inevitably be vague and only relevant to parts of the business. At too high a level there is little granularity and the lack of focus means it is easy to overlook relevant opportunities and threats and fail completely to identify those emerging trends.

The first challenge for marketers is to define carefully the industry and/or market they are analysing. That may sound reasonably straightforward but, unfortunately, it often is not.

Many organisations still fall into the trap of confusing industries and markets. Industry level analysis helps to define the supply/distribution chain and the various power relationships within it. However, to fully understand who your organisation is competing with you need to understand the customer's perspective – this is important because:

- If you define your business **by what you do**, the chances are your orientation will be internal rather than external and those **emerging trends can catch you unaware**.

- Your **customer is not buying a product but a solution to their problem.** If you fail to recognise this, your definition of competitors and substitute products may well be too narrow. It is not easy to get a clear view of what is happening in a market if you approach it with blinkers on ('marketing myopia').

Table 2.1   Examples

A CD manufacturer	Your local cinema	The local charity
The customer is buying personal entertainment and is happy to consider new technologies and formats including music downloads	Here the customer is looking for an evening's entertainment and the local theatre, wine bar or tonight's TV programmes are all potential competitors	The competition is for your discretionary pound and your support and empathy

Planning activity and strategy development starts by clarifying your market or business: your thinking could start with the phrase:

In this area of our activity, we are in the business of providing the following benefits to the following people…

The Chartered
Institute of Marketing

Look at the examples given and define their business in terms of the customer benefits being offered or the problem solved, and consider who might be competing in these markets other than the direct competitors.

Firm	They are in the business of:	They might be competing with:
1 An airline providing internal flights		
2 A manufacturer of plastic carrier bags		
3 A take away pizza restaurant		
4 Your local doctor		
5 The finance team in your organisation		
6 Your own business/organisation		

Check your answers with the feedback at the end of this chapter.

▶ **Assessment tip**

Make sure you are specific about your industry or market definition when preparing for your assignment. Being focused will make life easier for you and will generate more useful insights for your business.

Warning

Take care with international markets. While it is quite feasible to define a global industry in the way we have done above, your environmental analysis may differ across different geographies. There may be an emerging theme in Middle Eastern markets which is not apparent in the Far East. It is, of course, differences in the external macro environments that makes international marketing so challenging and the extent of those differences will determine how much your strategy has to be adapted to meet local needs.

1.1 Industries and markets

Once you have defined the business you are in, you have the scope for your analysis and can establish the players within that industry and /or market – other competitors, intermediaries and suppliers.

There are two models that can help you build this overview:

- Porter's (1979) five forces model – which is an industry level analysis tool
- McDonald and Dunbar's (2004) market maps – which is a more granular, or magnified, approach for looking at individual markets within an industry.

1.1.1 Porter's five forces

Figure 2.1   Porter's five forces

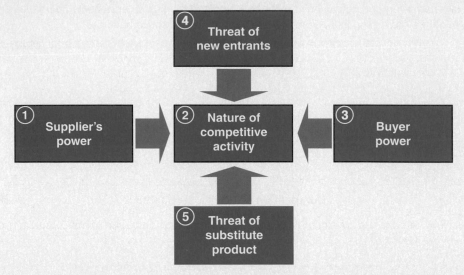

Michael Porter (1979) encouraged organisations to take a broad view of their markets, identifying the trends in five specific aspects of their industry. Note this is not simply about describing the current situation but forecasting changes in these aspects of the market activity. As you consider each of the five forces try and populate a model for your own industry. We return to this framework again in Chapter 6 when we cover changes in the competitive environment in more depth

1   **Supplier power** – consider how Intel used direct appeal to the end-user customer to change its power with computer manufacturers. The number and bargaining power of suppliers impacts on margins. What are the emerging trends in the supply side of your business activity?

2   **Nature of competitive activity** – how many competitors are there and how fierce is the competition between them – more significantly, how is that changing? Price wars and legislation can be the outcome if competitive activity becomes unbalanced. Governments tend not to approve of markets where there is limited competitive activity.

3   **Buyer power** – this is not just about purchasing power but also about knowledge and information. Over recent years customers across all sectors have become increasingly powerful.

4   **Threat of new entrants** – this is directly related to the barriers to entry and any trends that reduce or, indeed, raise these. New entrants may come from a new sector or new geography.

5   **Threat of substitute product** – this is often linked to new technologies and solutions being developed so trends in technical development need to be watched. Again remember substitutes are any other solution to the same customer problem and in some sectors a DIY option may be a competitor.

▶ **Assessment tip**

When using models like this, incorporate a traffic light system to help you identify where changes are happening and whether those changes are broadly good for your business or bad.

1.1.2 McDonald and Dunbar's market maps

Market maps are a development of Porter's five forces. Figure 2.2, below, is a simple illustration of the media competition for corporate advertising spend and it illustrates how different media owners are getting their solution to a specific market – corporate customers. You can see the additional detail – particularly in relation to competitive activity, and routes to market that this model offers when compared with the original five forces.

 The Chartered Institute of Marketing

Figure 2.2   Market map of media competition for corporate advertising spend

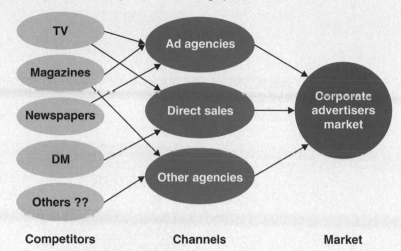

You can capture considerable amounts of information on a map like this, adding in revenues, the percentage of business going through different channels and which competitors are market leaders and followers.

McDonald and Dunbar (2004) provide a detailed overview of the theoretical and practical uses of market mapping. They look at how to define markets and have useful worksheets to help you work through your own mapping exercise.

2 Conducting a deeper analysis of macro-environmental factors

As we stated in Chapter 1, once you have established some facts about your market or industry, you need to analyse how changes to the macro-environment will affect this. We covered two initial steps in Chapter 1.

Step 1 involved identifying **drivers** and Step 2 identifying **key trends** through collection of both qualitative data in the form of market sensing and quantitative data from a range of sources. However, some environmental forces can be hard to predict so managers also need to be open to what Paul Schoemaker and George Day refer to as 'weak signals' (Schoemaker and Day, 2009). Step 3 of the process is therefore to identify **key uncertainties**. Combining the quantitative trend data and qualitative data with these uncertainties should be done based on a clear rationale in order to develop a series of scenarios. Step 4 is to develop some **rules of interaction** between the key forces you have identified. The simplest approach is often to consider what would happen in the worst and best case scenarios. Writing-up and sharing these scenarios with managers in the organisation and other relevant stakeholders is the final step in the process. These steps are outlined in more detail in the following sections:

- **Step 1** – Identify drivers of change   – 2.1
- **Step 2** – Identify key trends   – 2.2 – 3.2
- **Step 3** – Identify key uncertainties   – 4 – 5.1
- **Step 4** – Develop rules of interaction   – 5.2
- **Step 5** – Develop scenarios   – 5.2

Figure 2.3   Building blocks for scenarios

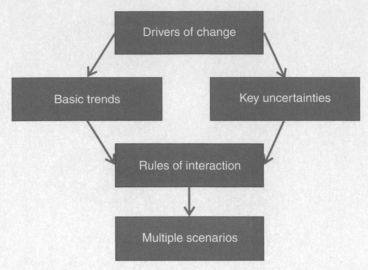

(Schoemaker, 1995)

2.1 Step 1 – identify key drivers

Start to build up a broad picture of the key drivers using your STEEPLE headings – do not worry about how these are changing at the moment, just consider what are the main factors that have or could influence the market in the future. These then become key factors for which you need to set up monitoring processes.

2.1.1 The market for confectionery and chocolate

The list below is a start at identifying the key drivers in a sector. We have chosen the confectionery market because it is one with which many people are familiar (you could probably add to the issues outlined).

Table 2.2   Key drivers identified in the confectionery market

Social and cultural	▪ Attitudes to health and obesity
	▪ Attitude to personal indulgences – the **'spoil yourself'** trend
	▪ The growth in connoisseur chocolate eating – a little, but high quality
Technological	▪ New methods of production – safer or longer shelf life, or 3D printing of food packaging
	▪ Added vitamins and minerals through mineral technology
Economic and demographic	▪ Demographic profile – chocolate is eaten more by women and the young
	▪ Disposable income levels
	▪ Pocket money trends
Environmental	▪ Issues related to the production of coco products
Political	▪ Pressure on the government to intervene – promoting healthy eating
Legal	▪ Legislation re packaging information and advertising to children
	▪ European legislation on use of the term 'chocolate'
	▪ Protecting brands from counterfeit products in some emerging economies
Ethical	▪ Fair trade
	▪ Pester power marketing
	▪ Encouraging excessive consumption – bigger bars and packets etc

The Chartered Institute of Marketing

Try and identify some of the key drivers in a market you are familiar with.

Social and cultural	
Technological	
Economic and demographic	
Environmental	
Political	
Legal	
Ethical	

2.2 Step 2 – Identify trends

▶ **Key term**

You can see that when you are looking at emerging themes you need to give some thought as to whether this is a **trend**, a **bend in a trend** or a **fad** because the strategic importance and implications differ.

Before we look at how you can collect information about the environment we need to consider whether forecasting and trend analysis have a place in such a fast moving world. This was the question addressed in a 2009 article in *Marketing Week* (Davies, 2009).

This article usefully differentiates between fads and trends. It is worth noting that even fads can generate opportunities and threats so still need to be identified and responded to. They may, however, be more difficult to predict and short-lived in terms of their impact on consumer behaviour.

- **Trends** are grounded in the fundamental forces shaping consumers' lives, capturing important shifts in consumer priorities. The Futures Company has identified Ten Global Energies it believes provide a comprehensive framework to explore the many ways in which consumer and brand behaviour is changing around the world and should have a significant shelf life. Two of these are 'Making a Difference' (the green agenda) and 'seeking Experiences' with customers shifting from demand for products and services to experiences. Such underlying trends are, according to The Futures Company, likely to survive despite the unexpected events of global financial crisis. You may be seeking more cost effective experiences if spending is cut, but your expectations are already established by the trend.

- However, **fads** come and go within weeks or months.

- **A bend in the trend?** Ged Davis, formerly Head of Scenario Planning at Royal Dutch/Shell is quoted by Davies (2009) in the *Marketing Week* article. '**a trend is a trend is a trend, until it bends**'. It is the bends in the trends that may prove to be the most interesting.

Companies that focus their resources on detecting and acting on these 'bends' will be better placed than those who hastily tear up and rewrite their strategies. Abandoning what we understood from the past will not help. Being open, sensitive and responsive to change will determine success.

Mintel is forecasting a more entropic society as you can see from the extract below:

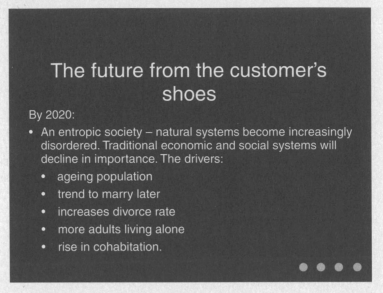

The future from the customer's shoes

By 2020:

- An entropic society – natural systems become increasingly disordered. Traditional economic and social systems will decline in importance. The drivers:
  - ageing population
  - trend to marry later
  - increases divorce rate
  - more adults living alone
  - rise in cohabitation.

Take a few minutes to consider the trend towards a more entropic society.

Take **two sectors** you are familiar with and consider the implications of the underlying trends. Choose which sectors you want but you will find feedback on Social Services and house-building at the end of this section.

Note: at this level, the Examiners are interested in your ability to use a longer time-frame when forecasting, and your ability to consider the impact at sector, not just at organisational, level.

Identifying trends starts with you having a sense of the market. What is happening today?

3 Collecting environmental information

Given the potential impact of environmental change on your business performance it is easy to appreciate why businesses ought to be organising themselves to monitor and anticipate sector changes, be they new trends, bends or fads.

In practice, few organisations pay as much heed to external monitoring as they do to internal analysis. Those with an external monitoring brief are often scattered across the business. You can find them in business intelligence, corporate planning, research and development and library functions. They are often frustrated by the apparent lack of pro-activity and interest from marketing planners about '**tomorrow's world**'.

There are, however, a number of methods for collecting environmental information and you may be able to utilise a number of them for your business and CIM assignment.

▶ **Assessment tip**

It is a good idea for you to try to use the following tools to assess your own organisation at the earliest possible opportunity. Once you have your assignment, you will then be in a prime position to start work promptly because you will be aware of the issues of most relevance to your market.

3.1 Market sensing

Market sensing is an approach to monitoring environmental change. It is a technique you already use and, indeed, may be quite expert in, without even recognising it as a technique. It is likely to be particularly useful in establishing emerging trends in your own market.

Market sensing is the result of your own observations and experiences in a market and environment you are familiar with. For example, over the last five years in the UK you would have a 'sense of' the increasing concern over obesity in children, the growing 'hostility' towards smokers and the increased interest in governance issues, bankers' pay or politicians' expenses. You will also recognise the '**feel the pinch**' effect of the emerging trend of '**back to basics**'.

Your sense of these and similar trends and themes comes simply from reading the papers, talking to friends, observing the behaviour of others.

The result of this '**market sense**' is that if I were to suggest a new business idea – perhaps a pre packaged 'at home spa break' or to take advantage of the demand for 'staycations' – (staying at home+vacations: economy driven experiences) you would have a '**sense**' of whether this may be an idea worth exploring further.

THE REAL WORLD

UK retail giant Marks and Spencer has a team of 27 trend-hunters who travel the world looking for the next 'big thing' in food. One of the best sources of inspiration for the team is the trends found in New York City. The combination of arts innovation and wealthy individuals has attracted creative chefs and food producers for generations. The team sample foods but also use their experience in the field to pick the new tastes and products that will appear on M&S's shelves.

However, whether a product makes it into the firm's shops is not just based on the team liking it. The trend-hunters also conduct continuous market research with M&S's customers and also take into consideration practical issues such as storage and the overall cost of sourcing and transporting the product.

The team's hot tips for 2011 included a wider range of flavoured popcorns, to move the product into the adult market in a big way; jellies were another product predicted to move from children's parties to having a wider appeal. Small versions of sweet desserts have become a trend for home consumption having seen significant growth in the restaurant business over the last few years.

(McDonald, 2011)

3.2 Industry level sensing

'**Sensing**' activity takes place at different levels. The manager who has worked in the sector for 20 years has a real 'sense' of the industry. What can look like 'gut feel' pronouncements may, in fact, be quite well-honed sensing skills at work.

If you work in pharmaceuticals you will probably be aware of changes in the NHS approach to procurement, have a sense of changing clinical priorities and how major works like The Darzi Review (2008) are influencing the organisation of healthcare. In this sector, the pathway's themes may become an established trend, or a change of government policy could leave it as a short-lived fad.

Note: The Darzi Review was a 10 year plan put forward by UK Government Health Minister, Lord Darzi in 2008. The review consisted of a series of reports which focused on patients' experience of the National Health Service and the quality of care being offered by hospitals and GP practices. The review covered everything from doctors' training to the length of time it takes to license medicines for use in the UK. The reforms proposed in the review have already had a significant impact on organisations in the health sector in the UK.

In some companies, specialist researchers may be briefed to monitor the various sources of industry information, attending events, seminars etc, to formalise the 'industry sense'.

Alternatively, you may informally provide feedback mechanisms and briefings to encourage your sales teams and client-facing staff to act as company '**streetscapers**'.

4 Trend analysis and adding key uncertainties to the mix

Whereas '**sensing**' may start off as broadly qualitative and based on observation, trend analysis adds to it the qualification and evidence of a pattern over time.

- The climate is getting warmer and summers are wetter with average temperature changes of *x* and rainfall of *y* compared with 10 years, 50 years or 100 years ago

- People are spending considerably more of their incomes per annum on entertainment. There is a trend for people to marry later, with the average age having risen from *x* to *y*.

The problems with trend analysis occur if you simply assume that the trend will continue with no bends. Trends have a life cycle so the pace at which a trend is happening can change, indeed the trends may cease.

Trends can be identified from your own internal sales and customer data.

- For example, a trend to sell more eco-friendly models.

Increasingly, external analysts and specialists are used:

- Organisations like The Futures Company, The Future Foundation, Faith Popcorn's Brain Reserve and Mintel provide trend reports and there are briefings services such as *U talk Marketing* and, of course, CIM White papers.

▶ **Assessment tip**

The challenge for you is to review some of the key sources of trend data available and choose those most relevant, accurate and reliable. Remember to keep focused on your market. There may be plenty of interesting information about 16-25 year olds but if your target audience is the over-60s you need reports that focus on the '**greys**'. You will not be short of data but you could end up swamped by it, if you are not clear about your scope and area of interest.

4.1 Expert forecasts

Because tomorrow may be very different from today, those trends may indeed bend. You need to take a fresh look at tomorrow's markets and what they may look like.

Forecasters in their various guises are '**experts**'. They may be experts in the industry, some aspect of the technology development or the customer. Their expertise gives them added credibility when they consider the 'picture' shape of the market or evolving customer behaviour.

An expert would be someone like Bill Gates. His forecasts about the intelligent house of the future are worth listening to.

Experts can often be heard at industry events, or they may be academics, publishing research papers and writing articles. Their views are, however, the views of individuals and so should be taken into consideration alongside other sources of information.

4.2 Jury forecasts

Jury forecasts are generated by a group of people who usually have knowledge, or experience of the sector or market. It could be as simple as your own management team pooling ideas and insights about changes in the marketplace.

Alternatively, you could convene a jury specifically to review and discuss this topic. You may choose representatives or suppliers and customers as well as your own team. Well-convened group discussions like this can generate considerable output and jurors can come to a consensus view about many issues.

ACTIVITY 2.4

You may like to try this yourself. Set up a '**jury**' at work, drawn from colleagues, or at home with friends and family. If you do not want to focus on your own market set an agenda others can contribute to. The changing market for out-of-home entertainment, or future trends in healthy lifestyles are possible topics.

What are the emerging themes?

The problems with the jury forecast include:

- Having to get a group of people together at a specific time.

- The potential for one person to dominate and bias the group view.

- The danger of '**group think**'. Because individuals are not responsible for the outputs, the group becomes rather more radical in its views than the individuals would be.

4.3 Delphi Oracle

The Delphi Oracle addresses some of the shortcomings of jury forecasts. This method allows you to select a diverse group of 'experts' who never meet, and so can come from different locations and sectors, disciplines or backgrounds. It usually utilises a number of stages.

Stage 1   This group agrees to take part in the process.

Stage 2   Each is sent a questionnaire with open questions that prompt participants to consider aspects of the future nature of markets and customer behaviour.

Stage 3   The results are consolidated and sent out to those involved, who are invited to comment, elaborate or amend their responses in light of the collective opinion. This stage can go on for a number of 'rounds' as the group moves towards a broad consensus.

Because they do not meet, a Delphi Oracle group does not get easily dominated and individually take responsibility for their responses.

4.3.1 What the experts say

Management guru Gary Hamel is dismissive of any notion of forecasting. He points out that organisations can very easily fall into the trap of coming to a single view of how the future will be and then planning for that single future. When things do not pan out as forecast the strategy fails.

Instead, Hamel (2000) talks of organisations developing **foresight** – the notion of trying to look ahead, being alert, but not kidding themselves they can see the future.

In agreement with Arie de Geus (1997) (formerly planning director at Royal Dutch Shell), Hamel (2000) promotes the benefits of scenario planning.

Scenarios are set up, based on alternative views of the future: what if this happens or what if that happened?

Figure 2.4 summarises the associated process.

Figure 2.4   Scenario planning

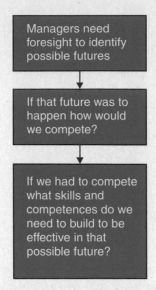

Managers need foresight to identify possible futures

↓

If that future was to happen how would we compete?

↓

If we had to compete what skills and competences do we need to build to be effective in that possible future?

Paul Schoemaker of Wharton School of Business, at the University of Pennsylvania, is also critical of only relying on a single view of the future. His advice, in an article written with George Day (2009), is to build on sensing and market intelligence by looking outside your industry and actively searching for potential problems and issues. However, managers should avoid turning this data into a single view of the future and a much stronger way of making use of trend analysis, forecasts and key uncertainties is to construct multiple, but separate narratives about the future. This is one way of overcoming the groupthink issues that can arise from techniques such as Jury forecasts. Encouraging disagreement about the future is a positive element of the process, as it can encourage managers to keep an open mind.

> ▶ **Assessment tip**
>
> The Examiners are looking for a critical discussion of the emerging theme you identify – so it is important to consider different potential views of how the theme will impact on your industry or market. Relying on a single source, or adopting a single view, of how the emerging theme will change the industry is unlikely to lead to a good paper. A good critical discussion will examine a number of possible outcomes and come to a clear conclusion, after a robust debate.

4.3.2 Futurology

> ▶ **Key term**
>
> So what is **futurology**?
>
> It is both an art and a science and some companies are taking it very seriously. It is based on putting forward possible and probable views of the future – it works with the patterns from trend analysis but also incorporates expert understanding and technology insights.

Finally, in our list of methods for considering the future there is *futurology*. A number of organisations, particularly in fast moving technology-based sectors, employ futurologists.

The Chartered Institute of Marketing

5 Making sense of the changes – mitigating risks and scenario planning

Once you have completed your environmental analysis, you need to 'sort' the factors identified.

You need to treat opportunities and threats differently to avoid confusing them later.

For each category and factor, you need to consider the:

- Likelihood that it will happen
- Significance to the business if it does

5.1 Risk matrix

Figure 2.5   Risk matrix

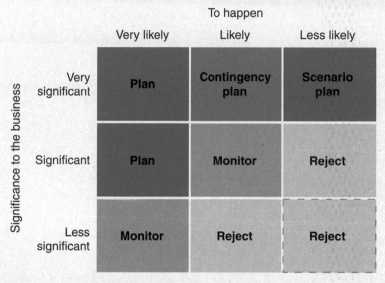

Produce separate **opportunity and threat risk matrices** and use these to help you identify those that you must build into your plan.

- **Plan for the 'likely'** or that which will probably have a significant impact

- Factors which would be significant to your forecast, but are not confirmed events, require **contingency plans**. You are already an expert contingency planner – it is a normal approach to planning If it is likely to be a nice day and you are having friends round you might plan to have a barbecue. The weather is, of course, a very significant factor in this decision, so you may have a contingency plan in case there is an unexpected rainstorm.

The unlikely, but significant, factors can be the focus of **scenario plans** – 'what would we do if?' As individuals, many of us have scenario plans in case we win the Pools or the National Lottery – unlikely, but it would have a significant impact on our lives. Some organisations have followed the lead of Shell, which developed scenario planning as a technique for improving planning skills amongst its managers.

> ▶ **Key term**
>
> **Scenario planning** is the development of plausible alternative futures in narrative form. It is different from forecasting, which extrapolates historical data. Scenario planning also includes the potential interactions between different elements of the macro-environment. For example, it allows marketers to plan for the impact that technological change might have on economic or socio-cultural factors. Scenario planning is normally used to test strategies rather than there being a blank canvas.

5.2 Interactions between key factors in the environment and developing scenarios

In order to develop a range of scenarios, planners will usually take a limited number of key factors (usually no more than two or three) and consider what might happen in the event of an extreme outcome. So, in an unpredictable economic environment, the impact of boom and of bust will be considered as part of the process of developing different scenarios. For some industries, a combination of extreme events can be used to develop several scenarios which are then used by firms to develop 'real options' to protect themselves against a number of options.

Scenario planning is particularly useful when addressing the question of emerging themes. They allow you the opportunity to consider not just a single forecast future but a number of alternative futures and so assess the implications and potential impact on your industry and sector and how an individual organisation might need to respond if it is to compete effectively.

THE REAL WORLD

The Austrian Tourist Agency developed a range of scenarios predicting the state of the market in 2015 with local ski-based businesses. By considering the impact of technological, social, economic and environmental changes it came up with four possible narratives:

'Good-bye snow': was one extreme scenario, which predicted that the loss of ski destinations due to climate change would transform the industry to one of exclusive, high-priced offerings.

'Heaven and Hell': economic polarisation between rich and poor would mean that demand would also polarise for high-end exclusive holidays and no-frills package offerings. Climate change would not have a significant impact on the number of viable ski-resorts in Austria.

'Ecological winter breaks': changes in social trends and environmental taxes would mean potential customers would come from neighbouring countries and be looking for environmentally sound holidays.

'Ski, snow and more': the use of technology would improve the tourist experience through use of virtual skiing and easy booking of holidays via the internet. Social changes would mean that visitors would combine skiing with a range of other activities.'

(Mittringer, 2011)

ACTIVITY 2.5

The changing pattern of higher education

Read the article 'End of empire for Western Universities' by Sean Coughlan on the BBC News website:

http://www.bbc.co.uk/news/business-18646423

What do you think are the other significant factors that university marketers should take into account when analysing their environment?

Choose two of these – and combining with the social/demographic trend outlined in the article – develop a range of brief scenarios – some with potentially positive outcomes for Western Universities and some more negative.

The Chartered Institute of Marketing

CHAPTER ROUNDUP

- In order to put key trends into context managers need first to identify the industry their organisation operates in and/or the markets the organisation serves.

- Porter's Five Forces Framework and McDonald and Dunbar's market maps provide a useful starting point.

- Once the industry or market has been defined managers can begin to conduct a deeper analysis of macro-environmental factors which affect their sector.

- This can be started by prioritising the STEEPLE factors identified in the activities in Chapter 1.

- However, in order to take into account dynamism in the environment, managers also need to collect information on key trends.

- Environmental information to support this kind of analysis can come from multiple techniques, including market and industry level sensing.

- In some sectors where it is harder to predict the future, key uncertainties need to be identified and analysed. Firms can use the services of experts, using jury forecasts and the Delphi technique or even futurology.

- In order to create a coherent narrative, drivers, trends and uncertainties can be synthesised through the development of rules of interaction and turned into a range of scenarios. Managers can use these to mitigate risks and consider an alternative range of futures rather than a single forecast.

FURTHER READING

Cornelius, P. *et al* (2005) Three decades of scenario planning in Shell. *California Management Review,* Vol48(1), pp42-109.

Coughlan, S. (2012) End of empire for Western universities? BBC, http://www.bbc.co.uk/news/business-18646423

Faith Popcorn's Brain Reserve, http://www.faithpopcorn.com/#home

For more details on scenario planning see: Schoemaker, P. (1995) Scenario Planning: a tool for strategic thinking, *Sloan Management Review*, Vol36(2), pp25-40, and Schoemaker, P. and Day, G. (2009) Why we miss the signs, *MIT Sloan Management Review*, Vol50(2), pp43-44.

Future Foundation, http://www.futurefoundation.net/

REFERENCES

Davies, S. (2009) Interpreting trends. *Marketing Week,* 20 February, London.

de Geus, A. (1997) *The Living Company*. Harvard, Harvard Business School Press.

Hamel, G. (2000) *Leading the Revolution.* Harvard, Harvard Business School Press.

McDonald, L. (2011) The tastemakers; how do food stores stay one step ahead of the trends. *i-Independent*, 20 January, p32.

McDonald, M. and Dunbar, I. (2004) *Market segmentation: how to do it – how to profit from it*. Oxford, Elsevier.

Mittringer, R. (2011) Austrian tourism 2015. EFMN, http://www.foresight-network.eu/index.php?option=com_docman&task=doc_view&gid=52 [Accessed 30 July 2012]

Porter, M. (1979) How competitive forces shape strategy, *Harvard Business Review.*

Porter, M. (1980) *Competitive advantage.* New York, Free Press.

Schoemaker, P. (1995) Scenario planning: a tool for strategic thinking, *Sloan Management Review*, Vol36(2) pp 25-40.

Schoemaker, P. and Day, G. (2009) Why we miss the signs, *MIT Sloan Management Review*, Vol50(2), pp 43-44.

ACTIVITY DEBRIEFS

Activity 2.1

Firm	They are in the business of:	They might be competing with:
1 An airline providing internal flights	Transporting people and goods over medium distances, quickly and safely	Railways, cars and video conferencing
2 A manufacturer of plastic carrier bags	Providing disposable and cheap solutions for packaging and transporting goods	Natural fibre bags and reusable carrier bags, boxes and alternative packaging
3 A take away pizza restaurant	Providing customers with the option of not cooking	Restaurants, other take away food providers and 'easy to make' pre-prepared food dishes
4 Your local doctor	Keeping you well and, if sick, helping you recover quickly	Alternative therapists and DIY or over the counter remedies as well as the temptations that might discourage you from a healthy lifestyle
5 The finance team in your organisation	Providing managers with accurate and timely financial analysis and information to support improved decision making	Gut feel decisions and DIY financial analysis
6 Your own business/organisation	(remember what benefits to whom)	

Activity 2.2

Your answer will depend on your own organisation.

The Chartered Institute of Marketing

Activity 2.3

An example of two sectors is shown below. Your answer may depend on the industries you chose.

Social services	House-building
Greater demand for services to support both the elderly and children from broken homes or living with single parents	Demand for features that support independent living for longer – wheelchair access and technology to aid everyday tasks
New methods of social support needed – communities and virtual support groups to keep costs low	Flexible property units to allow additional modules to be added as family sizes change – older children staying or returning home and single parents cohabiting and merging families
Less obvious authority sources may mean social unrest, crime and threats to the officers of the public sector increase	Greater interest in security features and community spaces to deal with isolation problems
More 'nannying' culture as the State tries to fill in the gaps left by the breakdown of more traditional family networks	

Activity 2.4

Your answer will depend on both the trend you are considering and also the make-up of the 'jury'.

Activity 2.5

You could choose any of the following:

- Increase in fee levels in UK HE from September 2012

- Changes in visa regulations making it harder for non-EU students to enter the UK and work after studying

- Slowing economic growth in India and China affecting the demand for HE overseas

- Availability of high quality online alternatives to Higher Education developing due to changes in technology

- Legal changes in the UK to allow more private colleges to apply for degree-awarding powers

- Concerns about the sustainability of travelling long distances to study abroad (carbon footprint etc)

The final set of scenarios you develop will depend on your choice of factors. Remember, you should explore extremes in each case – if, for example, you chose the increase in fees in the UK as one of your factors at one extreme you might consider that this would make very little difference to most UK universities and that students would continue to apply and take places at undergraduate level. On the other hand, it could lead to a dramatic fall in the number of applicants overall and pull new entrants into the UK market from other countries where undergraduate study is taught in English and still free or cheap relative to the UK – for example, the Netherlands and Sweden.

Once you have plotted this against the social cultural changes in the BBC news item, you should be able to develop four scenarios based on the two sets of extremes. If a marketer in the HE sector was thinking about how to respond to one of the changes in the environment, testing their strategy against each scenario would give them some idea what might work and what moves they would need to make, early in the process, to ensure they kept their options open.

The Chartered Institute of Marketing

CHAPTER 3

Macro-environment, political, ethical and economic factors

Introduction

This chapter, together with Chapter 4, is intended to give you an introduction to some of the key changes and emerging themes at macro level. As you have already seen, not all changes impact on all sectors or do so in the same way or to the same extent. The coverage of macro trends cannot be exhaustive but we examined one or two trends and changes in each of the core macro-environmental areas.

Topic list

Politics and the law   ①

Ethics   ②

Contemporary economic opportunities and challenges   ③

Syllabus references

1.1	Critically evaluate macro-environmental emerging themes and assess/forecast their potential impact upon one specific sector or industry:

- Changes in political governance systems and political focus
- Contemporary economic opportunities/challenges
- Social change (at local and global levels)
- Emerging technologies
- Environmental challenges
- Methods of forecasting/predicting change

1 Politics and the law

You might like to create your own 'maps' of the key themes emerging from each of the macro level areas covered in this chapter and the next – we have started one for politics and the law.

Figure 3.1   Political and legal emerging themes

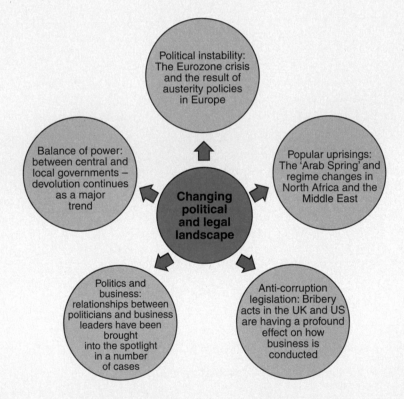

The Chartered Institute of Marketing

1.1 Relationships between politics and business

In 2009 the *Daily Telegraph* in the UK revealed the extent of the abuse of the expenses and allowances system operated for UK politicians. As the revelations became more wide-ranging the reputation of politicians as a whole appeared to reach an all time low. However, this was before the *News of the World* scandal broke in spring and summer 2011, with allegations made against some of the government's closest advisors, including the Prime Minister's former Director of Communications, Andy Coulson. The scandal centred on allegations that various staff employed by the newspaper had been involved in illegal phone hacking. Coulson was editor at the *News of the World* from 2003 to 2007 when he resigned following the conviction of one of the newspaper's reporters for illegal phone hacking. Coulson subsequently joined David Cameron's personnel until 21.01.2011, leaving his post due to the continued media coverage of the phone hacking scandal.

The Leveson inquiry and subsequent media reports also revealed how close some News International executives had been to members of the government when they were in opposition. The nature of the relationship between the business elite and politicians was further highlighted by a *Sunday Times* undercover operation, which revealed that the UK's Conservative Party former treasurer, Peter Cruddas, claimed he could arrange a private dinner between the Prime Minister and anyone willing to make a £250,000 donation to the party. The cash for access scandal is a further blow to politicians' efforts to rebuild their reputation with the public.

ACTIVITY 3.1

Take a few minutes to consider how the issue of politicians' behaviour is being played out today. Has it escalated and is starting to become an emerging theme or has it faded into yesterday's news?

If you are studying in a non-UK centre, consider similar themes within your current country of residence.

1.2 Changing political climate

While events such as those outlined above can clearly change attitudes, political climates alter with transitions in political leadership. Around the world there are regular changes in leadership in many countries. With those changes come new attitudes to international trade and relations, economic policy and local legislation. As a marketer working in the global marketplace you need to keep checking for adjustments in political climate.

How, for example, might the following political developments influence business in the coming years?

May 2012 François Hollande is elected President of France

Hollande is the first socialist to be elected as President of France since Mitterand in the 1980s. The parliamentary elections, which took place in June 2012 confirmed the country's shift to the left. The changes are likely to affect France's relationship with Germany and other European neighbours.

Change to the top leadership in China at the end of 2012

Seven of the nine members of the Chinese communist party's Politburo Standing Committee are due to retire at the end of 2012, so there will a new group of politicians leading the superpower in the New Year. However, their selection won't be decided by popular election, but through unknown processes by the senior party leaders, acting in secret. The make-up of the new leadership could have a profound effect on the world economy, the way business is conducted in China and the relations between it and other major powers, such as the US.

US presidential election in 2012

Americans will be electing a new president at the end of 2012. Whether they will stick with the liberal policies of Barack Obama, whose presidency appears to have failed to live up to its early promise, or vote in his Republican rival, Mitt Romney, remains to be seen. Whoever is in the Whitehouse for the next four years, there

will be alterations to US policy, especially given the continuing poor state of the economy and the high levels of unemployment.

1.3 Devolution changes political landscape

> ▶ **Key term**
>
> **Devolution** is the statutory granting of powers from the central government of a State to government at a subnational level, such as a regional, local, or State level. It differs from federalism in that the powers devolved may be temporary and ultimately reside in central government, thus the State remains, *de jure*, unitary.
>
> Any devolved parliaments or assemblies can be abolished by central government in the same way an ordinary statute can be repealed. Federal systems, or federacies, differ in that state or provincial government is guaranteed in the constitution. Australia, Canada and the United States have federal systems, and have constitutions (as do some of their constituent states or provinces). They also have Territories, with less power and authority than a state or province.
>
> The devolution can be mainly financial, eg, giving areas a budget that was formerly administered by central government. However, the power to make legislation relevant to the area may also be granted.

Key points about devolution in the UK

- Devolution has been relatively successful and popular in Wales and Scotland. The English seem content with continued, centralised government from Westminster and have not been persuaded of the benefits of regional government (with the exception of the Greater London Authority (GLA) in London where a similar model of regional government is now well-established, currently under the leadership of Boris Johnson as Mayor). There is a significant basis of support for devolution among citizens in both Protestant and Catholic communities in Northern Ireland – including Sinn Fein and Democratic Unionist Party (DUP) voters – though political elites there have shown little inclination, as yet, to respond to that support and make devolution work. However, the government has continued to decentralise administrative functions to appointed bodies in the regions. The growth of **'administrative governance'** has brought with it currently unresolved problems of accountability, duplication and inefficiency. This is because decentralisation of buying technically reduces buyer power, making it easier for suppliers to regional bodies and government to negotiate better deals.

- According to the UK's Economic and Social Research Council (ESCR) there is little evidence to suggest that an **'economic dividend'** should be expected from devolution, or has yet appeared. Devolution – even administrative devolution in England – appears to lead to a widening of regional economic disparities. The UK government only has limited ability to intervene to secure UK-wide economic balance.

- For companies trying to operate at a national level, devolution can make sales and marketing more difficult with variations in purchasing behaviours and protocols at regional level.

- According to the work on devolution undertaken by ESRC there has been surprisingly little conflict between the devolved administrations, central government and Westminster so far. There has been innovation and divergence of priorities and actions but little sharing and 'learning' across the authorities.

- The main reasons for this period of calm were temporary:

  - Labour's role as the leading partner in government in Westminster, Scotland and Wales;

  - A general growth in public expenditure which has limited distributional conflicts.

The Chartered Institute of Marketing

The election of a Conservative / Liberal Democrat coalition in May 2010 and the clamp down on public spending that is currently taking place is likely to cause many more disputes and mechanisms to handle these will be key.

1.4 The implications of changing political attitudes, climate or systems

The implications of big changes like devolution are felt at sector level. Decentralisation of decision-making becomes a theme which is reflected across health, education and other public service areas. Each of these changes will impact on organisations trying to provide services and support to public sector customers.

At a local level, changes in political attitudes can affect local government decisions including planning decisions. How the green belt is used, permission for road improvement schemes negotiated and new developments approved impact on many different sectors. One of the Coalition's initiatives is to allow local people to have far more say in planning decisions in their own communities.

You may be interested in reading the environment blog from *The Guardian* (UK) correspondent Adam Vaughan, which outlines the issues the new planning rules are likely to produce:

http://www.guardian.co.uk/environment/blog/2012/mar/27/planning-system-reforms-live-coverage

1.5 The Eurozone crisis and political instability in Europe

One of the key impacts of the crisis has been to create a great deal of political uncertainty in Europe. Events throughout the latter part of 2011 and 2012 have seen changes of government in countries at the heart of the crisis, such as Greece and Italy. Political parties whose manifestos have supported austerity measures, favoured by the German government, have found that this does not translate into electoral success. There is further uncertainty around whether all the current members of the Eurozone will retain the single currency. All this has a profound impact on the firms doing business in some of the Eurozone countries. Whether it is currency risk, or fear of rioting citizens, some firms may well decide that business in European States with problems is not worth pursuing, or that the terms on which that business is agreed are much tougher than in the past.

The crisis in the Eurozone is having an impact on banks and their willingness to lend to businesses and to individuals. Added to the credit crunch and the recession, this is likely to have far-reaching effects on a number of industries. For example, the lack of credit and difficulties for first time buyers in securing mortgages, affects not only the construction industry, but also estate agents, DIY chain stores, furniture manufacturers, and a whole range of other sectors that focus on this segment of the market. The cost of investment products, such as Government bonds will have an impact on the pensions industry as those offered by more stable governments become more expensive. (Peachey, K. 2012.)

The Senior Examiner has recommended a series of articles from *The Economist* magazine which provide a good explanation of the crisis and options for the future of the single currency. These can be found in *The Economist*'s three-part briefing on the Euro Crisis, May 12, 19 and 26 2012.

1.6 Popular uprisings: The Arab Spring

Although the causes of the popular uprisings in North Africa and the Middle East are complex and contentious, the first country to topple its leader was Tunisia, in January 2011, when Ben Ali fled the country. This was closely followed by the resignation of President Hosni Mubarak in Egypt. The Libyan revolution to remove Colonel Gaddafi was a longer, bloodier conflict and only ended after the death of the dictator. Other States have seen unrest but not changes in government. In Oman, Jordan and Bahrain there have been protests but, as yet, no full scale revolution. Syria is the most recent country to descend into civil war in July 2012.

The Arab Spring has produced a range of different outcomes, from a more Islamist regime in Tunisia to the first free presidential elections in Egypt. The results of the uprising will have a profound impact on business, whether it is through the adoption of Islamic structures and systems, such as Sharia Law, specific banking

rules concerning lending and borrowing, or increased levels of danger for doing business in countries because of the numbers of armed militias.

THE REAL WORLD

The Arab Spring has had a significant impact on the business community as well as on the balance of power in the region. The changes have produced a growth in the number of new ventures and highlighted some of the successful firms already operating in North Africa and the Middle East. Online start-ups such as Cinemoz in the Lebanon and Diwanee in Dubai are both focused on providing internet content for Arabic speakers. Other more established firms like Emirates airline and GEMS, an education company, are longer established and have customers around the world.

Other firms have found the political changes a threat rather than an opportunity. Travel agent Thomas Cook's recent poor performance has, in part, been blamed on the problems it encountered operating in Tunisia and Egypt during both countries' uprisings. Thomas Cook has recently been forced to sell its Spanish hotel subsidiary HVC to help repay its debts.

(Schumpeter, 2012; BBC, 2012)

1.7 The legal environment

The political climate will influence the priorities around new legislation but they are separate dimensions of the PEST environment. It is also important to remember that legislative changes can be generated at EU as well as Westminster level so a good environmental observer will be watching for emerging themes in the broader European context.

ACTIVITY 3.2

Legal changes that have had an impact

Take a few minutes to think about legal changes that have had an impact on specific sectors, consumer behaviour or marketing activity recently. Try to identify five examples from your own sector or broader business.

Your list will inevitably be different from ours but you can make the comparison at the end of the chapter.

THE REAL WORLD

The introduction of the Bribery Act, in July 2011, updated and extended the law on bribery and corruption in business and public life. The Act will have a profound effect on the way organisations do business both at home and abroad. The Act also covers foreign companies if they have any business operations in the UK.

Individuals and organisations are covered by the Bribery Act and the penalties are more severe than previous legislation with up to ten years in prison and unlimited fines being two of the sanctions available to UK courts. Although most corporate hospitality is not deemed illegal under the Act, previously common practices in some countries, such as facilitation payments, are outlawed. Companies are also responsible for developing systems to ensure bribery does not occur in their business dealings. The Act will mean Marketers and Senior Managers, particularly those involved in sales and business development may need to change the level and manner of control they exert on the sales force as well as training staff within the organisation about what is legal under the new legislation.

1.8 Marketing and the law

Legal issues have a direct influence on how we as marketers do our job. According to CIM's Hot Topic Paper **No Marketer is an Island: Marketing and the Law** (2006) there is no doubt that marketers face increasingly

restrictive legislation. Heavy-handed bills are regularly placed before governments in the UK, the US and further afield. Marketers face confusion over the number of laws, regulations and codes that they have to know about. Increasingly, marketers even need to know about laws that have been passed elsewhere in the world.

The days of *laissez-faire* marketing are long gone. We must work out how to market our products and services fairly and effectively. Since ignorance of the law is no defence, marketing teams need to be proactive in self-regulation in order to avoid brand damage and costly legal proceedings should they make a mistake.

ACTIVITY 3.3

Visit CIM's website and read its papers:

No Marketer is an Island: Marketing and the Law which considers how best to tackle such legal compliance.

The Long Arm of the Law. Marketers and Legislation asks marketers to question what they know, consider whether their legal compliance is all it should be – and think hard about the implications for the future.

---

2 Ethics

2.1 An overview of current ethical issues

As we have seen above, there is a growing trend to use legislation to ensure organisations behave in an ethical manner in their business dealings. Companies adopting a triple bottom line (Elkington, 1997) approach to measuring performance are increasingly conscious of the social impact of their activities as well as the economic and environmental. Figure 3.2, below, is a map of some of the current ethical issues facing organisations.

Figure 3.2   Current ethical issues facing organisations

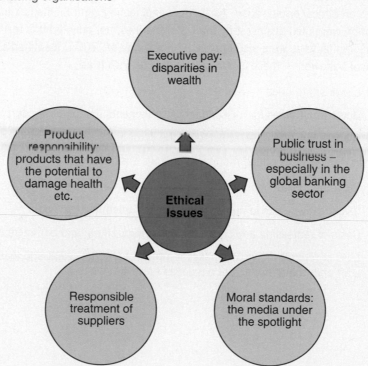

2.2 Business ethics

'Business ethics is the application of ethical values to business behaviour. It applies to any and all aspects of business conduct, from boardroom strategies and how companies treat their employees and suppliers to sales techniques and accounting practices. Ethics goes beyond the legal requirements for a company and is, therefore, about discretionary decisions and behaviour guided by values. Business ethics is relevant both to the conduct of individuals and to the conduct of the organisation as a whole.' (IBE, 2012)

2.3 Losing trust

One of the most important ways in which ethical issues impact on business is when consumers and customers lose trust in the firms they deal with. Nowhere is this more evident than in the banking sector. As we will see below, the LIBOR scandal is another major issue for banks to deal with, if they are going to rehabilitate their image with the public, following the credit crunch. As we saw above, the media has also come in for its share of criticism and the revelations from the *News of the World* affair and, more recently, the Leveson Inquiry have shown that some companies do not adhere to the ethical standards expected of them.

However, if good business is ethical business, it would make sense for all organisations to adopt an ethical approach to their operations. In Europe and North America, there are robust legal systems to provide redress if, for example, a firm's patents are infringed. This is not always the case in other parts of the world. There are also cultural issues to consider. Islamic banking operates under very different rules, in some Middle Eastern countries, bankruptcy is a criminal offence. There are also cultures where corporate hospitality is very different in nature to that of the UK or Western Europe. Scandinavian countries are amongst the least corrupt, with North Korea, Somalia, Myanmar and Afghanistan amongst the most corrupt according to Transparency International (2011).

2.3.1 The impact of unethical behaviour

Marketers need to consider the obvious and hidden costs of unethical behaviour as well as the benefits of being seen as an ethical organisation. As German engineering giant Siemens found after allegations of bribery and corruption were filed against it by the US authorities, not only did this result in the loss of key senior personnel, but substantial fines were also imposed. Thomas, *et al* (2004) identified a range of costs associated with unethical behaviour – these included tangible costs such as:

- Lower share price

- Government fines for misconduct or settlements made out of court

- Class actions by those affected by the company's actions and other legal costs

However, they also identified many less obvious costs which took time to come to the fore, including:

- Customer defections

- Investigative costs to pursue allegations of unethical behaviour

- Costs of redressing any problems, including training and administrative expenditure

- Loss of reputation, which makes it difficult to recruit talent and leads to lower morale amongst existing staff and, therefore, higher employee turnover.

 The Chartered Institute of Marketing

THE REAL WORLD

Recent events in the US and UK have further dented the public's trust in the banks and the banking system. On 27 June 2012, one of the biggest UK banking brands, Barclays, publicly admitted that its traders were involved in misconduct in the calculations of the LIBOR lending rate. LIBOR, the London Inter-Bank Offered Rate, underpins lending rates and trillions of pounds of loans and financial contracts. The knowledge that bank staff had been rigging the rate marked a new low in the reputation of the banks.

For Barclays, the fallout from the scandal has been wide-ranging. The bank was fined £290 million by US and UK government agencies and shortly after the revelations, both its Chairman, Marcus Agius and high profile CEO, Bob Diamond, resigned. As the scandal gathered pace, it soon became clear that Barclays traders had not acted alone. Royal Bank of Scotland sacked four of its staff for their alleged involvement in rate-fixing and, according to the Financial Services Authority investigation, the activity between traders had been going on since 2005.

The LIBOR scandal has had an impact on all banks, as it will mean the regulators take a much tougher stance on rules. For those involved in the rate-fixing, it is likely they will face ongoing lawsuits in the US from investors, including hedge and pension funds, who believe they have lost out. However, the LIBOR scandal and the credit crunch have not been bad for all financial institutions. Those banks that have based their strategy on transparency and an ethical stance have benefited from the public's disenchantment with the high street lenders. The Charity Bank has reported a 200% increase in new customers during 2012. Other providers of financial services which cut out banks altogether, such as peer-to-peer lending sites like Zopa has now lent more than £200 million since it started in 2005.

(BBC, 2012)

3 Contemporary economic opportunities and challenges

3.1 An economic overview

The following overview of the key economic changes is a little light on opportunities. The near collapse of the international banking system and subsequent credit crunch is going to create long-term challenges that will affect every sector of the economy. In Europe, the Eurozone crisis has tipped several countries into double-dip recessions and the slowdown of the Chinese economy also has the potential to impact on the economic health of countries whose firms are dependent on China as an export market.

In the public sector, the purse strings have tightened as the UK Government works to rebalance the books. The Bank of England's predictions of low or no growth in the economy will mean government income is likely to remain static, or fall. However, it is possible that the worsening economic conditions may prompt a re-think and result in the government spending more to stimulate the economy.

Figure 3.3 summarises some of the likely changes.

Figure. 3.3   Overview of current economic themes

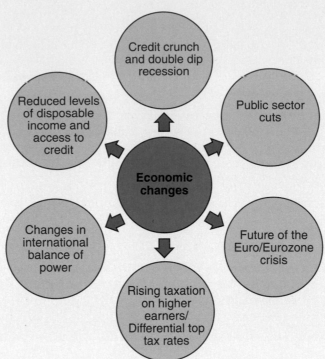

This is not just a localised challenge. Across the globe, governments are addressing the fall-out from the near collapse of the banking system. Some countries have already suffered badly, for example, Iceland. Others like China have seen their rapid growth-rate slowing and some commentators are predicting a potential crash, as the troubles in the Eurozone and US economies affect their exports. China's growth rate dipped to 8% in 2012 and its construction sector has been badly hit by slowing demand and taking on too much debt. Although, recent inflation figures of 1.8% (July 2012) mean that the Chinese Government has scope to intervene if the economy does slip.

The economic environment is particularly important in forecasting future activity levels because demand has to be backed by the ability to pay, for it to be relevant. Alterations in that ability to pay are caused by changes in:

- The level of economic activity determined by the level of employment and productivity

- The size of the population affecting average incomes

- Inflation impacting on the purchasing value of income nationally

- Exchange rates impacting on purchase values between countries

- Tax policy and the tax burden influencing the balance of public and private sector expenditure and the distribution of income

- The availability of, or social attitude to, credit and savings which impact on the marginal propensity to spend or save.

All of these factors will alter the economic health of customers, be they business or household customers and so the marketing professional needs to be able to understand how they impact on their customers. There are plenty of statistics available to help which will provide regional insights as well as national ones.

3.1.1 Example

The Office for National Statistics (ONS) is the executive office of the UK Statistics Authority, a non-ministerial department which reports directly to Parliament. ONS is the UK Government's single largest statistical producer. The National Statistician is also the UK Statistics Authority's Chief Executive and principal statistical adviser.

The Chartered
Institute of Marketing

Note: In most European countries you will find the National Statistics Institute performs similar functions at country level.

ACTIVITY 3.4

Visit National Statistics Online *'UK Snapshot'* to get an up-to-date picture of the current state of the economy. Remember that even if your target markets are other companies (eg, B2B) their demand will be influenced by end-user demand: in other words, theirs is derived demand, so forecasts of consumer changes will provide you with insights about emerging themes which may impact on your business later.

Have a look around the site to familiarise yourself with the sort of data that is available.

3.1.2 The impact of economic changes

It is important that you can make use of economic trends and changes. Being able to gather information and data is the first step in this process, but to be really useful, the impact of that information has to be assessed. In crude terms, it is a matter of identifying which economic factors present threats for an industry, or organisation, and which represent opportunities. The Senior Examiner has recommended a recent report (December 2011) by consultancy firm PwC as a good source of economic information, see Activity 3.5 below.

ACTIVITY 3.5

Visit the PwC website and look at the *Economic Views* report.

http://www.pwc.co.uk/economic-services/publications/economic-views-global-december-2011.jhtml

What are the key trends that you think will affect your industry?

Decide if each one is an opportunity or a threat (or both)

3.2 The recession and its impact

> ▶ **Key term**
>
> **Recession**
>
> A recession is a period of economic decline, normally lasting for at least two quarters. It is characterised by higher levels of unemployment and lower levels of economic activity. A double dip recession is when the period of decline is followed by a brief recovery and growth for a few months, but then a further two quarters of trough.

The important thing about emerging themes, as you have already seen, is how changes at the macro level impact on how markets behave and influence customer needs and behaviours.

The credit crunch/recession has already been featured in examples earlier in this text. It has caught the headlines for a number of reasons:

- The speed of events
- The global nature of those events
- The wide impact of problems in the core financial sector
- The seriousness of the legacy of events and the actions taken to deal with them both nationally and internationally.

There is no shortage of information about the causes of the crash, nor a shortage of forecasts about its long-term shape and severity. This is a good example of how it will be important to examine a number of sources when trying to assess the severity and implications of change.

3.3 Recession at sector level

There is no doubt that the recession has impacted on some sectors more seriously than others. The global car industry and construction have been hit hard but also have benefited from direct government support to try to help them.

To date, those whose main customers have been in the Public Sector, such as, for example, the pharmaceuticals industry, have been relatively unaffected, but, as we have indicated, cuts in public sector finance have to follow.

ACTIVITY 3.6

You need to do some research to find sources of information that can help you evaluate the credit crunch and global recession (in the context of your own sector and industry). Spread your research net wide and include the media, BBC and newspapers as well as YouTube and, of course, your own trade association and industry bodies. Try talking to colleagues and do your own jury forecasting.

3.4 Changes for marketing

3.4.1 A more strategic role for marketing

Within sectors the pain of recession has not been felt equally. However, as your saw in Chapter 1, recession forces the pace of change to become a '**buyer's market**'. With less active customers in the market and less disposable income, competition to win custom intensifies.

Strategic marketing activity has accordingly started to move centre-stage. There is evidence that the need to be customer-focused and really understand customer needs and deliver solutions they value has been accepted. This change, altering the role of marketing within organisations, is still an emerging theme, but one that marketers have been arguing for and one you need to monitor within your sector and organisation. Certainly, the most forward looking organisations do not appear to be using the recession as a reason to slash marketing activity, though they may be reappraising it.

The longer lasting changes in marketing behaviour may involve a speedier adoption of new media opportunities for communication (with a knock-on impact on advertising incomes) and greater innovation in segmentation and developing customer solutions.

3.4.2 Changes in customer behaviour

The emerging themes that we cannot yet be sure about are those that will impact on longer-term customer behaviour. They could include the rise of the careful customer, the increased propensity for shopping around, negotiating deals and accepting non-branded alternatives. These changes will make it more challenging to establish and build long-term customer relationships. An increase in transactional behaviour will have a negative impact on return on marketing investment.

In business-to-business sectors, the pressure on budgets is likely to intensify and encourage the professionalisation of buying through procurement managers, tendering processes and so on. Again these developments would not make the marketers' job easier but would make it difficult to build relationships with customers and users and add to the cost of the sales process.

The Chartered
Institute of Marketing

- Politics and the Law have a profound effect on business both domestically and globally. Some key issues to consider currently include:

    - The impact of the Arab Spring

    - Instability in the Eurozone and the ongoing crisis over the Euro (also linked to economic factors)

    - The continuing trend of devolution and decentralisation of power in many countries in the developed world

    - The nature of relationships between politicians and business leaders

    - Increased legislation covering business behaviour – such as the Bribery and Corruption Act in the UK

- Ethics is also an increasingly important part of the business landscape and, as more is revealed about the way businesses behave and the rewards their executives receive, public trust appears to be declining

- Economic trends are more long term in nature, so many of the key issues are not new and include:

    - Ongoing shift in the balance of economic power between developed nations and emerging economies

    - The continuing recession in the UK and other parts of Europe, now termed 'double dip'.

    - The impact of public sector cuts as the promised reforms and austerity budgets are put into action.

FURTHER READING

BBC News website: Robert Peston's blog on Business issues is often a source of good information on a range of events: http://www.bbc.co.uk/news/correspondents/robertpeston/

BBC News website: Stephanie Flanders, the Economics editor, is a useful source of news and explanation about the UK Economy: http://www.bbc.co.uk/news/correspondents/stephanieflanders/

Schwartz, M. (2005) Universal moral values for corporate codes of ethics, *Journal of Business Ethics*, Vol59(1), pp 27–44.

Anon (2011) 2011 corruption perceptions index – results. Transparency International, http://cpi.transparency.org/cpi2011/results/ [Accessed on 20 August 2012].

Anon (2012) Frequently asked questions. Institute of Business Ethics, http://www.ibe.org.uk/index.asp?upid=71&msid=12#whatbe [Accessed on 20 August 2012]

Anon (2012) Libor – what is it and why does it matter?. BBC News, http://www.bbc.co.uk/news/business-19199683 [Accessed 20 August 2012].

Anon (2012) Struggling Thomas Cook reports quarterly loss. BBC News, http://www.bbc.co.uk/news/business-19091289 [Accessed 20 August 2012].

CIM (2006) No marketer is an island: marketing and the law. *CIM Shape the Agenda Nº.9*, Cookham, CIM.

Elkington, J. (1997) *Cannibals with forks: the triple bottom line of 20th century business*. Oxford, Capstone Publishing.

Peachey, K. (2012) Eurozone crisis explained: impact on you. BBC News, http://www.bbc.co.uk/news/business-18287476 [Accessed on 20 August 2012].

Peachey, K. (2012) Eurozone crisis explained: causes. BBC News, http://www.bbc.co.uk/news/business-16290598 [Accessed on 25 October 2012].

Schumpeter (2012) The other arab spring. *The Economist,* August, p62.

Thomas, T. *et al* (2004) Strategic leadership of ethical behaviour, *Academy of Management Executive* Vol18(2), pp56–68.

Vaughan, A. (2012) Planning system reforms as it happened. The Guardian, http://www.guardian.co.uk/environment/blog/2012/mar/27/planning-system-reforms-live-coverage [Accessed on 20 August 2012].

ACTIVITY DEBRIEFS

Activity 3.1

These activities will depend on your own research. A good starting point is the various news websites: especially those that cover politics in an independent manner. In the UK, the BBC News and ITN websites have good coverage of politics, but so also do many of the national newspapers. Political blogs can be a useful source of information, but the quality of these may be variable and they may also be rather partisan. In the US, the Huffington Post is one widely quoted site and in the UK conservativehome.blogs, order-order.com and leftfootforward.org are well regarded.

The Chartered Institute of Marketing

Activity 3.2

Legal changes that have had an impact

Our list includes:

- Legislation in Scotland setting minimum prices for alcohol, which has had an impact on the pub industry, supermarkets and the alcohol producers

- The UK's Bribery and Corruption Act, which will have an impact on international firms that do business in the UK as well as those based in the UK

- Banning smoking in public places which has had a significant negative impact on the pub industry and certainly contributed to an estimated closure of five pubs a week in 2008.

- The London Olympic Games and Paralympic Games Act 2006 which specifies that only companies which have been awarded official sponsorship status can make explicit reference to the Olympics in their promotions. According to a CIM poll, some 40% of marketers surveyed were unaware of the provisions of the Act or the potential £20,000 fine. To prevent ambush marketing and to protect exclusivity of official sponsors, the organiser of the Games, The London Organising Committee of the Olympic Games Limited (LOCOG), trading as '**London 2012**', has special statutory marketing rights under The London Olympics Association Right. It also has special legal rights under The London Olympic Games and Paralympic Games Act 2006 and The Olympic Symbol etc (Protection) Act 1995.

- Data protection legislation which has had considerable implications for what data companies hold about customers and how they use that information.

- Freedom of Information Act which has opened up a number of areas of government to scrutiny and thus has been a catalyst for improved governance.

- A raft of Health and Safety legislation which has impacted many sectors and influenced the environments in which customers can interact with organisations.

Activity 3.3

This activity will depend on your own research.

Activity 3.4

This activity will depend on your own research.

Activity 3.5

You might have focused on any of the five trends highlighted in the report, such as market volatility, the continuing Eurozone crisis and potential of the break-up of the single currency, or business and trade opportunities from emerging economies. However, the effect these might have and their relative importance will depend on your own industry: so it is important for you to make a judgement based on your knowledge of the sector.

Discussion point: How relevant do you think some of the predictions/trends are in the PwC report? Some, such as stability in the Middle East, could be seen as being out-of-date due to recent events in Syria and other parts of the Arab world.

Activity 3.6

This activity will depend on your own research – but there are some good potential starting points for your research in the Further Reading section above.

The Chartered Institute of Marketing

CHAPTER 4

Emerging themes in organisations' environment

Introduction

Chapter 3, together with this chapter, is intended to introduce some of the key changes and emerging themes at macro level. As you have already seen, not all changes impact on all sectors, or do so in the same way, or to the same extent. The coverage of macro-trends cannot be exhaustive but we examined one or two trends and changes in each of the core macro-environmental areas.

Topic list

Demographic change   (1)

Social and cultural change   (2)

Technological change   (3)

The environment   (4)

Assessment advice   (5)

1.1	Critically evaluate macro-environmental emerging themes and assess/forecast their potential impact upon one specific sector or industry:
	▪ Changes in political governance systems and political focus
	▪ Contemporary economic opportunities/challenges
	▪ Social change (at local and global levels)
	▪ Emerging technologies
	▪ Environmental challenges
	▪ Methods of forecasting/predicting change

1 Demographic change

▶ **Key term**

Demograhics

Demographics are current statistical characteristics of a population. These types of data are used widely in sociology (and especially in the subfield of demography), public policy, and marketing. Commonly examined demographics include gender, race, age, disabilities, mobility, home ownership, employment status, and even location. Demographic trends describe the historical changes in demographics in a population over time.

1.1 Consumer markets

It is easy to overlook demographics, but the subject is important. Marketers use demographics when building customer profiles and as one of the criteria for segmenting markets. In October 2011 the world's population reached the seven billion mark. The growth in human population is arguably one of the biggest problems facing mankind today. This pattern of growth is set to continue and cautious estimates are that growth rates will peak at eight billion by the end of the century or continue to swell beyond ten billion into the 22nd century. That is equivalent of twice the present population of China added in just two generations. This presents many challenges, not the least of which is how to feed this growing population.

THE REAL WORLD

At the John Innes Centre for plant research, work is being carried out to develop a strain of wheat that is resistant to the fungus called stem rust, a disease that affects many crop species and has been responsible for many of the world's famines. The new strain of wheat is not only immune to stem rust it is also highly drought-resistant. The technology takes protective genes isolated in existing wheat varieties, cultivates them in bacteria and then inserts them into the DNA of target plants. At John Innes, they are also growing blight resistant potatoes and nitrogen-fixing wheat that would remove the need for costly fertilisers. However, this development is currently being resisted by pressure groups, as it uses Genetically Modified (GM) technology and Greenpeace, Friends of the Earth and Gene watch UK have conducted a number of successful campaigns against transgenic crop development. Transgenic crops have been grown commercially in America for 15 years and, to date, there have been no major side effects reported. Hostility may be waning in Africa as Kenyan Biologist, Felix M'mboyi asked for Europe to end its opposition to GM foods as they represent, he claims, the only chance Africa has of feeding itself.

Figure 4.1   Key factors influencing demographic change

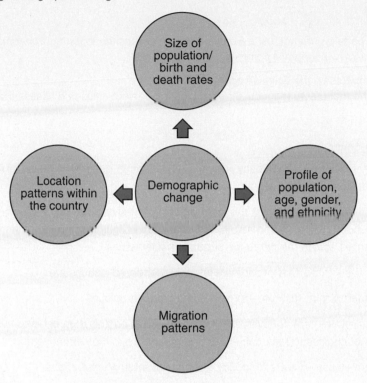

1.1.1 What about migration?

▶ **Key term**

Migration

Human migration is physical movement by humans from one area to another, sometimes over long distances or in large groups. Historically this movement was nomadic, often causing significant conflict with the indigenous population and their displacement or cultural assimilation. Migration for work in the 21st century has become a popular way for individuals from developing countries to obtain sufficient income for survival.

Would an increase in levels of immigration be a good or bad thing? A weakened UK economy with high levels of unemployment may make the UK a less attractive destination for economic migrants. There is evidence of Polish and other Eastern European workers quitting the UK, but what would the impact of this be?

Headline migration figures

- Estimated total long-term immigration to the UK in the year to June 2011 was 593,000. This compares to 582,000 in the year to June 2010 and has remained at a similar level since 2004

- Estimated total long-term emigration from the UK in the year to June 2011 was 343,000. This is similar to 347,000 in the year to June 2010 and a decrease of 32,000 from the year ending June 2008

- Net migration was 250,000 in the year to June 2011. Since the year to June 2010 when net migration was 235,000, it has peaked at 255,000 in the year to September 2010 and remained steady since

- Long-term immigration of New Commonwealth citizens has reached 170,000. This is the highest recorded estimate. Two-thirds have migrated to the UK to study

- Study remains the most common reason for migrating to the UK at 242,000 in the year to June 2011

(Office for National Statistics, 2012)

Changes in migration patterns are not just a European trend, access the following *Economist* article about changing migration patterns in China http://www.economist.com/node/21548273 and:

1   Consider the impacts on the Chinese economy.
2   Select one of the manufacturing industries eg, clothing or electronics and assess the impacts on that industry.

Think Tanks

The Institute for Public Policy Research is a leading, progressive think tank, producing cutting-edge research and innovative policy ideas for a just, democratic and sustainable world.

Since 1988, it has been at the forefront of progressive debate and policy-making in the UK. Through independent research and analysis, it defines new agendas for change and provides practical solutions to challenges across the full range of public policy issues.

Other think tanks that provide useful insight and publications are:

The Adam Smith Institute – promotes free market policies

Demos – think tank for everyday democracy. This organisation believes everyone should be able to make personal choices in their daily lives that contribute to the common good.

Chatam House – centre for policy research on international affairs

1.2 Business markets

Demographics are not restricted to the consumer markets. Changes in the number of firms, their average size, location and sector are equally valid and important if you are working in the business-to-business sector. These are structural changes that can have major implications for the success of nations and the performance of specific sectors. For example, there is concern about London's ability to retain its prominence as a global financial service centre following the worldwide collapse of the banking systems and the UK's role in that.

Recession and high levels of unemployment are typically catalysts for increased business start-ups and a boost to innovation.

Banks can still be a useful source of information and data. Try http://www.business.barclays.co.uk.

THE REAL WORLD

More than 450,000 extra primary pupils will need places in England by 2015 as schools face a surging birth rate, government figures reveal.

In Barking there is a forecast for the primary school population to increase by more than 40% – the equivalent of dozens of new schools.

The UK government has released its latest figures on school capacity – including local authority forecasts for how demand for places is set to change between the school years 2010 – 2011 and 2015 – 2016.

Population boom

This shows a picture of soaring demand for primary places in some areas, within a projected national increase in the number of primary-age pupils of 454,800.

This reflects a sustained population boom – with the birth rate in 2010, 20% higher than in 2002.

Barking will need to accommodate more than 8,000 extra primary pupils; Brent and Newham more than 6,000.

The Chartered
Institute of Marketing

County Councils, often with more pupils than urban authorities, also face big increases – Lancashire is forecasting demand to rise by 13,000, Hampshire by 11,000 and Kent is expecting to need places for more than 9,000 extra pupils.

Despite the shortage of places in some areas, there are still large numbers of unfilled places elsewhere – either because of demographic changes or because parents are not sending their children to unpopular schools.

The latest figures show that there are nationally more than 444,000 empty primary places – but not necessarily in the places where there is the growing demand.

This will be a tough planning challenge for national and local government, against a background of spending constraints and growing numbers of schools moving outside of local education authority control.

(BBC, 2012)

Take the time to find out how the demographics of your sector have changed recently. Your trade association or sector bodies may be a useful starting point.

To find a relevant trade association you could try the UK Trade Association Forum. The website can be found at http://www.taforum.org.

2 Social and cultural change

Social and cultural changes go straight to the heart of customer needs and behaviours. Changes here can directly impact on the basis of market segmentation and the ways in which organisations engage with their markets, by, for example, addressing concerns about obesity, community engagement and the 'Big Society', In China alone, ten to fifteen million people are predicted to move to cities, in a massive move to urbanisation. There will be global population increase – the UK population is set to increase 24% by 2050, with continued disparities in wealth and rising obesity. All this will impact on marketing in the future. (Business in the Community, 2011)

Figure 4.2   Key factors influencing social and cultural change

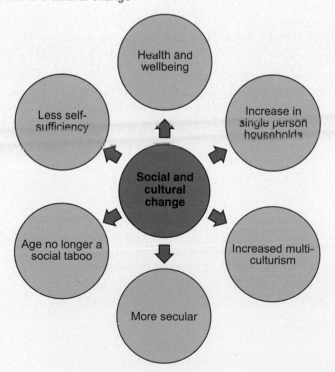

2.1 Headline trends

1   In January 2012, the Office for National Statistics (ONS) reported that unemployment had risen to an 18-year high of 2.68 million, while 1.3 million people were working part-time because they were unable to find a full-time job (the highest number since records began in 1992).

2   Ten million people in the UK are over 65 years old. The latest projections are for 5.5 million more elderly people by 2032 and the number will have nearly doubled to around 19 million by 2050. (www.parliament.uk)

3   Traditional household structures are changing with family sizes generally decreasing. The biggest change is the increase in single person households. By 2031, 18% of English households are expected to consist of just one person, compared to 13% in 2006. (Household Projections 2031, England)

4   If current trends continue, by 2050 about 60% of men, 50% of women and 25% of children in the UK will be clinically obese – so fat that their health is in danger. The analysis indicates that the greatest increase in the incidence of disease would be for type 2 diabetes (a >70% increase by 2050) with increases of 30% for stroke and 20% for coronary heart disease over the same period.

5   The pressure to achieve an unrealistic 'body ideal' is now an underlying cause of serious health and relationship problems, according to a study from the all-party parliamentary group on body image. A report by UK MP's and Central YMCA (2012) concludes that a toxic combination of the media, advertising and celebrity culture account for almost three-quarters of the influence on body image in society, yet the 'body ideal' typically presented was estimated to be not physically achievable by nearly 95% of the population. To read the full report access the following link: http://www.ymca.co.uk/news/body-image-report-launched

---

THE REAL WORLD

In Yorkshire, the communities of Hebden Bridge and Todmorden are at the vanguard of a movement that is picking up momentum across a UK disillusioned with corporate business, government and cuts. Community empowerment, social enterprise, co-operative, it has various titles, but it's quietly getting huge, said Mike Perry of the Plunkett Foundation. 'It starts with food, then it is taking over a shop that's closing. Then it is getting fired up about broadband and renewable energy, taking over the infrastructure of the community'.

There are nine community-run pubs and three hundred shops in the UK. It may not create many jobs but it does glue communities together and keeps money circulating locally. In London, Streetbank.com has begun organising people to share everything from a lawnmower to a DVD with others within a mile radius. DIY retailer B&Q has a pilot scheme in Reading on tool sharing, to ease the environmental damage caused by people buying power tools they may use only once or twice.

(Observer, 2012)

ACTIVITY 4.2

Select the National Health Service (NHS), private cosmetic surgery clinics and retail supermarkets and assess the impact of these social changes.

Sector	Positive impacts	Negative impacts
NHS		
Cosmetic surgery clinics		
Retail supermarkets		

The Chartered Institute of Marketing

3 Technological change

▶ **Key term**

Disruptive innovation

This is an innovation that helps create a new market and value network, and eventually goes on to disrupt an existing market and value network (over a few years or decades), displacing an earlier technology. The term is used in business and technology literature to describe innovations that improve a product or service in ways that the market does not expect. First, typically, by designing for a different set of consumers in the new market and later by lowering prices in the existing market: for example, digital photography, downloadable digital media, plastic replacing natural materials.

Technological and disruptive technologies is the macro-environment factor that is having the widest global impact eg, mobile banking, nanotechnology, product innovations, additive manufacturing.

Figure 4.3   Impact of technological change

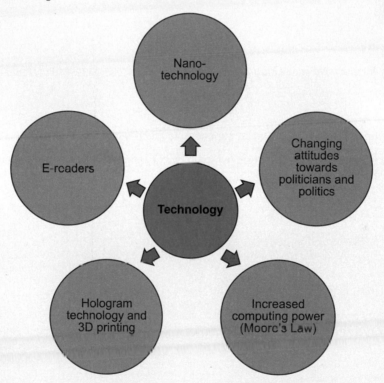

Nanotechnology

Nanotechnology, shortened to **Nanotech**, is the study of the control of matter on an atomic and molecular scale and involves developing materials or devices within that size. It is referred to sometimes as a 'general-purpose technology'. That is because, in its advanced form, it will have significant impact on almost all industries and all areas of society. It will offer better-built, longer-lasting, cleaner, safer, and smarter products for the home, communications, medicine, transportation, agriculture, and industry in general.

'Imagine a medical device that travels through the human body to seek out and destroy small clusters of cancerous cells before they can spread. Or a box, no larger than a sugar cube, that contains the entire contents of the Library of Congress. Or, materials much lighter than steel that possess ten times as much strength.' (U.S. National Science Foundation, 2009)

ACTIVITY 4.3

Find out more about nanotechnology on You Tube (http://www.youtube.com).

For an overview of the world of these very small developments use the search term '*Nanotechnology Takes Off - KQED* QUEST

You should also watch *Nokia Morph Concept* (long), one of a number of Nokia clips. This one takes a look at how nanotechnology might change the world of communication.

You might also take a sneak preview at the world of 3D printing. Visit http://www.clipser.com and search for '*3D printing*'. You will find a number of clips that show you how this technology might revolutionise product development and communication. The barriers to technology access could be removed with individuals able to print their own developed products from a cocktail glass to an iPod cover or watch strap.

What would be the implications for your sector?

ACTIVITY 4.4

The magazine industry

Access the following link: *Non News is Good News* http://www.economist.com/node/21556635 and answer the following questions.

Questions

1 Analyse how the magazine industry has responded to the threat of the internet.

2 Research the UK magazine industry and compare, with examples, how it has responded to the challenges and opportunities that the internet poses.

THE REAL WORLD

Robots and the car industry

The automotive industry is one of the biggest users of robots in the manufacturing process but much of the final assembly is still done by humans. But the next generation of robots will be cheaper and easier to set up and they will work with humans rather than replacing them. They will fetch and carry parts pick up tools, sort items and clean up. Germany's Fraunhofer Institute is involved in a European initiative to develop robots that can work alongside humans and understand simple voice commands.

(The Economist, 2012)

Look at the following link for other trends in the car industry: http://www.smmt.co.uk/about-smmt/what-is-smmt/

Additive manufacturing

3D printing or **additive manufacturing** is a process of making three-dimensional solid objects from a digital file. 3D printing is achieved using additive processes, where an object is created by laying down successive layers of material. 3D printing is considered distinct from traditional machining techniques (subtractive processes), which mostly rely on the removal of material, by drilling, cutting.

One-off prototypes are expensive to produce and 3D printing can significantly reduce these costs. Many consumer goods such as mechanical parts, shoes, and the models used by architects now appear in 3D printed form. 3T RPD, a British firm that offers additive manufacturing services, printed a gearbox with smooth internal pathways that was 30% lighter thus allowing faster gear changes.

The Chartered Institute of Marketing

3D printing also contributes to savings in material costs and minimising the impact on decreasing sustainable resources required for manufacturing. In the aircraft industry, metal parts such as extrusions are machined from solid billets of costly high-grade titanium, which can result in 90% waste. Titanium powder can be used to print brackets and these can be as strong as machined parts but use only 10% of the raw materials, according to researchers at EADS, the European aerospace consortium which is the parent of Airbus (*The Economist*, 2012).

Product innovation – graphene

Graphene is a form of carbon that comes in sheets a single atom thick, 40 times stronger than steel and the best conductor of heat at room temperature. It is also a semiconductor whose electrical conductivity is 1,000 times better than that of silicon. Many people predict that graphene will be the choice of the future for computer chips. Other applications are: low cost photodetectors, which convert light into electricity and are used in digital cameras, telecommunications, pollution sensors and biomedical images.

Watch the following YouTube clip to see a lecture at Manchester University where the scientists and Nobel prize winners Prof. Andre Geim and Prof. Konstantin Novoselov discuss this ground-breaking development:

http://www.youtube.com/watch?v=yVNkrEb6Ydw

ACTIVITY 4.5

The future of shopping

Every 50 years or so, retailing undergoes some kind of disruption. A century-and-a-half ago, the growth of big cities and the rise of railroad networks made possible the modern department store. Mass-produced automobiles came along 50 years later and soon, shopping malls lined with specialty retailers were dotting the newly forming suburbs and challenging the city-based department stores. The 1960s and 1970s saw the spread of discount chains – Walmart, Kmart, and the like. Soon after, big-box 'category killers' such as Circuit City and Home Depot arrived, all of them undermining or transforming the old-style mall. Each wave of change does not eliminate what came before, but it reshapes the landscape and redefines consumer expectations, often beyond recognition. Retailers, relying on earlier formats, either adapt or die out as the new ones pull volume from their stores and make the remaining volume less profitable.

Like most disruptions, digital retail technology got off to a shaky start. A bevy of internet-based retailers in the 1990s – Amazon.com, Pets.com, and pretty much everythingelse.com – embraced what they called online shopping or electronic commerce. These fledgling companies ran wild until a combination of ill-conceived strategies, speculative gambles, and a slowing economy burst the dot-com bubble. The ensuing collapse wiped out half of all e-commerce retailers and provoked an abrupt shift from irrational exuberance to economic reality.

Today, however, that economic reality is well established. The research firm Forrester estimates that e-commerce is now approaching $200 billion in revenue in the United States alone, and accounts for 9% of total retail sales, up from 5% five years ago. The corresponding figure is about 10% in the United Kingdom, 3% in Asia-Pacific, and 2% in Latin America. Globally, digital retailing is probably headed towards 15% to 20% of total sales, though the proportion will vary significantly by sector. Moreover, much digital retailing is now highly profitable. Amazon's five-year average return on investment, for example, is 17%, whereas traditional discount and department stores average 6.5%.

What we are seeing today is only the beginning. Soon it will be hard even to define e-commerce, let alone measure it. Is it an e-commerce sale if the customer goes to a store, finds that the product is out of stock, and uses an in-store terminal to have another location ship it to his home? What if the customer is shopping in one store, uses his smartphone to find a lower price at another and then orders it electronically for in-store pickup? How about gifts that are ordered from a website but exchanged at a local store? Experts estimate that digital information already influences about 50% of store sales, and that number is growing rapidly. (Rigby, 2011)

Questions

1   Evaluate this application of disruptive technology to the retail sector in your country.
2   Predict how you think this trend will develop and evolve.

4 The environment

The environment is a topic that has attracted considerable media and popular interest. The rise of the 'green consumer' has been a trend that has been observable for many years. It is linked closely to the response from business in the form of Corporate Social Responsibility strategies. An overview of some of the key macro trends under the environment heading includes:

Figure 4.4   Key macro trends for the environment

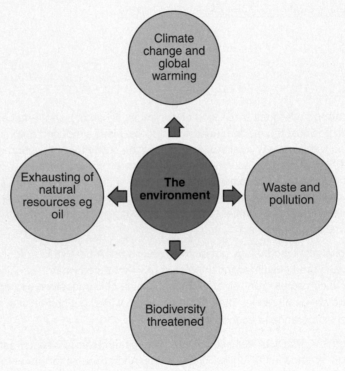

4.1 Climate change

▸ **Key term**

Climate change

This is a significant and lasting change in the statistical distribution of weather patterns over periods ranging from decades to millions of years. It may be a change in average weather conditions, or in the distribution of weather around the average conditions (ie, more or fewer extreme weather events).

This is one of the biggest changes with implications for how we live and work.

The Chartered
Institute of Marketing

Weather forecast

Find out about the forecast changes on http://www.bbc.co.uk/climate/evidence/uk_change.shtml and then tackle the questions below.

While visiting the site, take the time to listen to and review the content about the UKCIP02 scenarios. These are real examples of scenario planning in practice with a 100-year planning horizon.

1 What is the greenhouse effect?
2 What are the UKCIP02 scenarios and what do they say?
3 What would be the potential impact of increased precipitation?
4 What opportunities would a warmer UK offer?
5 What are some of the key changes you may expect to emerge from the real concerns about the climate?

4.2 Waste and pollution

This aspect of environmental concerns is of direct concern to marketers who may be responsible for packaging decisions.

According to a YouGov poll, in 2008 we got through 9.9 billion plastic bags, which equate to 162 bags per person and is enough to fill 188 Olympic-sized swimming pools. They only account for 3.5 to 5.3% of the total plastic packaging used but they are everywhere and take 400 years to break down.

Changing customer behaviour regarding plastic bags is possible. Some countries are making it a political decision with taxes and bans – others are relying on the retailers to 'market' the behaviour change to customers. In Ireland, a tax on plastic bags in 2002 resulted in the number of plastic bags given out dropping by 90% in just one year.

San Francisco and Paris have already banned plastic carrier bags, so has the Devon town of Modbury.

In 2006, the Australian state of Victoria became the first on the continent to ban free plastic bags.

Further afield, China banned shops from handing out free plastic bags in June 2008.

In April 2009, as part of the Government and the British Retail Consortium's *Get a bag habit* campaign, UK's leading seven supermarkets made a further commitment to halve the number of bags they give away by the end of May 2009.

(BBC, 2009)

THE REAL WORLD

The UK has relied on retailer actions rather than taxation. When Sainsbury's launched the cotton *I am not a plastic bag* carrier designed by Anya Hindmarch in April 2007 as an alternative to plastic bags, there were queues for a style accessory that became a collector's item.

- In February 2008 Marks & Spencer began charging customers 5p per plastic bag, with the money raised going to an environmental charity.

- In 2007 Asda agreed to cut packaging by 25% on its own-brand packaging by 2008.

- The Co-op introduced the first biodegradable carrier bag in 2002 and uses degradable netting and trays for some of its organic fruit and vegetables.

- By 2012 Marks & Spencer says all its packaging will be recyclable or compostable.

- Morrison's introduced compostable packaging to its own-brand organic produce in 2007.

- Tesco's less ambitious target is to reduce packaging, by 25%, on own-brand and branded products by 2010.

- Sainsbury's is stepping up the proportion of fruit and vegetables it sells loose and pledged to reduce by 25% the amount of packaging on fruit and vegetables by 2008. Its new carrier bags are made with one-third recycled material.

- Waitrose introduced the reusable '*bag for life*' in 1997 (customers buy a bag for 10p, which is replaced for free when it wears out. Returned 'bags for life' are recycled into furniture). Fifty per cent of its organic range of fresh produce is available in degradable, biodegradable and compostable packaging.

- The number of single-use plastic bags handed out to shoppers by UK supermarkets has risen for the second year running, new figures from the government's waste reduction body Wrap have revealed. The figures will be a huge disappointment to the government, which backed a voluntary scheme to cut the use if throwaway bags. A total of 8bn thin-gauge bags were issued in the UK in 2011 – a 5.4% rise on the 7.6bn in 2010 – and with every shopper now using an average of almost 11 a month.

(Smithers, R. (2012) Plastic bag use up for second year running. The Guardian, http://www.guardian.co.uk/environment/2012/jul/05/plastic-bag-use-rise-supermarkets)

ACTIVITY 4.7

1   Access the *Guardian* article, referenced above, and analyse why there has been an increase in plastic bag usage.
2   Keep a record of your own plastic bag usage? How does this compare with the average?
3   Recommend how the retail sector and governments can change consumer behaviour.

4.2.1 The recession and waste

There is already evidence that the recession is having a stronger impact on our behaviour as we are being extolled to:

- **Reduce** – for example '*Love Food Hate Waste'* campaign', launched by the government watchdog Waste Resources and Action Programme (Wrap) in November 2007, has raised awareness of the £10.2bn of food waste we throw away each year.

- **Reuse**

- **Recycle** – Defra's figures show a surge in recycling. Britons recycled 36.3% of their rubbish last year, up from 30.9% in 2007.

Local councils and waste management companies across the whole country are reporting a drop of up to 10% in waste collection in recent months, a fall that the UK environmental charity Waste Watch estimates could result in a massive reduction of 2.5 million tonnes in waste production in 2009 – enough rubbish to fill Canary Wharf five times over.

A number of factors have contributed to this:

- The shift in public attitudes away from profligate living and the disposable economy
- A drop in the amount of white goods, such as washing machines and TVs, being thrown out
- A fall in construction waste, as the recession affects the number of building projects.

Again the question is how sustainable is this trend? To maintain this fall there is a need to decouple economic growth from waste growth (which may be less easy to achieve).

Corporate social responsibility

Corporate social responsibility (CSR), or corporate citizenship, entails companies behaving in a socially responsible manner, and dealing with other business parties who do the same. With growing public awareness

and demand for socially responsible businesses, it is little wonder that companies of today take corporate social responsibility into account when planning future, socially responsible, business operations.

Using Fair Trade ingredients.

According to the Starbucks website, in order to purchase Fair Trade Certified™ coffee as part of its supply chain strategy, Starbucks pays a minimum of $1.26 (U.S.) per pound ($2.77 per kilogram) for Fair Trade certified ingredients such as non-organic green Arabica coffee and $1.41 per pound ($3.10 per kilogram) for organic green Arabica coffee, which are substantially over and above the prevailing commodity-grade coffee price.

Community engagement

One approach to engaging in corporate social responsibility is through community-based development projects. Community-based and community-driven development projects have become an important form of development assistance among global socially responsible companies. An economic relationship implies a strategy of engaging the wider community into the core business activity of the company so that communities become embedded in corporate supply chain strategy to create a sustainable business.

An example of this approach can be seen in the development project CARE International Starbucks started in 2007 in Ethiopia in the Gewgew Dingete villages in West Harrarghe, Ethiopia. The project aims to provide farmers and their families with better food, safe drinking water and greater income, as well as diversified income opportunities. Through the project, community warehouse facilities were built, a haricot bean loan scheme and vegetable seed bank were initiated and farmers were trained in crop husbandry and marketing. These would thus help the farm become a more sustainable business for each farmer in the village.

Corporate philanthropy

Starbucks also donates a portion of its pre-tax profits as corporate philanthropy as part of its efforts to be more socially responsible. Starbucks makes charitable contributions through the Starbucks Foundation created in 1997 with and/or a direct giving programme in communities in which it operates and in countries where its coffee is sourced.

Read more at Suite101: *Corporate Social Responsibility at Starbucks: (Bilson, 2010.)* http://suite101.com/article/corporate-social-responsibility-at-starbucks-a211758#ixzz1yLZrJ69s.

Before you move on to the next chapter and a look at the emerging themes, take time to apply your macro level thinking to your own sector. Create your map of the key macro trends driving your sector and note any useful sources of information that will help you assess these.

5 Assessment advice

As the unit covers 'emerging themes' the themes chosen should, by definition, be contemporary, in the context of the sector and country. For example, mobile money transfer is developed in some African countries but is relatively new in the UK.

The theme should be justified and backed up by national/industry statistics or other suitable sources, such as academic journal papers. The macro theme should be applied to the sector as a whole and the implications examined.

In this section, it is vital that the candidate demonstrates in-depth research of the emerging theme, as this will underpin the rest of the discussion paper. Hence, sources in task 1 should be referred to support the justification.

Below, an A grade answer is included in relation to technology, namely telematics and the motor insurance industry. This is a truly emerging theme in this sector and the candidate has explained the theme, justified it as the basis of the discussion paper, and analysed some of the impacts.

3. Discussion Paper

3.1 The Macro Environment: Telematics

Telematics devices are an in-vehicle technology which uses a "black-box" to facilitate date transmission from a vehicle for aspects such as usage, geographic positioning and timing information. This enables countless services including emergency and breakdown, intuitive satellite navigation and traffic reporting, security and tracking, logistics for fleet managers, remote diagnostics for motor manufacturers and, most prudently, 'pay as you drive' capabilities for motor insurers.

Insurance-based telematics is in essence, the application of such data in the pricing and rating of motor products. This data can assist insurance companies with tracking stolen vehicles and providing more timely and accurate accident information, but the most noteworthy industry transformation will originate from advancements in driver risk profiling (Allianz Insurance p.c. 2012). Visibility of factors such as driver attitudes to speed limits, vigour of acceleration and braking, types of roads typically taken, and length of journeys will almost negate the need for insurers to utilise traditional rating factors such as driver age, driving experience and vehicle type. Instead, they will be provided with a means to rate drivers according to their actual driving mileage and behaviour.

This considerable advancement in motor risk rating is defined by many industry professionals as revolutionary (Evershed, 2012; Khan, 2012; Morrison, 2012). Sirota (2011) similarly refers to telematics as the most recent step in the evolution of insurance. He describes the industry's historical evolvement towards individualised premiums as "leading up to this technology breakthrough"; something that is clearly illustrated in his depiction of the evolution (Figure 3).

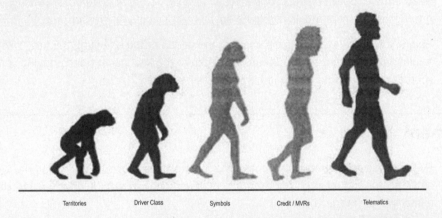

| Territories | Driver Class | Symbols | Credit / MVRs | Telematics |

Figure 3: The evolution of motor risk rating (Sirota, 2011)

The concept of telematics is certainly nothing new (Horrocks and Bellamy, 1997; Inayatullah, 2004; Rodriguez-Casal, 2005), yet it is only the past two years which have seen the 'blue sky' concept become any sort of reality within the insurance industry. There is a plethora of evidence indicating a growing interest in telematics propositions amongst consumers and insurers alike and, moreover, a handful of insurers have begun "dipping [their] toes in the telematics water" via small research trials (Barket, 2012 p.30).

The Chartered Institute of Marketing

There are a number of macro-environmental factors currently emerging which, collectively, are prompting this accelerated interest. Motor manufacturers and insurers are beginning to discuss 'mutually beneficial' opportunities stemming from the 2015 Intelligent Transport Directive, which will require all new private and light-commercial vehicles to have emergency call telematics capabilities as a minimum. Further EU legislation, in the form of the recent Gender Directive, dictates that as of 21st December 2012 insurers will no longer be permitted to use gender as a rating factor (FSA, 2012), and subsequent concerns over the potential for premiums increases for female drivers have been widespread (Denton, 2011); Bennett, 2012). This, when considered in conjunction with the general rising cost of motor insurance, particularly for young drivers is pushing consumers to seek premium-lowering propositions (King, 2011; Neligan, 2011), and has prompted UK government officials to 'call to action' insurers in facilitating premium cuts (Cockburn, 2012).

Barker (2012) believes that escalated interest in telematics is due to an increasingly prominent market trend: 'non-insurers' such as supermarkets and motor manufacturers beginning to offer their own insurance proposition; longstanding industry players looking for new opportunities to differentiate themselves in a tough economic climate. When coupled with shifting socioeconomic attitudes towards more tolerance for 'intrusive' technology (Howard et al., 2011), it seems that the time really could be right for telematics.

Though certainly an industry hot topic, the fact remains that telematics is sitting firmly within the 'emerging' realm; industry professionals advocate that the key issue is not whether telematics is a 'game changing' development for UK insurers, but rather how it will unfold and what exactly it will mean for the consumer (Brodie, 2012; Khan, 2012; Morrison, 2012).

BPP
LEARNING MEDIA

CHAPTER ROUNDUP

- Key trends and impacts in relation to demographic, social, technology and the environment were explained.

- A range of key demographic trends, for example ageing population and migration, were explained with examples.

- Social and cultural changes such as increasing obesity, body image and community engagement were explained with examples.

- Emerging technologies were explained, for example Grapheme and nanotechnology. Impacts of digital technology were considered for the retail and publishing industries.

- Key environmental concerns for example climate change, pollution, recycling were explained. Responses to this key environmental factor were explained in the context of Corporate Social Responsibility.

FURTHER READING

Anon (2011) *Financial services, consumers and new technology*, Mintel.

Anon (2012) *Healthy lifestyles,* Mintel.

Blayney, S. M. (2011) The good, the bad and the indifferent: marketing and the triple bottom line. *Social Business*, Vol1(2), pp173–187.

BBC (2012) Click, http://news.bbc.co.uk/1/hi/programmes/click_online/ [Accessed on 29 October 2012].

Crowther, D. and Reis, C. (2011) Social responsibility or social business? *Social Business*, Vol1(2), pp129–148.

Holmes, J. (2011) Cyberkids or divided generations? Characterising young people's internet use in the UK with generic, continuum or typological models. *New Media & Society.* November, Vol13(7), pp1104–1122.

Le Masurier, M. (2012) Independent magazines and the rejuvenation of print, *International Journal of Cultural Studies*, 15: 383.

Trend watching.com (2012) http://trendwatching.com/ [Accessed on 29 October 2012].

World Economic Forum (2012) The future of manufacturing opportunities to drive economic growth. http://www.weforum.org/reports/future-manufacturing [Accessed on 29 October 2012].

The Chartered Institute of Marketing

Anon (2009) Household Projections to 2031, England. Communities and Local Governments, http://www.communities.gov.uk/publications/corporate/statistics/2031households0309 [Accessed 29 October 2012].

Anon (2010) The ageing population. Parliament UK, http://www.parliament.uk/business/publications/research/key-issues-for-the-new-parliament/value-for-money-in-public-services/the-ageing-population/ [Accessed 29 October 2012].

Anon (2011) Visioning the future – transforming business – the forces for change – drivers & trends. Business in the Community, http://www.bitc.org.uk/resources/publications/visioning_the_future.html [Accessed 29 October 2012]

Anon (2012) A third industrial revolution. The Economist, http://www.economist.com/node/21553017 [Accessed on 29 October 2012].

Anon (2012), Body image report launched. Central YMCA, http://www.ymca.co.uk/news/body-image-report-launched [Accessed 29 October 2012].

Anon (2012) Changing migration patterns. The Economist, http://www.economist.com/node/21548273 [Accessed 29 October 2012].

Anon (2012) Non-news is good news, The Economist, http://www.economist.com/node/21556635 [Accessed 29 October 2012].

BBC (2009) Packaging. BBC Food, http://www.bbc.co.uk/food/food_matters/packaging2.shtml [Accessed on 21 June 2009]

Bennett, J. and Dixon, M. (2006) *Single person households and social policy: looking forwards*. York, Joseph Rowntree Foundation.

Bilson, J. (2010) Corporate responsibility at Starbucks. 101. http://suite101.com/article/corporate-social-responsibility-at-starbucks-a211758 [Accessed 29 October 2012].

Coughlan, S. (2012) Birth surge 'means 450,000 more primary pupils'. BBC, http://www.bbc.co.uk/news/education-16486747 [Accessed 29 October 2012].

Hanlon, M. (2011) How to feed the world's population. *The Observer*.

McVeigh, T. (2012) Free food, sharing and caring; the spirit of community is reborn in the Yorkshire Hills *The Observer*.

Rigby, D. (2011) The future of shopping, *Harvard Business Review*, Vol89 Issue 12 pp64-75

Smithers, R. (2012) Plastic bag use up for second year running. The Guardian, http://www.guardian.co.uk/environment/2012/jul/05/plastic-bag-use-rise-supermarkets 21556635 [Accessed 29 October 2012].

Activity 4.1

Discussion points

1   Summarise the changing migration patterns

2   Discuss how they will affect the Chinese economy and Labour supply.

3   Changes in migration patterns may disrupt availability of labour and thus the clothing and electronic manufacturers may have to look to alternative suppliers and thus this will have major implications on the supply chain. Evaluate what these may be.

4   Improvements in welfare, conditions may lead to demands for higher wages, which will impact on pricing strategies.

5   These manufactures may seek alternative alliances and partnerships to ensure supply, which will result in different business models. Suggest what you think these may be.

Activity 4.2

Sector	Positive impacts	Negative impacts
NHS	Global promotion of the NHS brand to provide funds	Shortage of specialist care provision for the ageing population Increased public sector cost
Cosmetic surgery clinics	Growth in this sector Increased social acceptability of non-essential cosmetic surgery procedures	Increased regulation Media backlash as too much focus on perfect body image
Retail supermarkets	Higher levels of online shopping could result in reduction in outlets and hence business costs	Smaller households smaller spend and lifetime customer value so customer loyalty becomes fundamental

Activity 4.3

Discussion points

1   Discuss the technological developments in your own industry.

2   Are there any significant emerging technologies such as nanotechnology that will have impacts? What are these impacts?

Activity 4.4

1   Why do you think the some genres in the magazine industry have been successful despite the digital threat? You might want to discuss the profile of readers, preferences, title loyalty, subscription offers?

2   How does the UK magazine industry compare – what new titles have been launched, which genres are successful, how do circulation and readership compare year on year?

3   How has the digital threat affected the competitive nature of the UK magazine industry?

Activity 4.5

Discussion points

1   Assess retail development in your own country. Consider the type and patterns of retail outlets on the high street, the balance of independent and branded retailers, out of town shopping developments, global retailers. How has this changed in the last ten and five years?

2   How has e-commerce impacted on the retail sector in your country? Evaluate the long-term consequences.

3   Consider the impacts of Smartphone technology on the retail sector and the consumer behaviour of customers.

Activity 4.6

Discussion points

1   The greenhouse effect is central to the climate change debate. The greenhouse effect is the natural process by which the atmosphere traps some of the Sun's energy that warms the Earth enough to support life. Most mainstream scientists believe a human-driven increase in greenhouse gases is increasing the effect artificially. Identify and discuss some of the impacts of climate change.

2   The UKCIP02 represent four different scenarios for UK climate change over the next 100 years. Evaluate the scenarios – how realistic and useful are they?

3   Globally there have been a number of devastating floods eg, Australia, UK and Philippines. Long-term flooding had impacts on urban development, insurance industries.

4   The UK may experience a surge in the tourist industry. Which other industry may benefit from a warmer climate in the UK?

5   Many UK organisations have introduced recycling policies, are considering energy use and how to conserve energy. In addition, sustainability is a key consideration when new buildings are planned. How is your organisation responding to energy conservation?

Activity 4.7

Discussion points

1   In the UK there have been three main approaches to plastic bag use: charging to encourage re-use, awarding points for re-using and free bags. Is this approach too tactical and should retailers adopt a more strategic approach to recycling issues?

2   Recommend how retailers could change consumer use and perception of plastic bags.

The Chartered
Institute of Marketing

CHAPTER 5

Consumer behaviour insights

Introduction

An understanding of how consumers respond to changes in the marketing environment is fundamental to an organisation's success. The ability of the related industry to adapt to these changes in a proactive manner will ensure the long-term viability of the particular industry. Hence, marketers can adapt and improve their marketing campaigns and strategies to reach the consumer more effectively. Data about consumers helps marketers to define the market and to identify opportunities and threats in relation to current and future marketing activity. This chapter provides an overview of **some** key models and concepts and introduces more contemporary thinking.

Topic list

Consumer behaviour	1
Consumers' impact on marketing strategy	2
Consumer decision-making	3
Culture	4
Reference groups	5
Business-to-business buyer behaviour	6
The assessment	7

1.2	Critically evaluate meso-environmental themes and assess/forecast their potential impact upon a specific sector or industry:
	▪ Changes in consumer behaviour
	▪ Changes in nature/structure of competition
	▪ Changes in nature/structure of supply chains

1 Consumer behaviour

The study of consumers helps organisations improve their marketing strategies by understanding issues such as:

The psychology of consumers in terms of how they think, feel, reason and select between different alternatives eg, brands, products, and retailers and how consumers are influenced by their environment eg, culture, family, signs and media. Consumer behaviour also considers decision-making behaviour for both individuals and organisations. Thus, consumer behaviour is the product of the interrelationship between individual influences, group and situational influences and this coupled with purchase behaviour and marketing influences determines product/service choice.

Figure 5.1   Consumer decision-making overview: processes and influences

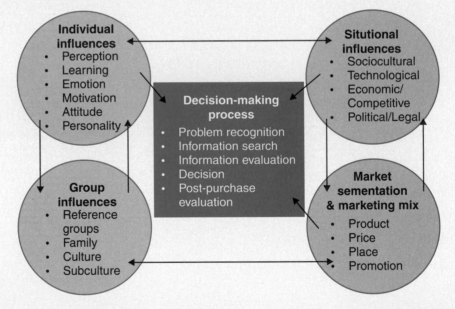

(Adapted from Brassington and Pettitt, 2006)

2 Consumers' impact on marketing strategy

Understanding consumer behaviour is essential for good business. The fundamental definition of marketing relates to satisfying consumer needs and this is governed by the extent to which marketers understand the people or organisations that use their products and services.

2.1 Segmentation

In order to fully understand their customer marketers use a range of segmentation variables such as demographics, geo-demographics, lifestyle and benefits sought in order to identify common variables, which allow them to group customers together and develop targeted strategies and campaigns. At George at Asda (a clothing sub-brand of UK Asda Walmart) customers are profiled according to their lifestyle interests and demographics, for example:

Table 5.1   Customer profiles segmented for a clothing sub-brand of a large UK supermarket

Customer profile	Characteristics
Frugal fashionistas	Age: 25–44 Gender: M–22% F–78% Social class: C2DE Want trendy items at bargain prices. Read: *The Sun, Look, Cosmopolitan, Grazia, Glamour* Watch TV: *Desperate Housewives, This Morning, X Factor* Celebrity influences: Cheryl Cole, Coleen Rooney
Comfy casuals	Age: 35–54 Gender: M 40% W 60% Social class: D Reads: *The Sun, Company, Essentials* Watch TV: *Dave, Sky One, Eastenders, TV Burp, Come Dine With Me* Influences: Comfort, practicality, does not look for sources of inspiration
Savvy shoppers	Age: 45+ Gender: M 35% W 65% Social class: ABDE Read: *Daily Mail, Take a Break, Bella, Good Housekeeping* Watch TV: *BBC News, Midsomer Murders, Strictly Come Dancing* Influences: Quality, instore displays, shop windows, little influence from outside sources.

2.2 Relationship marketing

As technology has improved and databases have become more sophisticated, Relationship Marketing (RM) has evolved and developed and is key to building a lifetime relationship between brands and customers. Various types of membership schemes demonstrate this and, in the UK, the use of the Tesco Clubcard pioneered this method of building customer relationships. The information provided by Clubcard data at store level can be used to identify large spenders and target specific offers. For example, Tesco encourages parents-to-be to sign up to its Baby Club at a point in time when they are likely to considerably increase their spending in this area. In an attempt to build a profitable long-term relationship with this group, Tesco provides them with a targeted magazine and special customised offers. At the individual store level, this relationship can be even further developed, as it pays to target this valuable group on a more individual basis (eg by sending birthday cards, organising special events, etc). Based on store-level Clubcard information, store managers can also telephone defecting or dissatisfied customers.

2.3 Virtual brand communities

A brand community is a community formed based on attachment to a product or marque. Recent developments in marketing and in research in consumer behaviour have resulted in stressing the connection between brand,

individual identity and culture. Among the concepts developed to explain the behaviour of consumers, the concept of a brand community focuses on the connections between people. A brand community can be defined as an enduring self-selected group of consumers sharing a system of values, standards and representations (a culture) and recognising bonds of membership with each other and with the whole.

ACTIVITY 5.1

Access the following journal article and read more about virtual brand communities at Zara.

The influence of belonging to virtual brand communities on consumers' effective commitment, satisfaction and word-of-mouth advertising: The ZARA case, *Online Information Review*, Vol 35(4), pp517–542. (Marcelo Royo-Vela, Paolo Casamassima, 2011)

▶ **Assessment tip**

A useful tip is to produce a 300 to 500 word summary of journal articles where you consider key findings, models used, insights and the usefulness of the article. You need to reflect on the findings: don't just accept what they say. Ask questions such as 'How do you know', 'What are the reasons?' and 'Is that a good source of information?' Explore reasons for your views and seek reasons for others' views. Look for alternative hypotheses, conclusions, explanations, sources of evidence, points of view and plans.

THE REAL WORLD

Discount supermarkets and the middle classes.

A supermarket is a large form of the traditional grocery store, but operating as a self-service shop offering a wide variety of food and household products, organized into aisles.

The supermarket typically comprises meat, fresh produce, dairy and baked goods aisles, along with shelf space reserved for canned and packaged goods, as well as for various non-food items such as household cleaners, pharmacy products and pet supplies. Most supermarkets also sell a variety of other household products that are consumed regularly, such as alcohol (where permitted), medicine, and clothes, and some stores sell a much wider range of non-food products. Examples are Tesco, Sainsbury's and Asda in the UK and Walmart in the USA.

With their no-frills range of obscure brands and the promise of permanent discounts, German supermarkets Lidl and Aldi have brought a compelling efficiency to the weekly shop for millions of Britons. More middle class customers who traditionally shop at Waitrose are 'trading down' and choosing to shop at discount supermarkets as rising fuel costs, and the recession continue to reduce disposable income.

Data from market analysts IGD found that 39% of families from ABC1 households will use the stores in the year ahead compared with 30% of those from the lower-income C2DE groups.

The analysts also found that both major budget chains had invested in the quality of their products, which had helped to reverse any stigma associated with shopping there.

(Brown, 2012)

ACTIVITY 5.2

How e-readers took the embarrassment out of erotic fiction (*The Independent*, 2012)

Fifty Shades of Grey has become the best-selling book in Britain since records began, surpassing *Harry Potter and the Deathly Hallows* with sales of 5.3 million copies. It began life as a viral word-of-mouth hit, selling more than 250,000 copies, as a download, before it had even been published as a conventional book.

The e-reading phenomenon has led to a rise in the sales of erotic and romantic fiction that readers may previously have felt too inhibited to buy and read in public.

Fifty per cent of the erotica market is in e-books, compared to around 20% of general fiction. Mills & Boon, the long-established publisher of paperback romances, has not only brought out a 'steamier' series, but 40% of their trade is now electronic. The fact that racier texts, and garishly packaged 'bonk-busters' (a pun on 'blockbusters') can be downloaded, has removed the embarrassment factor in buying them.

James conceived her novel on an internet 'fan fiction' forum. As an avid reader of Stephanie Meyer's vampire trilogy, *Twilight*, she began writing the book as an imaginative off-shoot to the vampire series.

Read the full article at: http://www.independent.co.uk/arts-entertainment/books/features/how-ereaders-took-the-embarrassment-out-of-erotic-fiction-7743289.html and answer the following questions.

Questions

1 Evaluate the impacts of the *Fifty Shades of Grey* publishing phenomenon in terms of audience taste, distribution and consumer behaviour.

2 Identify and explain how macro changes have affected the publishing industry.

3 Explain and justify three future scenarios for the publishing industry.

3 Consumer decision-making

Figure 5.2   Consumer decision-making process

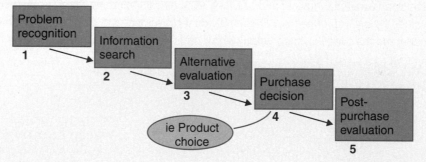

(Adapted from Soloman *et al*, 2010)

The five-stage model of decision-making is a classic view of consumer behaviour and, as a linear model, assumes Stage 1 precedes 2, and 2 precedes 3 etc. It is useful in that it structures and sequences purchase behaviour but it is too simplistic in explaining real-life purchase behaviour. The model assumes each stage takes place in isolation without the impact of external influences. However, it is a useful basis on which to explore and analyse consumer behaviour.

Research that is more recent, carried out by McKinsey (2009), attempts to explain purchase-decision behaviour from a more contemporary perspective. With the explosion of product choices and digital channels, coupled with the emergence of an increasingly discerning, well-informed consumer, a more sophisticated approach is required to help marketers navigate this environment, which is less linear and more complicated than the funnel suggests. We call this approach the **consumer decision journey**. This thinking is applicable to any geographic market that has different kinds of media, internet access, and wide product choice, including large cities in emerging markets such as China and India.

Access the following YouTube video and evaluate the suggested consumer decision journey model and assess whether or not it explains the purchase behaviour in your industry.

http://www.youtube.com/watch?v=EfRrD3we0Hg

Access the following link *Winning in Japan's Consumer Electronics Market* (McInerney, P. *et al*, 2009) which relates the consumer decision journey research to a specific market and country, then answer the questions:

http://www.csi.mckinsey.com/knowledge_by_topic/packaged_goods_consumer_electonics

1   Evaluate the consumer decision journey model in this context.
2   Consider the implications for the retail industry in Japan and your own country.

---

4 Culture

'Culture is a concept crucial to the understanding of consumer behaviour and may be thought of as the collective memory of a society. Culture is the accumulation of shared meanings, rituals and norms and traditions among the members of an organisation or society. It includes abstract ideas, such as values and ethics and material objects and services, such as cars, clothing, food, art and sports that are produced or valued by a group of people. Thus, individual consumers and groups of consumers are but part of culture, and culture is the overall system within which other systems are organised.' (Solomon, 2010, p506)

THE REAL WORLD

It is being called 'snow White syndrome' in India, a market where sales of whitening creams are far outstripping those of Coca-Cola and tea. Fuelling this demand are the country's 75-odd reality TV shows where being fair, lovely and handsome means instant stardom. As a result, the Indian whitening cream market is expanding at a rate of nearly 18% a year. The country's largest research agency, AC Nielsen, estimates that figure will rise to about 25% this year – and the market will be worth an estimated $432m, an all-time high. With the Indian middle class expected to increase ten-fold to 583 million people by 2025, it looks as if things will only get better for the cream makers.

The implicit assumption by many is this: the whiter the skin, the more attractive you are.

'India is on a fairness hook, everyone wants to look fair,' says Mohan Goenka, director of the Calcutta-based Emami group, whose *Fair and Handsome* brand for men was the first of its kind in the market.

A recent study by Hindustan Unilever showed how men in southern States like Tamil Nadu, Kerala, Andhra Pradesh and Karnataka are fervent purchasers of whitening creams. For example, Tamil Nadu has been recording – for the past year – the highest number of sales for Narayanan, a skin-whitening cream from the Unilever range.

(Adapted from Ray, 2010)

5 Reference groups

'A reference group is an actual, or imaginary, individual or group conceived of having significant relevance upon an individual's evaluations, aspirations or behaviour. The term "reference group" is often used to describe any external influence that provides social cues. The referent may be a cultural figure eg, a footballer or pop star, or a person or group whose influence only operates in the consumer's immediate environment. Some groups and individuals exert a greater influence than others and affect a broader range of consumer decisions. Normative influence helps to set and enforce fundamental standards of conduct. In contrast, Manchester United Fan club exerts comparative influence, whereby decisions about specific brands or activities are affected. (Solomon, 2010, p 384)

5.1 Membership reference groups

Before the internet was widely accessible, most membership reference groups consisted of people who had face to face contact. The internet has changed that and now virtual communities are emerging and their impact on individuals' product choice can be significant. These consumers are working together to form their tastes, evaluate product quality and negotiate deals with producers. The opinions of the members are extremely influential and marketers need to be aware of this, when devising their marketing campaigns.

THE REAL WORLD

Popular parenting website Mumsnet has taken a significant step into expanding its brand by creating a series of workshops, courses and other events across the UK. With the new experiential venture Mumsnet Academy, site owners will be hoping for more direct engagement between the audience and the events being facilitated.

Several partners are already on board including the Faber Academy, which offers courses in creative writing and Great British Chefs (www.greatbritishchefs.com), which offers cooking courses. The courses, which are evenly spread across the country, have been well matched to the upmarket and generally affluent Mumsnet audience, be it garden design, small business management or writing classes. This effective matching will help Mumsnet deliver revenues from this activity.

Mumsnet already has a solid business proposition, with big advertisers such as Marks & Spencer and Unilever spending hundreds of thousands of pounds to reach the site's two million monthly users. The users are an active group, consuming nearly 40m pages of content each month and contributing more than 25,000 content posts. This level of engagement suggests that offline learning events are likely to resonate well with, at least a part of, the site's users.

The creation of these offshoots from companies that were born digitally is nothing new: with other web 2.0 darlings such as Spotify and Last.fm arranging music gigs in their own right, it represents a trend for the consolidation of a strong digital base with low-risk expansions. In a world where users are increasingly hard to reach with traditional advertising this offers brands a way to communicate with potential consumers in a more informal, but deeply engaged, way.

(Adapted from Carat, 2012)

---

6 Business-to-business buyer behaviour

Business buyers usually face more complex buying decisions than do consumer buyers. Purchases often involve large sums of money, complex technical and economic considerations and interactions among many people at many levels of the buyer's organisation. Because the purchases are more complex, business buyers may take longer to make their decisions. For example, the purchase of a large information technology system might take many months, or more than a year to complete and could involve millions of pounds, thousands of technical details, and dozens of people ranging from top management to lower-level users.

Model of business buyer behaviour

At the most basic level, marketers want to know how business buyers will respond to various marketing stimuli. Figure 5.3 shows a model of business buyer behaviour. In this model, marketing and other stimuli affect the

buying organisation and produce certain buyer responses. As with consumer buying, the marketing stimuli for business buying consist of the four Ps: product, price, place, and promotion. Other stimuli include major forces in the environment: economic, technological, political, cultural, and competitive. These stimuli enter the organisation and are turned into buyer responses: product or service choice; supplier choice; order quantities; delivery; service; and payment terms. In order to design good marketing mix strategies, the marketer must understand what happens within the organisation to turn stimuli into purchase responses.

Within the organisation, buying activity consists of two major parts: the buying centre, made up of all the people involved in the buying decision, and the buying decision process. Figure 5.3 illustrates that the buying centre and the buying decision process are influenced by internal organisational, interpersonal, and individual factors as well as by external environmental factors.

Figure 5.3 Model of business buyer behaviour

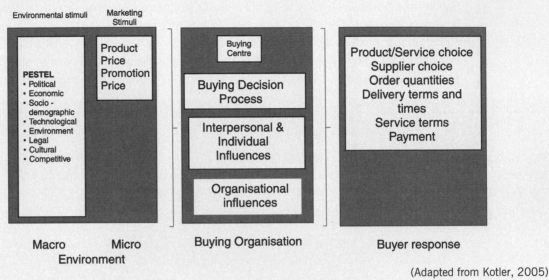

(Adapted from Kotler, 2005)

7 The assessment

When considering how your selected theme relates to the micro-environment it is critical to select the correct micro aspect of consumer behaviour, competition or supply chain and consider how this relates to your macro theme. For example, if you were discussing ethical consumption, then clearly consumer behaviour would be an appropriate aspect to discuss. If you were discussing how nanotechnology and the impacts on differential advantage, then competition would be an appropriate micro area to explore.

Ensure that you select and apply the most relevant models to underpin your explanation and justification. If possible try to research more contemporary models and assess how these apply.

Finally, do not just describe the micro aspects but evaluate the impacts. Postgraduate study is more than amassing information: it should challenge conceptual thinking and encourage you to assess things from various perspectives, and develop (and justify) your own opinions in connection with these concepts. In applying theories to different contexts you will see that 'one size does not fit all' and have to be able to adapt your conceptual thinking.

In the following example, which is from an A Grade paper, the student is focusing on the impact of technology in the retail sector and the potential of Intelligent Retailology. In this excerpt, the impact of technology on the consumer behaviour of customers is discussed. They have analysed some of the implications, underpinned their explanation with a relevant model, namely Kotler's Buyer Decision Process Model that would have resulted in a good pass. However, this particular candidate has also used more contemporary theory to expand their analysis and this relates to their technology theme and explains what future consumer behaviour may be. Moreover, their explanation is critiqued throughout and a high level of critical evaluation skills is displayed. The answer is correctly referenced throughout. Overall, this was an excellent answer.

The Chartered Institute of Marketing

The Impact on Consumer Behaviour

"Customer's want everything. They want the advantages of digital... They want the advantages of physical stores, and shopping as an event and an experience... all are likely to want perfect integration of the digital and the physical" (Rigby, 2011).

Increased Sophistication

As technology continues to evolve consumers are becoming increasingly sophisticated and demanding; "Tools and technology will change the balance of power in retailing. Consumers will have almost perfect information access about products and pricing" (Russo and Clarke, 2008).

The consumer of the future will expect everything quicker, more personalised, convenient and aligned with their lifestyle. It's not just what they will purchase but how they will purchase it. Consumers are using technology to bring the retail experience to life; there is a convergence between on-line and off-line purchasing (Marketing Week, February 2011).

"In today's decision journey, consumer-driven marketing is increasingly important as customers seize control of the process and actively "pull" information helpful to them" (Court et al 2011).

Historically marketing information has been 'pushed' to consumers through the use of traditional channels such as advertising and direct mail. In recent years, with the advantages of new technology, this has turned on its head and consumers are now pro-actively 'pulling' their own marketing information together to make informed buying decisions. The "Super Digital Consumer" (Retail is Detail, 2009) is emerging. Successful retailers need to empower consumers with the ability to find out the information that they need themselves, rather than assume that they want, or need, the information to be force-fed.

Traditional Consumer Behaviour

Whilst Kotler's (1999) Buyer Decision Process model is still relevant in terms of the stages that consumers pursue, it is linear in its approach and created at a time when retailers marketed to the generic mass market. Technology has made the process more complex and dynamic and time-starved consumers are demanding empowerment and effectively becoming 'prosumers' (Tapscott and Williams, 2008)

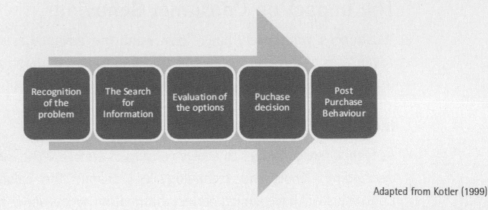

Adapted from Kotler (1999)

Consumer Buying Decision Process of the Future

Court et al (2009) have researched consumer buying behaviour and suggested that it should now be referred to as a 'journey'. The model created below highlights the impact that technology is having on consumer buying behaviour and introduces the concept of "intelligent retailology";

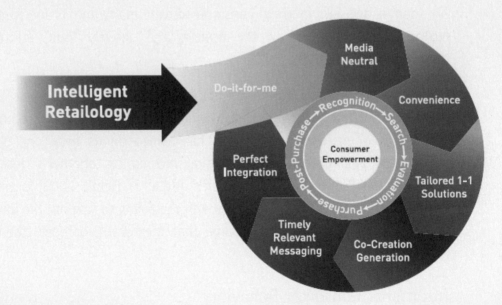

Perfect Integration

Whilst consumers are moving to buying on-line for a selection of products - sales have more than doubled in the last five years to £25.3bn and analysts expect them to grow further to £40bm by 2015 - consumers do still 'enjoy' the physical shopping experience. With an estimated 90% of sales revenue being generated through 'physical' stores, there is an active choice by consumers to shop in this manner and this creates an ideal opportunity for retailers to embrace new technology and look at innovative ways to converge it with the physical (Butler, 2012).

The Chartered
Institute of Marketing

The consumer is making buying decisions through information across channels and as digital retailing continues to advance the ability to define exactly when the final purchase decision was made becomes blurred. In a recent article in the Harvard Business Review, it was suggested that the term omni-channel better reflects the wealth of different channels that now exist, from physical stores, traditional direct mail, social media and gaming consoles (Rigby, 2011).

"Different customers will value parts of the shopping experience differently, but all are likely to want perfect integration of the digital and physical" (Rigby, 2011, P72).

Convenience

Convenience of pre-purchase and the purchase itself is expected as standard in today's world; if it is seen as a 'hassle' for consumers they will go elsewhere. This rings true across all channels. Retailers are delivering real value equity to consumers when the time, cost and effort of doing business with that retailer is reduced (Marketing Management, Spring 2001). Consumers will be increasingly be interested in technology that will save them time.

Empowerment

The consumer of the future will expect to be empowered by retailers to find information for themselves and to have 'intelligent' information passed to them. The buying process will become increasingly fragmented and compressed as consumers 'weave' in and out of it (Schaefer, 2011) completing their journey in the most convenient way for them. Retailers need to 'reach-out' and influence consumers at the most relevant touch points.

In the future we will be able to explore consumer behaviour more scientifically through Neuromarketing (Journal of Marketing Management, 2011). It enables marketers to look beyond asking people directly about their purchasing decisions to discovering the truth behind consumers hidden emotions. This has already become a booming industry (growing by over 100% in the last year) with retailers, brands and advertisers all wanting to understand what drives buyer behaviour. Gemma Calvert who founded Neurosense, clams that the technology is becoming so advanced she is "able to predict how customers will behave" (The Observer, 2012). The impact for retailers could be massive giving them the ability to predict how consumers will behave.

CHAPTER ROUNDUP

- The importance of relationship marketing was explained in the context of consumer behaviour and in order to build relationships with consumers it is essential to understand consumer lifestyles.

- Segmentation and customer typologies were explained with a retail store example.

- Key concepts and models were introduced such as the Five Stage Decision Process Model, B2B Buyer behaviour Model. More contemporary models such as the Mckinsey Consumer Decision Journey were explained.

- The importance of situational influences was explained for example membership reference groups, environmental and cultural.

- The increasingly influences of digital communication on consumer behaviour was explained for example Brand communities and Mumsnet.

FURTHER READING

Anon (2011) *Online Spending Habits,* Mintel.

Anon (2011) *Women's Fashion Lifestyles,* Mintel.

East, R. *et al* (2008) *Consumer Behaviour: Applications in Marketing*. London, Sage Publications.

Journal of Consumer Culture

Journal of Consumer Research

Parsons, E. and Maclaran, P. (2009) *Contemporary Issues in Marketing and Consumer Behaviour*. Oxford, Butterworth Heinemann.

Phillips, B. J. and McQuarrie, E. F. (2011) Contesting the social impact of marketing: a re-characterization of women's fashion advertising. *Marketing Theory*, 11: 99.

Rafferty, K. (2011) Class-based emotions and the allure of fashion consumption. *Journal of Consumer Culture,* 11: 239.

Salsberg, (2010) The New Japanese Consumer. *McKinsey Quarterly*. Issue 2, p80-87.

REFERENCES

Akbar, A. (2012) How e-readers took the embarrassment out of erotic fiction. The Independent, http://www.independent.co.uk/arts-entertainment/books/features/how-ereaders-took-the-embarrassment-out-of-erotic-fiction-7743289.html [Accessed on 18 October 2012].

Brassington, F. and Pettitt, S. (2006), *Principles of Marketing*. 3rd edition. Prentice Hall, London.

Brown, J. (2012) Every Lidl helps: bargain hunters flock to German masters of no-frills shopping. The Independent, http://www.independent.co.uk/news/business/news/every-lidl-helps-bargain-hunters-flock-to-german-masters-of-nofrills-shopping-7888984.html [Accessed on 29 October 2012].

Court, D. *et al* (2009) The consumer decision journey, *McKinsey Quarterly*.

Kotler, P. *et al* (2005) Principles of Marketing, Harlow FT Prentice Hall.

McInerney, P. *et al* (2009) *Winning in Japan's consumer electronics market*. McKinsey Asia Consumer and Retail

Humpage, A (2012) Mumsnet Academy set for success. Carat, http://www.carat.co.uk/blog/mumsnet-academy-set-for-success/ [Accessed July 2012].

Ray S. G., (2010) *India's unbearable lightness of being* http://news.bbc.co.uk/1/hi/world/south_asia/8546183.stm [Accessed July 2012]

Royo-Vela, M. and Casamassima, P. (2011) The influence of belonging to virtual brand communities on consumers' affective commitment, satisfaction and word-of-mouth advertising: The ZARA case. *Online Information Review,* Vol 35(4), pp517–542.

Solomon, M.R. *et al* (2010) *Consumer behaviour – a European perspective*. 4th edition, Harlow Prentice Hall.

Sparke, T. (2011) McKinsey consumer decision journey. Youtube, http://www.youtube.com/watch?v=EfRrD3we0Hg [Accessed on 25 October 2012].

ACTIVITY DEBRIEFS

Activity 5.1

It is important to access journal articles as part of your research into the macro and micro impacts and also gain insights into contemporary thinking.

Discussion points

1   Discuss the findings of the journal article with your fellow students.

2   Evaluate the findings – do you agree or disagree with them?

3   What are the potential implications of these findings for marketers? Do they only apply to the fashion industry?

Activity 5.2

Discussion points

1   The *Fifty Shades of Grey* publishing sensation has revolutionised the erotic fiction genre just as *Harry Potter* did with children's fiction. Compare and contrast these two: the impacts of *Fifty Shades of Grey* and *Harry Potter*. Did they both create new genres or revitalise existing ones?

2   Evaluate the impact that technology has had on distribution of e-books, (marketing – social media, blogs and consumer behaviour – lack of embarrassment).

3   Can e-books and printed titles co-exist? Examine your own consumer behaviour in relation to book purchase.

4   Have your consumption habits changed? Why is this?

5   Have your consumption habits changed in relation to any other media eg films, newspapers?

6   Evaluate the macro impacts on the publishing industry. What are the most significant impacts?

7   In terms of the scenarios you can develop, one could be that in ten years' time all books are read as an e-book. Reading books may increase among teenagers, as a new genre emerges. Perhaps, bookshops will disappear from the high street as consumers demand more interactivity.

8   The development of two alternative scenarios: from where things remain as they are now and one where the worst case scenario is possible.

Activity 5.3

Discussion points

1   Evaluate the McKinsey findings: are they a viable alternative to more linear consumer behaviour models?

2   Compare the McKinsey findings with a consumer behaviour model of your choice.

3   Which model best describes your behaviour as a consumer?

Activity 5.4

Discussion points

1   Discuss the criteria you will use to evaluate the consumer decision journey model.

2   How can organisations ensure they feature in the consumer's initial consideration set?

3   How fundamental is multi-channel marketing in the consumer decision journey?

4   Evaluate the significance of post-purchase behaviour.

The Chartered Institute of Marketing

CHAPTER 6

Competition

Introduction

Identifying, monitoring and responding to competitors are critical activities for most organisations. However, in many industries, the competitive structure is something which changes rapidly and adapting to these shifts can be demanding for all but the best prepared organisations. Marketers are often given the task of interpreting industry data and responding to the manoeuvring of competitors, potential new entrants to the industry and substitutes. Increasingly, especially in high velocity markets, marketers are also being asked to take the lead in developing pro-active strategies designed to help their organisation enter new industry areas or build barriers to prevent potential competitors from entering their sector. This chapter covers some of the classic frameworks for identifying competitors and monitoring the competitive environment of the organisation as well as introducing some newer ideas which provide more dynamic approaches to the challenges of the contemporary marketplace.

Topic list

Identifying competitors   ①

Strategic groups   ②

Addressing complexity – interrelationships between different elements of the industry and beyond   ③

Dynamic industry analysis   ④

1.2	Critically evaluate meso-environmental themes and assess/forecast their potential impact upon a specific sector or industry:
	▪ Changes in consumer behaviour
	▪ Changes in nature/structure of competition
	▪ Changes in nature/structure of supply chains

1 Identifying competitors

Understanding which organisations are direct competitors starts with defining the industry in which they operate. For the purposes of this text an industry is defined as 'a group of firms producing products that are close substitutes for each other' (Porter, 1980). An industry or sector is distinct from a market in that it is principally characterised by the attributes of the producers rather than those of customers. Industries can serve many different groups of customers or markets. For example, tyre manufacturers supply their products to car drivers through a number of channels, including automobile manufacturers, chains such as Kwik Fit, and wholesalers supplying independent garages. They also supply tyres to other businesses such as road haulage firms, truck manufacturers, agricultural machinery specialists and a host of other B2B buyers.

According to Porter (2008) industries can also be defined on a geographic basis. While some will serve global customers and operate on a similar basis worldwide, others will have distinctive regional or local features.

A skilled analyst will be able to determine industry boundaries effectively. To do this they need to understand that the product or service their organisation is selling is often treated by customers as a solution to a problem (see Chapter 5). There is usually a balance needed between defining an industry too broadly, in which case analysis becomes over-generalised, or too narrowly, which brings the dangers of missing a group of competitors, substitutes or potential entrants to the sector. Knowledge of customers and their reasons for buying the product or service are thus an important further element in understanding any industry. In some cases, such as the tyre sector mentioned above, it may be desirable to treat some of the markets as distinct industries in their own right.

Once the industry has been defined, marketers need to identify the actors in that sector and divide them into groups. Here, one of the classic theories, the five forces (Porter 2008) can provide a useful framework for understanding the role of each group of participants in an industry (Figure 6.1 below). Most managers are familiar with this concept, first introduced in 1979 by Harvard Professor, Michael Porter. However, the framework is much misunderstood and often not well applied.

Figure 6.1   The five forces that shape industry competition

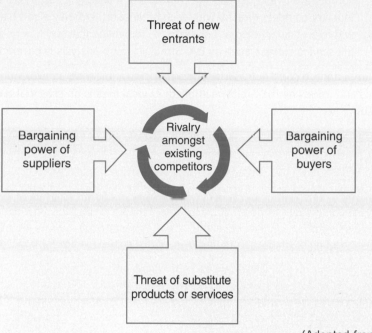

(Adapted from Porter, M., 2008)

1.1 Industry analysis

Applying the five forces to an industry helps marketers to understand the level of competition and ultimately its profitability. Consider each of the five factors in relation to your own industry.

- **Bargaining power of suppliers** – tends to be stronger when there are few large organisations controlling supplies, switching costs are high, or there are a large number of smaller customers.

- **Bargaining power of buyers** – the balance of power generally sits with buyers when there are few of them buying in large quantities. For example, supermarkets in the UK have significant bargaining power over wholesalers and farmers. Buyer power is also strongest when the products the industry supplies are standardised and undifferentiated, where it is easy to change suppliers or where they can produce the product themselves.

- **Threat of new entrants** – this is determined by the barriers to entry in an industry. The threat is highest where barriers to entry are low. Significant barriers to entry include, capital requirements, economies of scale and scope, access to distribution channels, likely response of incumbents in the industry and government regulations and policies. Apple has made use of patent protection to challenge new entrants to the smartphone market, such as Samsung and HTC, in recent years.

- **Threat of substitute products or services** – substitutes are determined by customers, so this is one of the hardest elements of industry analysis to get right. Understanding buyer behaviour is critical to this aspect of applying the framework. Substitutes are products or services which customers consider to be equivalent in value to those produced by the industry. In practical terms, these products limit the price firms in the industry can charge for their goods. Some substitutes can be relatively straightforward to identify – for example, honey can be seen as a substitute for sugar as they both can be used as a sweetening ingredient. Other substitutes are trickier to capture because they may be more generic. A trip to the cinema could be substituted with anything a customer considered to be an evening's entertainment.

- **Rivalry amongst existing competitors** – analysis of this element of the framework should reveal the intensity of competition in the sector. This will be related to a number of factors, including the relative size of competitors, the level of fixed costs in the industry, the stage in the industry life cycle (see below), and barriers to exit. The culture and history of an industry can also play a role in the nature of competitive rivalry, as can the character of the leading executives in the sector. Not all competitors in an industry compete directly with each other and there may also be evidence of different strategic groupings within particular sectors. For example, the airline industry has no-frills operators, such as Ryanair and full service carriers such as BA. Strategic group analysis is covered further below.

It is important to carry out your analysis in a critical manner, so evaluating what factors are driving each of the forces and assessing their relative strength or weakness is an essential part of the process according to Porter (2008).

THE REAL WORLD

Budget gyms

The recession has produced many changes to the way business is done and the way some markets respond. New entrants with a no-frills approach have targeted a wide range of industries from airlines to grocery shopping. Most recently, the fitness sector has seen a growth in budget gyms offering basic facilities to cost conscious consumers.

The UK fitness industry was worth £2.7 billion in 2011 sufficient to attract the likes of Sir Stelios Haji-Iaonnou, the founder of EasyJet, who has set up EasyGym as an extension of his existing brands. Other entrants include Pure Gym and FitSpace. The new entrants offer less added extras but their monthly fees are as little as £15, compared to the £40 to 50 charged by mainstream players such as LA Fitness and Virgin Active. Although some commentators believe the budget gyms are targeting a separate market to the main players, some firms are so concerned that they have set up their own low cost brands to compete.

Fitness First was an early convert in 2011 with the launch of their Klick Fitness brand.

(Johnston, 2011; Walsh, 2011)

1.1.1 Refining your analysis

There are also a number of other ideas that can help to refine your industry analysis. Organisations are increasingly managing networks of suppliers and rather than the zero-sum outcome, which is envisaged in the five forces framework, there are groups of firms which work closely together and have a relationship-driven rather than a transactional approach to supply chain management (this is covered further in the next chapter). The same is true of distribution chains. In some instances, buyers may supply retailers, who supply end consumers. In a competitive sector, close co-operation is often necessary to ensure sales volumes achieve target. Consumer power is also something marketers need to consider when analysing the distribution element of the industry. As firms such as Intel have found, acknowledging the needs of, and appealing to, end consumers can change the balance of power between supplier and buyer.

1.1.2 Identifying different types of competitors

As we have seen, the Five Forces Framework encourages managers to think beyond their direct competitors by considering latent competition in the form of buyers and suppliers. Both these groups can compete for profits in an industry, but they can also move forward, or backward down the supply chain to become direct competitors. Similarly, there are a range of firms offering substitute products or services or posing a threat as potential new entrants to an industry or market. The Five Forces Framework is less useful in helping managers to identify specific organisations as indirect or potential competitors. Bergen and Peterhaf (2002) proposed a method for refining this analysis by taking account of the resources and competencies of other organisations and the markets they served (Figure 6.2 below).

 The Chartered Institute of Marketing

Figure 6.2   Mapping the competitive terrain

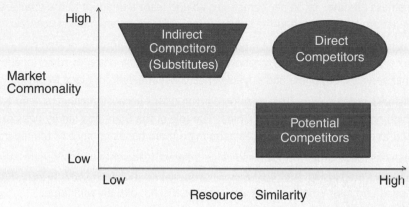

(Bergen and Peterhaf, 2002)

Potential competitors are classed as those whose resources and competences have a high degree of similarity with those in the industry, but who are currently not serving the same markets. These organisations are those which are most likely to become new entrants. Indirect competitors (or substitutes) will typically serve many of the same markets as the firms in the industry, but will have very different resources and competencies (further coverage can be found in Chapter 8).

ACTIVITY 6.1

Read Porter's most recent article on the five forces; (Porter, M. (2008) The five competitive forces that shape strategy, *Harvard Business Review*, January, pp78–93) and answer the following questions:

(a)   What are the common mistakes strategists make when analysing their industry?
(b)   How can analysts use the five forces framework in a more dynamic manner according to Porter?
(c)   How does the knowledge generated by a five forces analysis help organisations to develop their strategy?

1.1.3 Problems with the five forces framework

Since it was first published in 1979, Porter's framework has been praised and criticised by practitioners and academics. The ideas are based on concepts from industrial economics which was in vogue from the 1930s to the 1970s. While Porter's framework simplifies relatively complex economic ideas into a practical and usable model, some commentators have questioned his definition of industry, competition and competitive advantage (Meyer and Volbeerda, 1997). In practical situations, managers are the ones that define industries rather than economists.

The framework was developed at a time when industries were more stable and competitive moves more predictable (el Namaki, 2012). Since 1980, the growth of competition on a global basis; the increasing influence of capital markets on how firms develop their corporate strategy; and the appearance of emerging market firms who have different approaches to business; have all challenged the fundamental assumptions on which the framework was founded. For example, the de-regulation of capital markets and ready access to funds for mergers and acquisitions has made it easier for new entrants to an industry to overcome financial barriers to entry and concentrated power with suppliers and/or buyers due to consolidation (el Namaki, 2012).

A recent study in China (Wang and Chang, 2009) found that very few Chinese executives had either heard of, or used, the five forces for developing their strategies. The researchers put forward an alternative set of five forces that were seen as more appropriate for the Chinese market:

Business purpose: Companies with a win-win approach to business did better than those solely focused on profit. A key criticism of Porter's five forces framework is that it fails to appreciate the collaborative possibilities for gaining and sustaining competitive advantage. In China, co-operation is a given, not an optional extra.

Business climate: In China, companies able to learn and adapt to the changes in the environment, such as regulation, technology and the values of their customers are more successful.

Business location: China is a huge country and where a firm is located can have a profound effect on the success of its enterprises. Transport links are very much better in some locations than others and access to other services, suppliers and buyers varies substantially from place to place.

Business organisation: This new force is important because managers need to understand the different way in which organisations operate in China. The role of the State and family ties are just two of the elements that need to be appreciated as well as adopting a more hands-on style of management.

Business leadership: The Chinese value different leadership characteristics and successful enterprises are seen as those with leaders that are wise, sincere, and courageous. Leaders who are perceived as reckless, hot headed and over-emotional will not earn the respect of their workforce.

(Adapted from Wang and Chang, 2009)

One of the other issues with the five forces framework is its incompatibility with corporate social responsibility (Maxfield, 2008). The imperatives that often come from industry analysis and a desire to gain a sustainable competitive advantage does not always sit well with CSR principles. As outlined below, perfect markets, where all competitors have the same access to resources and customers and are about the same size, deliver poor returns to organisations. Imperfect markets are better for profit levels over a sustained period of time. However, imperfections are often based on control or exploitation of scarce resources or information asymmetries between buyers and suppliers. The transparency and the sustainable use of resources demanded by CSR present firms with a paradox because their very source of competitive advantage may derive from an activity that is not considered to enhance their CSR credentials.

The five forces framework should, therefore, be considered as a starting point for analysing industry and the changing nature of competition. It is important to understand the concept, but there are also other factors which need to be taken into account, a number of these are examined below.

1.2 Complementers – a sixth force?

Porter (2008) argues that any other factors affecting an industry, such as macro-environmental changes and pressures from stakeholder groups, should be included through the way they influence the five forces. Other commentators, most notably Brandenburger and Nalebuff (1995), consider that in many industries the producers of complementary products or services can have a positive or negative influence on the level of profits within the sector. For the customer, complementary products increase the value of the basic product and are widespread in most consumer and many business markets. A smartphone (product) without apps (complementary products) is less valuable to the owner of the phone than one with these additional features, supplied by other firms. Increasingly, as organisations use platforms and systems – made up of a combination of products and services – to compete rather than single products, complements are an increasingly important part of the mix.

Who profits from a complementary relationship will depend on the power balance between the supplier of the original product and the complementary product. In the smartphone industry the power currently sits with the handset manufacturers, especially where they control the software behind the apps through licensing. However, more open architectures may well lead to the power balance shifting as in the PC industry in the 1980s when Microsoft became a dominant supplier of a complementary product with its Windows software.

Brandenburger and Nalebuff's value net framework (Figure 6.3) provides a tool for assessing with which organisations a firm can collaborate. When you analyse your own industry, the value net can be used to understand what co-operative relationships exist in the sector.

The Chartered Institute of Marketing

Figure 6.3   The value net

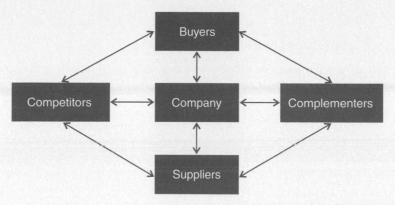

(Adapted from Brandenburger and Nalebuff, 1995)

ACTIVITY 6.2

Think about the following industries and identify at least one complementary product or service in each and comment on where the power rests in the relationship between product and complementer.

Once your five (or six) forces analysis is completed it should be clear how your industry is structured. There are four generic structures put forward by economists, few industries conform to these exactly but most can be assigned to one of the types.

1.3 Industry structure

Table 6.1   Types of industry structures

Structure characteristics	Monopoly	Oligopoly	Monopolistic competition	Perfect competition
Number of firms	One	A few large organisations	Some larger firms and many medium-sized and smaller organisations	Many firms of a similar size
Sustainability of competitive advantage	Total	Longer term	Possible	None
Degree of competition	Low	Low/Medium	Medium	High
Marketplace stability	High	High/Medium	Low/Medium	Low
Typical strategic stance	Defensive	Defensive	Aggressive	Aggressive
Pricing implications	*Carte blanche* on pricing (but usually regulated by governments	Strategic pricing possible – determined by responses from other players	Some discretion with pricing	Firms must take market price
Examples	Utilities, Railways	Commercial aircraft, Supermarkets, Banking	Beauty therapists, Restaurants, Dentists	Commodity industries such as wheat, oil, milk etc

Industries located to the right of the table will tend to be less attractive for firms, competition is often based on price and barriers to entry are low. Firms enter and leave the industry frequently. Unless the industry is experiencing high growth these sectors are unlikely to produce high levels of profit.

THE REAL WORLD

Internet companies in China – a world of perfect competition?

Despite giant firms such as Alibaba (owner of China's equivalent of eBay, Taobao), Tencent, and Baidu, low barriers to entry and easy access to venture capital have made certain parts of the internet in China resemble a state of perfect competition. In July 2011, there were over 2,000 online coupon websites, 200 online video services and over 80 social networks operating on China's internet.

All this has made the internet in China into a highly competitive, gladiatorial environment according to Richard Robinson, a Beijing-based American entrepreneur. The sheer size of the Chinese market and the rapid growth in online retailing and advertising means that many of these firms are able to make substantial profits for their owners.

(Adapted from The Economist, 2011)

1.4 Hypercompetition

Richard D'Aveni coined the phrase hypercompetition in 1994 to describe industries where changes are so rapid and competition so intense that it is impossible for firms to gain a sustainable competitive advantage. The idea of rapidly changing industry structures driven by new entrants and disruptive innovation is nothing new and was first highlighted by Joseph Schumpeter (1976) and the Austrian school of economics in the 1940s. However, D'Aveni argues that the frequency of such disruptions is increasing dramatically due to globalisation, advances in technology and socio-cultural changes. Although hypercompetition is a contested concept, it could be seen as a fifth generic industry type. It can be just as likely to occur in an industry with an oligopolistic structure – such as mobile handsets, as it is to be found in a state of perfect or near perfect competition.

2 Strategic groups

Groups of firms following the same basic strategy in a range of areas including product range, pricing, market coverage, R&D focus etc.

Segmenting customers into groups using various factors from simple demographics to behaviours and values is something marketers should be familiar with. Segmenting competitors is often less practiced or well understood. One way of classifying competitors in an industry into different groups is to look at the strategies they are following. This can be useful in identifying the strategic niches being followed by different firms and can sometimes also provide evidence of which strategies are the most successful in an industry.

▶ **Assessment tip**

Identifying the strategic groups in your own industry can be a valuable exercise when you are thinking about which strategic marketing responses to discuss in you assignment. It may also provide strong evidence when you need to provide justification for your recommendation.

2.1 Mapping strategic groups – selecting relevant dimensions

Firms in the same strategic group are not necessarily direct competitors, though they could be. In some cases, firms in different regions of countries will be pursuing similar strategies but not actually competing directly for the same customers. To conduct a strategic group analysis you need to select at least two dimensions as a basis for your comparison. These might include the extent of a firm's product range or geographic scope, which distribution channels they use, how vertically integrated they are, the level of product quality, choice of technology etc. It is important to choose divergent dimensions to give a more insightful analysis. Another way of structuring your analysis might be to look at the best and worst performing firms in your industry and see which dimensions they have in common as important aspects of their strategy.

The Chartered Institute of Marketing

THE REAL WORLD

Strategic groups within the global hotel industry

Figure 6.4 below represents a partial analysis of the global hotel industry in 2012. There are a wide range of players operating with very different strategies. Some are focusing on dominating a national market with a specific brand, such as Whitbread with their Premier Inn offering. Some of the Global multi-brand operators will certainly be competing with this group – even though their strategy is different. Accor's Ibis brand could be considered a direct competitor to Premier Inn in the UK. At the other end of the scale Accor's Sofitel brand of luxury hotels competes with the likes of Fairmont. However, the strategies being followed by each organisation are very different. Accor has a very broad range of customers and also mixes franchising with owned hotels. Their strategy is segmented as opposed to the Luxury Hotel firms who are more focused on a high-end niche.

Figure 6.4   Map of strategic groups in the global hotel industry

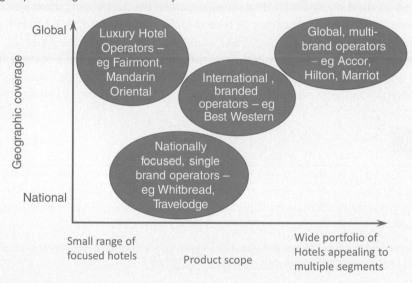

3 Addressing complexity – interrelationships between different elements of the industry and beyond

By using the various frameworks to analyse an industry and markets we can gain a clear picture of the individual elements that shape competition. However, to gain real insight into the industry, and more importantly to be able to generate possible future scenarios, you will need to take a holistic approach to your analysis. Synthesising the results of each piece of analysis is a good starting point for this, but you will also need to think about the interrelationships between the different players in an industry. For example, powerful suppliers can encourage new firms into an industry in order to enhance their bargaining power with buyers. They might do this by offering favourable credit terms or access to rare raw materials etc.

3.1 Interdependencies between different industry forces

Tony Grundy of Cranfield School of Management argues (2006) that there are significant interdependencies between each of the five competitive forces in Porter's model. The actors within the industry, such as buyers and suppliers, are actively changing their positions to gain advantage and may be the source of significant change. For example, buyers may actively search for substitute products – especially if they are not satisfied with the existing products or services being produced by the industry. Suppliers may seek to bypass the existing players in the industry by forward integration or developing their own substitute products. Both groups can also be active in encouraging new entrants to the market or becoming new entrants themselves through backward or forward integration.

THE REAL WORLD

Bands such as Groove Armada and the Arctic Monkeys have been able to bypass record labels and much of the traditional music business by using the internet to communicate directly with their fans. Music buyers have also encouraged substitutes by being willing to illegally download tracks rather than buy music through traditional channels. The dominance of the iTunes service from Apple has encouraged the record labels to work with a wider range of organisations including new entrants to the digital music industry like streaming service Spotify.

3.2 Actors outside the industry

There is a range of organisations and individuals that fall outside the boundaries of an industry, but can still have an effect on the nature of competition within the industry and the manner in which firms conduct themselves. Some of these may be related to the macro-environmental factors you have already covered in previous chapters. For example, trade unions can have a significant impact on how industries operate. Universities and research institutes may already be working on some of the technological advances that will render an industry obsolete or change it beyond recognition. Forging links with some of these actors or understanding their aims and objectives can give firms a competitive advantage over their rivals.

ACTIVITY 6.3

At the beginning of July 2012, UK dairy farmers blockaded the plants of their key customers, the supermarkets and milk processing companies, such as Robert Wiseman Dairies (owned by Muller). The demonstrations were a protest in response to cuts in the price being paid to the farmers for their milk, Many farmers now claim they are being paid less than it costs to produce the milk in the first place.

Read the following item on the BBC News website: BBC News (2012) Farmers demand reversal of milk price cuts, BBC News online, available at: http://www.bbc.co.uk/news/business-18733248

Questions

(a) Analyse the UK dairy industry using the five forces and the value net frameworks. Who are the most powerful players in the industry? Why do they have significant power? What scope is there for more co-operative relationships in the industry?

(b) What actions could buyers and suppliers take to change the dynamic of the dairy industry?

(c) What are the most important external factors affecting the industry in 2012?

(d) Which actors outside the industry might have an influence on how the sector operates?

4 Dynamic industry analysis

All the frameworks we have covered so far could be criticised as being too static. They tend to be used to capture the nature of competition at a particular point in time. However, the emerging themes unit is focused on changes in the environment so, for the purposes of the assignment, you will need to move beyond this basic starting point and ensure that your analysis is dynamic and future focused.

4.1 Industry life cycle

There is strong evidence that like products, industries also have a life cycle with different stages over a period of time. Each stage has specific characteristics when it comes to competition and typical industry structure. Understanding which phase of the life cycle an industry is in can help to predict what might occur in the future. When analysing your own industry you need to consider that it may not follow the typical pattern. The emerging theme you are investigating may actually change the life cycle stage of the industry. For example, the introduction of a new technology may take a mature industry back into a growth phase again. Some of the explosive growth seen in the sales of mobile handsets in the 1990s has been seen again in many markets with the introduction of smartphones. Industries may also be at different stages of their life cycle in different countries or regions. Understanding what has happened in other geographies can also help to predict some of the potential changes that an industry may face in another country whose industry is in an earlier phase of the life cycle. The introduction of mobile number portability (the ability to keep the same number when switching networks) has increased churn and competition each time it has been introduced into different markets (usually through legislation).

Figure 6.5 Typical Industry life cycle stages

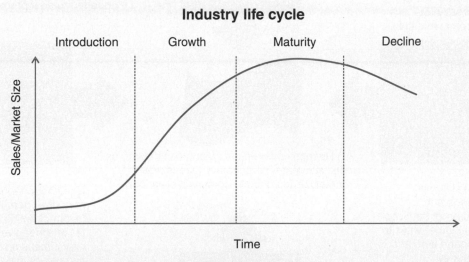

Table 6.2 Industry features at different stages of the life cycle

Stage feature	Introduction	Growth	Maturity	Decline
Competition	Low, as there are few companies, mainly intent on establishing an industry	Entry of new competitors, beginning of merger activity and some exits. Still more buyers than sellers	Increasing rivalry due to lower growth and more powerful buyers. Price competition. Some consolidation likely	Fierce competition often in the form of price wars, many exits from the industry
Key success factors	Ability to innovate and differentiate	Ability to sustain growth and scale-up production and distribution	Managing costs and processes, economies of scale, financial strength	Rationalisation and aggressive cost management. Commitment to the industry

4.2 Making the five forces or other industry frameworks dynamic

Having identified the key macro-environmental factor that you predict will have a significant impact on your industry; you will need to think about how this will change the forces within the sector individually and what impact this will have overall on firms. Some changes may tip an industry from one phase of its life cycle to another. For example, increased knowledge of the health impacts of smoking, combined with government campaigns and bans have contributed to the decline of the tobacco industry in the UK.

Figure 6.6 below shows the predictions made by managers in the magazine industry in Finland of the impact the internet would have on their sector. Most believed the most significant change would be an increase in rivalry between existing competitors

Figure 6.6   The impact of the internet on the five-forces of the magazine publishing industry in Finland

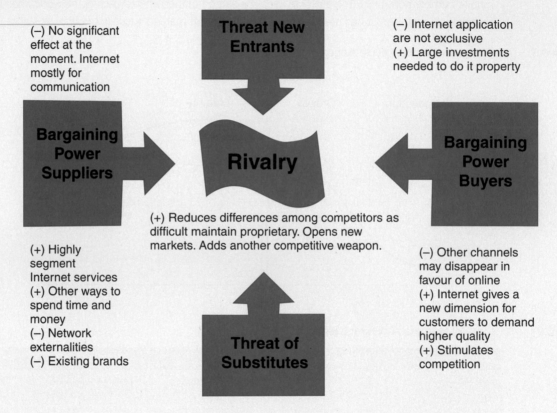

(–) No significant effect at the moment. Internet mostly for communication

(–) Internet application are not exclusive
(+) Large investments needed to do it property

(+) Reduces differences among competitors as difficult maintain proprietary. Opens new markets. Adds another competitive weapon.

(+) Highly segment Internet services
(+) Other ways to spend time and money
(–) Network externalities
(–) Existing brands

(–) Other channels may disappear in favour of online
(+) Internet gives a new dimension for customers to demand higher quality
(+) Stimulates competition

(Adapted from Ellonen, H-K. *et al*, 2008)

This technique of predicting the changes to the different forces in the industry can be applied to other frameworks, such as the value net or to anticipate changes to strategic groups within the industry.

▶ **Assessment tip**

Using graphics such as Figure 6.6 above or radar plots can be an effective way of showing the impact of changes on an industry over time and can also help you to maximise your word count in the assignment.

The Chartered Institute of Marketing

- Porter's five forces framework is a traditional way of analysing competition in an industry.

- The five forces framework has been widely criticised but can still provide a useful starting point.

- The growth of CSR and emergence of new economies with other ways of doing business need to be considered in contemporary industry analysis.

- Other concepts for looking at the competitive landscape include the value net, which looks at opportunities for collaboration and introduces a sixth force, complementers.

- There are four generic industry types, monopoly, oligopoly, monopolistic competition, and perfect competition.

- A further industry type has been put forward by Professor Richard D'Aveni, hypercompetition, where disruptive innovation is a constant factor.

- Competitive structure can also be analysed be identifying groups of companies who are following similar strategies.

- Some of the criticisms of the five forces framework can be addressed by analysing the interrelationships between and the impact of external actors on each of the forces.

- A more dynamic form of competitive analysis can be achieved through taking account of the life cycle of the industry and how changes to the macro-environment will affect different components of the sector.

FURTHER READING

Bodily, S. and Venkataraman, S. (2004) Not walls, windows: capturing value in the digital age. *Journal of Business Strategy*, Vol25(3), pp15–25.

Brandenburger, A. and Nalebuff, B. (1995) The right game. *Harvard Business Review*, July–August 1995, pp57–71.

Ellonen, H-K. *et al* (2008) The strategic impact of the internet on magazine publishing. *International Journal of Innovation and Technology Management*, Vol5(3), pp341–361.

Grundy, M. (2006) Rethinking and reinventing Michael Porter's five forces model. *Strategic Change*, Vol15, pp213–29.

Huyett, W. and Vigurie, S. (2005) Extreme Competition. McKinsey Quarterly, February 2005 online, https://www.mckinseyquarterly.com/Extreme_competition_1564

McKinsey (2008) How companies respond to competitors: A McKinsey Global Survey. *McKinsey Quarterly*, May 2008, online, https://www.mckinseyquarterly.com/How_companies_respond_to_competitors_2146

Or apply the framework to a specific sector:

Others provide alternatives:

Porter has answered his critics on numerous occasions – apart from the most recent (2008) restatement of the framework, it is also covered in:

Porter, M. (2001) Strategy and the internet. *Harvard Business Review*, Vol79(3), pp63–78.

Porter, M. and Kramer, M. (2006) Strategy and society; The link between competitive advantage and corporate social responsibility. *Harvard Business Review*, Vol84(12), pp78–92.

Practitioners have also provided a good range of ideas on the changing nature of competition:

Several authors provide enhancements to the five forces framework, these include:

Vining, A. *et al* (2005) Building the firm's political (lobbying) strategy. *Journal of Public Affairs*, Vol5, pp150–175.

Wang, W. and Chang, P. (2009) Entrepreneurship and strategy in China: why 'Porter's five forces' may not be. *Journal of Chinese Entrepreneurship*, Vol1(1), pp53–64.

REFERENCES

Anon (2011) An internet with Chinese characteristics. *The Economist*, July 30 2011, pp55–56.

Anon (2012) Farmers demand reversal of milk price cuts. BBC News, http://www.bbc.co.uk/news/business-18733248 [Accessed 8 July 2012]

Bergen, M. and Peterhaf, M. (2002) Competitor identification and competitor analysis: a broad-based managerial approach *Managerial and Decision Economics*, Vol23 pp157-169.

Brandenburger, A. and Nalebuff, B. (1995) The right game. *Harvard Business Review*, July–August 1995, pp57–71.

D'Aveni, R. (1994) *Hypercompetition: Managing the Dynamics of Strategic Maneuvering*. New York, The Free Press.

El Namaki, (2012) Does the thinking of yesterday's management gurus imperil today's companies? *Ivey Business Journal*, March/April.

Ellonen, H-K. *et al* (2008) The strategic impact of the internet on magazine publishing. *International Journal of Innovation and Technology Management*, Vol5(3), pp341–361.

Grundy, T. (2006) Rethinking and reinventing Michael Porter's five forces model. *Strategic Change*, Vol15, pp213–29.

Johnston, C. (2011) It's no stretch for budget gyms to flex their muscles. *The Times*, Monday, 22 August, pp32–3.

Maxfield, S. (2008) Reconciling corporate citizenship and competitive strategy: insights from economic theory. *Journal of Business Ethics*, Vol80, pp367–377.

Meyer, R. and Volbeerda, H. (1997) Porter on corporate strategy. *In* van den Bosch, F. and de Man, A. (eds) *Perspectives on Strategy*. pp25–33, Antwerp, Kluwer Academic Publishers.

Porter, M. (1980) *Competitive Strategy*. New York, Free Press.

Porter, M. (2008) The five competitive forces that shape strategy. *Harvard Business Review*, January 2008, pp78–93.

Schumpeter, J. (1976) *Capitalisation, Socialism and Democracy*. London, George Allen & Unwin.

Walsh, D. (2011) Flotation means new approach to fitness. *The Times (London)*, 2 July.

Wang, W. and Chang, P. (2009) Entrepreneurship and strategy in China: why 'Porter's five forces' may not be. *Journal of Chinese Entrepreneurship*, Vol1(1), pp53–64.

 The Chartered Institute of Marketing

Activity 6.1

(a) What are the common mistakes strategists make when analysing their industry?

One of the key mistakes Porter covers at length is defining an industry too broadly or too narrowly. But he also covers a range of other ways in which strategists can miss the point in analysing an industry. The analysis needs to consist of more than lists and should be used to inform strategic options. To do this the analysis needs to give an overview of the industry as well as analyse the component parts. Porter also points out that analysis using the five forces framework should be dynamic and take account of changes in the environment.

Discussion point: Does Porter make valid points about the way in which the framework is used or does this criticism of strategists covering the inherent flaws in the concept?

(b) How can analysts use the five forces framework in a more dynamic manner, according to Porter?

The Framework can be used to factor in the impact of changes from the macro-environment (for example, the introduction of a new technology) and also changes internal to the industry (for instance the merger of two large competitors). It can also be used to predict changes in the future. In both cases the impact of the change on each force is assessed.

(c) How does the knowledge generated by a Five Forces analysis help organisations to develop their strategy?

The Framework doesn't just provide an assessment of industry attractiveness but it can explain why profit levels are as they are. It can help managers to understand the strengths and weaknesses of an organisation and to develop a stronger competitive position. Analysis using the Five Forces – especially using the dynamic approach recommended by Porter can help firms to exploit changes to the industry

Activity 6.2

Sector/Industry	Complementer?	Power?
Video Games	Console manufacturer/Movie firms and other owners of characters	
	Power – Console manufacturer	

Discussion points: if you chose the console manufacturer as the main firm then the games designers would be the complementer. The console manufacturers have the power, currently, but how do you think the rise of on-line gaming, such as World of Warcraft, Social Network games such as Farmville or mobile gaming, such as Angry Birds will affect this relationship?

Automobile manufacture: Oil companies (fuel) /Garage services power – depends – if the garage is franchised to the manufacturer then the power sits with the automobile brand.

Discussion points: what will happen as more hybrids and cars fuelled with alternatives to petrol come onto the market? Who will be the new complementers (electricity firms, for example) and how will the power shift between the players?

Coffee machines: Cartridge manufacturers, suppliers of filters and ground coffee. Power is most likely to rest with the cartridge manufacturers as they have the ongoing relationship with the customer through retail outlets.

Discussion points: If one of the manufacturers of coffee machines invents a universal adapter that allows users to access the other ranges of cartridges, how will this change the relationships in the industry?

Your own sector – this will depend on your industry and who you identify. However, do remember that the relationships are not static and just as external forces can change the other five forces, they can also impact on complementers and complementary products.

Activity 6.3

(a) Analyse the UK dairy industry using the five forces and the value net frameworks. Who are the most powerful players in the industry? Why do they have significant power? What scope is there for more co-operative relationships in the industry?

You might conclude that the processors are the most powerful players or the supermarkets. Why would this be the case? If you look at the key factors that drive advantage between suppliers and buyers, one reason is that they are more concentrated than the dairy farmers and also have a direct link to the customer (in the case of the supermarkets). The power also comes from the fact that milk is largely a commodity product – so it is relatively easy for the processors to switch suppliers and they have plenty of choice. Finally, you could also think about the fact that there is an oversupply of milk in Europe, which again, reduces the power of the suppliers.

Discussion points:

Although it appears that the supermarkets and the processors have the upper hand, how does the blockade of their plants and the 'hard-luck' story being told by the farmers, impact on their reputation? Is this a case of competition clashing with the social element of CSR? Consider how supermarkets such as The Co-operative, Asda and Morrisons have responded to the crisis by increasing the prices they pay directly to farmers for their milk. Is this the best option for a successful long-term strategy? Further coverage of this and other aspects of the crisis can be found at: BBC News (2012) "Q & A: Milk prices row and how the system works" BBC News on-line 23rd July 2012 available at: http://www.bbc.co.uk/news/business-18951422 [accessed 4th October 2012]

(b) What actions could buyers and suppliers take to change the dynamic of the dairy industry?

Some of the points you could have noted down include:

- Farmers could band together and form co-operatives or merge to form larger businesses with more clout

- They could also try to go directly to the supermarkets or the end consumers

- The farmers could add value by putting their milk into other products themselves and move forward up the supply chain by producing yoghurt or cheese or flavoured milks or ice cream etc.

- The processors could import milk from mainland Europe and effectively end the relationship with their troublesome suppliers

- Both the supermarkets and processors could pass on the higher costs to their customers or accept lower profits for this one product and gain through an enhanced reputation and CSR credentials

Although many of these points appear to be logical moves, how many of them are realistic? Would the farm businesses be able to access sufficient capital to build their own plants or bypass the retailers? Would the shareholders of the processors and the supermarkets allow them to lower their expected profits?

(c) What are the most important external factors affecting the industry in 2012?

Some of the points you could have made include:

Economic: The fall of the price of cream on commodity markets is cited as one factor affecting the price offered to the farmers

Political: In the UK the Conservative and Liberal Democrat Politicians are more likely to represent rural constituencies – so farmers have a disproportionately loud voice.

Legal: the dispute could trigger more regulation through monopolistic bodies or government intervention because the market is deemed to be failing.

Ethical: Given the current climate with the banks and other businesses under the spotlight for their behaviour, it may be very dangerous for the supermarkets and processors to continue to act in a way that will damage their reputation with their end customers.

Discussion points: Which do you think is the most important of these factors? If you applied this factor to each of the five (or six) forces in turn, how would it change the nature of competition in the UK dairy industry?

(d)   Which actors outside the industry might have an influence on how the sector operates?

Your list could have included:

- The UK Government
- The European Union
- The National Farmers Union
- The UK Media – BBC, ITN, Sky, newspapers, radio etc
- Commodity speculators
- Producers of milk substitutes – such as soya or almond-based liquids
- Health organisations (which have encouraged the switch to skimmed and semi-skimmed milk to reduce fat in the diet and thus meant a larger role for processors)
- Lobby Groups – from anti-supermarket websites such as tescopoly.com – to anti-farming/animal rights groups such as PETA

Discussion points: From your own list decide who you thought were the most significant and why?

The Chartered
Institute of Marketing

CHAPTER 7

Supply chain insights

Introduction

Supply markets are becoming increasingly volatile with wildly fluctuating commodity prices in oil, copper and cotton. Research by MIT and Accenture, has shown that while disruptions in the balance between supply and demand due to geopolitical events and natural disasters get the most press, disruptions due to volatility from everyday occurrences like poor supplier performance, forecast inaccuracy and slow, or inconsistent performance actually cause more lost profits.

(Accenture, 2012) http://www.accenture.com/us-en/consulting/Pages/index.aspx

Topic list

What is supply chain management?	1
The concepts of 'lean and agile'	2
Porter's value chain (1985)	3
The assessment	4
Kraljic portfolio purchasing model	5
Supplier relationships	6
Sustainable SCM	7
Technology and SCM	8

1.2	Critically evaluate meso-environmental themes and assess/forecast their potential impact upon a specific sector or industry:
	■ Changes in consumer behaviour ■ Changes in nature/structure of competition ■ Changes in nature/structure of supply chains

1 What is supply chain management?

There are numerous definitions of the supply chain and supply chain management (SCM). The Chartered Institute of Purchasing and Supply (CIPS) gives a definition of a supply chain as:

'The supply chain conceptually covers the entire physical process from ordering and obtaining the raw materials through all process steps until the finished product reaches the end consumer. Most supply chains consist of many separate companies, each linked by virtue of their part in satisfying the specific need of the end consumer.'

(CIPS Intelligence, 2009-2012)

SCM may be thought of as the management of all activities aimed at satisfying the end consumer. As such, it covers almost all activity within the organisation. It has been suggested that it incorporates a number of key success factors, which include a clear procurement strategy, effective control systems, and development of expertise. SCM therefore represents and reflects a holistic approach to the operation of the organisation. Hence, SCM relates to the entire procurement cycle and not just at the end (which is the commonly held view). In particular, it has a pivotal role to play in the development of an initial sourcing strategy.

A further definition is that SCM is the management of a network of interconnected businesses involved in the provision of product and service packages required by the end customers in a supply chain. Supply chain management spans all movement and storage of raw materials, work-in-process inventory, and finished goods from the point of origin to point of consumption.

Figure 7.1   Six Markets Model

(Adapted from Payne *et al*, 2005)

In the six markets model (Payne *et al*, 2005) the importance of supplier/alliance markets in achieving long-term, sustainable relationship marketing is highlighted. Suppliers provide physical resources to organisations and these are typically, the upstream source of raw materials, components, products or other tangible goods. Alliance partners are also suppliers but they will be typically supplying competences and capabilities that are more knowledge-based. They may provide logistics and these type of alliances are usually created for the

perceived need to outsource an activity within the company's value chain This chapter provides an overview of some key models and concepts and introduces more contemporary thinking.

2 The concepts of 'lean and agile'

'Lean', in this sense, means developing a value stream to eliminate all waste, promote innovation and enable a level schedule. The five principles of 'lean' (Womack and Jones, 2003) are:

- Specify what creates value, as seen from the customers' perspective
- Identify all steps across the value stream
- Make those actions that create that value flow
- Only make what is 'pulled ' by the customer
- Strive for perfection by continually removing successive layers of waste

'Agile' means using market knowledge and a responsive supply network to exploit profitable opportunities in the marketplace.

Criticisms of 'lean' (Hines, Howle, Rich, 2004)

- There is a lack of inbuilt contingency, which does not allow for flexibility
- Inability to cope with variability
- Tactical shopfloor focus rather than strategic
- Mechanistic, thus ignoring the human factor
- Low-volume industries
- Global aspects
- E-business

3 Porter's value chain (1985)

Figure 7.2   Porter's value chain

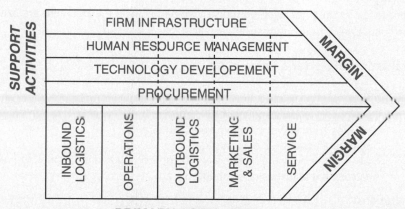

A value chain is a set of activities that an organisation carries out to create value for its customers. Porter (1985) proposed a general-purpose value chain that companies can use to examine all of their activities, and see how they are connected. The way in which value chain activities are performed determines costs and affects profits, so this tool can help you understand the sources of value for your organisation that determine competitiveness.

Primary activities

Primary activities relate directly to the physical creation, sale, maintenance and support of a product or service. They consist of the following:

Inbound logistics – These are all the processes related to receiving, storing, and distributing inputs internally. Supplier relationships are a key factor in creating value here.

Operations – These are the transformational activities that change the inputs into outputs sold to customers. Here, operational systems create value.

Outbound logistics – These activities deliver your product or service to your customer. These are things like collection, storage, and distribution systems, and they may be internal or external to your organisation.

Marketing and sales – These are the processes you use to persuade clients to purchase from you instead of your competitors. The benefits the organisation offers, and how well you communicate them, are sources of value here.

Service – These are the activities related to maintaining the value of your product or service to your customers, after purchase.

Support activities

These activities support the primary functions outlined above. In Figure 7.2, the dotted lines show that each support, or secondary, activity can play a role in each primary activity. For example, procurement supports operations with certain activities, but it also supports marketing and sales with other activities.

Procurement (purchasing) – This is what the organisation does to get the resources it needs to operate. This includes finding vendors and negotiating best prices.

Human resource management – This is how well a company recruits, hires, trains, motivates, rewards, and retains its workers. People are a significant source of value, so businesses can create a clear advantage with good HR practices.

Technological development – These activities relate to managing and processing information, as well as protecting a company's knowledge base. Minimising information technology costs, staying up-to-date with technological advances, and maintaining technical excellence are sources of value creation.

Infrastructure – These are a company's support systems, and the functions that allow it to maintain daily operations. Accounting, legal, administrative and general management are examples of necessary infrastructure that businesses can use to their advantage.

Evaluation of Porter's value chain

Advantages:

- Develops an understanding of how internal business activities add value
- Identifies source(s) of competitive advantage
- Analyses a company's cost position
- Makes better outsourcing decisions by optimising and co-ordinating linked activities
- Analyses the activities of competitors

Limitations:

- Many people find it difficult to use identifying linkages and cost drivers and to calculate costs
- It presents a static picture of a dynamic situation
- There are dangers in applying it in isolation from the value system
- It ignores the importance of information to maximise value and create virtual value chains

THE REAL WORLD

Ryanair and EasyJet are good examples of airlines that operate with a lost cost strategy and high operational efficiency to achieve this. They operate from lower cost airports such as Luton, Stansted, Marseille and Milan Bergamo. These are not normally the major airports serving any destination and can be some distance from the capital city. Aircraft are tightly scheduled. They are allowed only 25 minutes to off-load one set of passengers and load another, less than half the time of scheduled full-fare rivals. There is no 'slack' in the system. EasyJet admits to having one-and-a-half planes' worth of spare capacity compared with the dozen planes BA has on standby at Gatwick and Heathrow. There are fewer cabin crew than full-fare rivals and staff rostering can be a major logistical problem. In terms of customer service, it means there are not the 'frills' of other airlines, such as free drinks, meals or assigned seats. There is no compensation for delays or lost baggage. The low-cost airlines do not guarantee transfers as the planes could be late. The low-cost airlines concentrate on point-to-point flights, whereas the full-fare airlines tend to concentrate on hub-and-spoke traffic. Thus, through a combination of stripping out cost from the primary and support activities, the low cost operators developed a new business model for the airline industry. This low-cost strategy has clearly paid off and, while national carriers such as BA and American Airlines are struggling with the impact of the recession an increase in the volume of its business and the number of European travellers helped Easyjet report increased profits for 2011.

Easyjet announced a pre-tax profit of £248m for the year to 30 September 2011, in line with expectations, up from a profit of £154m in 2010. The improvement was led by an 11.8% increase in passenger numbers, with one million more people using the airline for business travel. In September, Easyjet announced a £150m special dividend for shareholders. The special dividend brings the total cash return to shareholders to £195m, or 45.4 pence per share, for the year. Easyjet chief executive, Carolyn McCall, said the results were achieved, 'despite the headwinds of higher fuel costs and a weak and uncertain economic outlook'.

(BBC, 2011)

ACTIVITY 7.1

Evaluate how MacDonald's has configured its supply chain in India.

Access the following link:

http://www.logisticsweek.com/feature/2011/07/the-big-idea-mcdonalds-unravels-its-supply-chain/

ACTIVITY 7.2

1 Analyse the value chain of your own organisation and evaluate how it contributes to its overall competitiveness.
2 How does the value chain for your organisation compare with your competitors?
3 How does the purchasing and supply strategy for your organisation compare with your competitors?

The key to developing purchasing and supply strategies is the issue of the influence of the balance of power between a company and its key suppliers. This depends on the organisation's approach to purchasing: whether it be 'adversarial' or more of a partnership-type approach and this will be determined by the availability of the product/service being purchased. It is vital that the purchasing strategy supports the overall corporate strategy and meets the long-term requirement of the organisation.

4 The assessment

Analysis of supply chains as a micro theme is the least popular. When selecting this theme candidates need to ensure that it relates to their macro theme, for example, the growth in demand for organic food and the tea industry in Sri Lanka. This emerging theme is clearly concerned with the agriculture — the primary stage in the supply chain for the tea industry and thus the selection of SCM is a relevant aspect to explore.

Candidates may use value system concepts from the 1990s to underpin their explanations but may choose to consider a wider range of models that take account of network level strategies, developments in vertical integration and outsourcing and more open organisations.

Candidates need to ensure that they have a working knowledge of how supply chains operate in their industries so they can conceptualise the models and apply to the context they have selected. Thus their exploration and critical evaluation will be from a professional perspective rather than a generic theoretical discussion.

The example below relates to ethical consumerism on the UK fashion and clothing industry. Here the candidate has contextualised their analysis to green supply issues, which relate to their macro theme. They have included a relevant model and there is good evaluation throughout.

The Chartered Institute of Marketing

3.3 Change in the nature of supply chains

The UK fashion and clothing market is linked with developing countries as 90% of clothing consumed in the UK is imported from China, India, Bangladesh and Sri Lanka (Department for environment, food and rural affairs, 2011). Therefore environmental and ethical improvements across the international clothing supply chains are essential.

The fashion industry is characterized by high volatility, high competition and high impulse purchasing. This nature of the industry has resulted in clothing suppliers operating within tight deadlines. The sector comes under substantial criticism for worker abuses, forced labour and unethical environmental practices. These criticisms have influenced both high-street and luxury fashion brands' supply chains. This is evident in the survey results that 92% of the UK consumers expect companies to be responsible for their supply chain (Ramrayka, 2006).

The nature of the fashion and clothing supply chains has changed dramatically during last decade. Firms have identified the benefits of green supply[2] implementation for purchasing and supply processes (Bowen et al, 2001) and these initiatives occur as a response to ethical consumerism.

These initiatives can be evaluated using the framework of SSCM by Bowen et al. (2001) (Figure 1)

(See appendix c for framework)

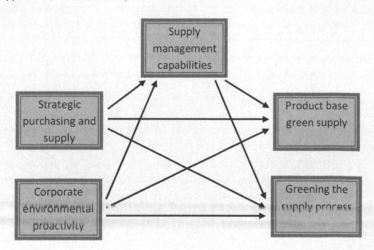

(Figure 1) Frame work of SSCM by Bowen et al. (2001)

Supply management capabilities

Firms liaise between purchasing and other divisions. Policies and procedures are established for purchasing as well as improving the technical skills of professionals. Partnership approaches with

---

[2] The term 'green supply' denotes 'supply management activities that are attempts to improve the environmental performance of purchased inputs, or of the suppliers that provide them. They might include activities such as co-operative recycling and packaging waste reduction initiatives, environmental data gathering about products, processes or vendors, and joint development of new environmental products or processes. (Bowen et al. 2001: 175).

stakeholders are also followed by most of the fashion brands. One industrial example is that began to deal with dyeing and finishing issues in its supply chain and launched a green process guide, which it has used to educate suppliers about every aspect of its green supply chain (WGSN, 2011).

Corporate environment proactivity enhancement

Companies have identified the need to prioritize and manage environmental risks effectively beyond basic compliance. As an example, UK supermarket retailer Tesco is aiming for a 30% reduction in its clothing carbon footprint by 2020, targeting "greener" garment production in its supply chain. This reflects that companies have changed their supply chain strategies to address global environmental issues (WGSN, 2011).

Strategic purchasing and green supply

Companies are considering implementing sustainable sourcing strategies. Some luxury fashion brands have adapted to ethical and innovative procurement strategies. This has also resulted in creating new elements in the fashion supply chain. For example Stella McCartney is one brand that introduced anti fur fashion to the market.

Product- based green supply

Recycling is one initiative that firms implement as a way of adapting to ethical supply chains. Many retail fashion brands collaborate with their suppliers to eliminate waste. This has also created a new business entity in the fashion industry introducing "up cycling and recycling". Donation based recycling such as the initiative run by Marks and Spencer in collaboration with Oxfam is one of the best examples that reflects the reshaping of supply chains with innovations in waste management.

Greening the supply process

Fashion retailers like M&S use ranking systems based on environmental and sustainability performance to select their suppliers.

> "Factories are allowed to move up the sustainability ladder, with the starting point categorized as bronze, followed by silver, gold and ultimately platinum performance level" - Mike Barry, head of sustainable business at Marks & Spencer (Nichols, 2010).

These promote suppliers to have an environmental management system integrated in to their business processes.

Despite the initiatives taken by the firms to change the nature of their supply chain, there are several concerns remain:

- Many fashion companies with the exception of a few large retail fashion brands find difficult to involve in sustainable supply chains due to economic challenges. This is most significant during the prevailing economic recession. Small and medium fashion firms cannot afford the large capital investment that need for initial implementation of sustainable supply chain processes. Even if these firms adapt to ethical initiatives they find difficult to compete with big retail chains due to their lack of convincing power over consumers.

Page | 11

The Chartered
Institute of Marketing

- Although fashion companies highlight the need for responsible procurement processes some practical limitations can be observed in the industry. Companies are meant to be transparent with regard to their supply chain. But the traceability of the raw materials and the compliance of labour are still beyond the control of retail brands due to tendency for corruption over the results by supplier audits (The Economist, 2012).

- The product life cycle of a garment is becoming shorter and replenishments ideally need to be back in store within a very short time. In some instances this becomes less than four weeks (Just-style, 2011). Fashion brands find it difficult to achieve elements of sustainability such as ethically sourced raw materials and unforced labour conditions when operating within tight deadlines.

5 Kraljic portfolio purchasing model

The Kraljic portfolio purchasing model was created by Peter Kraljic and first appeared in the *Harvard Business Review* in 1983. Despite its age, it's a popular and useful model, used in companies worldwide. Its purpose is to help purchasers maximise supply security and reduce costs, by making the most of their purchasing power. In doing so, procurement moves from being a transactional activity to a strategic role. Kraljic's portfolio purchasing model involves four key stages, which are discussed below.

Figure 7.3   Kraljic portfolio purchasing model

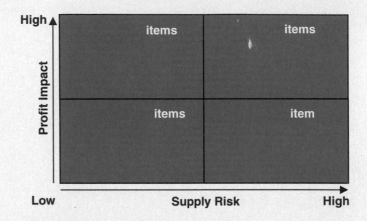

**Kraljic Model
Purchasing Portfolio Management**

5.1 Purchase classification

Step 1   Start by classifying all of the commodities, components, products, and services that you buy according to the supply risk and potential profit impact of each.

Supply risk is high when the item is a scarce raw material, when its availability could be affected by government instability or natural disasters, when delivery logistics are difficult and could easily be disrupted, or when there are few suppliers.

Profit impact is high when the item adds significant value to the organisation's output. This could be because it makes up a high proportion of the output (for example, raw fruit for a fruit juice maker) or because it has a high impact on quality (for example, the cloth used by a high-end clothing manufacturer).

Then, mark each item in the appropriate place on the product purchasing classification matrix. Kraljic recommends the following purchasing approaches for each of the four quadrants:

Strategic items (high profit impact, high supply risk). These items deserve the most attention from purchasing managers. Options include developing long-term supply relationships, analysing and managing risks regularly, planning for contingencies, and considering making the item in-house rather than buying it, if appropriate. Examples are engines and gearboxes for car manufacturers, bottling equipment for breweries.

Note that Step 3, below, provides detailed options for the best purchasing approach for these items, after considering other factors.

Leverage items (high profit impact, low supply risk). Purchasing approaches to consider here include using your full purchasing power, substituting products or suppliers, and placing high-

volume orders. Examples are bulk chemicals and standard semi-manufactured components. Using e-auctions may be a useful way to arrive at competitive prices in an efficient way.

Bottleneck items (low profit impact, high supply risk). Useful approaches here include over-ordering when the item is available (lack of reliable availability is one of the most common reasons that supply is unreliable) and looking for ways to control vendors. Examples are aircraft aluminium, natural flavourings and vitamins for the food industry.

Non-critical items (low profit impact, low supply risk). Purchasing approaches for these items include using standardised products, monitoring and/or optimising order volume, and optimising inventory levels. Examples are office supplies, cleaning materials.

Market analysis

Step 2 Here, you investigate how much power your suppliers have and how much buying power you have as their customer. A good way of doing this is to use **Porter's five forces analysis**.

Strategic positioning

Step 3 Classify the products or materials you identified as 'strategic' in Step 1, according to the supplier and buyer power analysis you drew up in Step 2. To do this, simply enter each item in the purchasing portfolio matrix, shown below.

Figure 7.4   Purchasing portfolio matrix

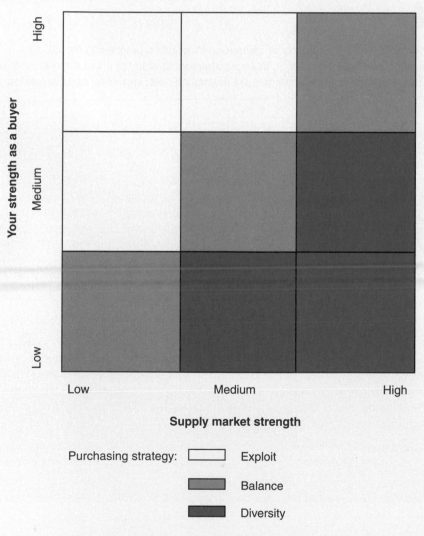

Purchasing strategy: ☐ Exploit

■ Balance

■ Diversity

Action plans

Step 4   Finally, you should develop action plans for each of the products and materials you need on a regular basis according to where those items are placed in the matrix in Figure 7.4.

The three purchasing strategies indicated are:

Exploit – Make the most of your high buying power to secure good prices and long-term contracts from a number of suppliers, so that you can reduce the supply risk involved in these important items. You may also be able to make 'spot purchases' of individual batches of the item, if a particular supplier offers you a good deal.

The only real caution is not to take any adversarial approach too far, just in case circumstances change.

Balance – Take a middle path between exploitation and diversification.

Diversify – Reduce the supply risks by seeking alternative suppliers or alternative products. For example, in our logistics example, could you use the road to ship some of your overland freight instead of relying solely on haulage companies?

You can also increase your buying power by consolidating to a single supplier. In other situations, you could bring the production of the item in-house.

ACTIVITY 7.3

1   Analyse your organisation's purchasing by using Kraljic's portfolio purchasing model.
2   Is your organisation adopting the most suitable procurement strategy or could it reduce risk and increase profit?
3   Evaluate which macro-environmental themes are having the most impact on procurement in your industry sector.

THE REAL WORLD

Britain's biggest clothing retailer Marks and Spencer said it had not only been caught out by the cold snap in February, which sparked a late run on winter coats and woollens, but had failed to buy enough stock in hot trends such as tribal print fabrics and coloured chinos. Chief executive Marc Bolland said M&S sold 100,000 cardigans and jumpers from its core M&S Woman collection in the fourth quarter – but could have sold three times that number. That was a miss, he said, blaming a temporary buying issue. Women's ballet pumps, he added, could have sold at double the quantity.

The stock shortages meant like-for-like clothing and homewares sales at M&S fell 2.8% in the fourth quarter, missing City forecasts. While sales of lingerie and childrenswear held up, the patchy performance of its important women's division depressed the retailer's overall growth in the fourth quarter, with its shares the second biggest faller in the FTSE 100, closing down more than 2% at 358.7p.

With much of M&S's knitwear made in Asia, the retailer was unable to repeat orders fast enough to meet the demand sparked by the cold weather. The length of its lead times meant it missed the opportunity to sell another 25,000 coats and jackets. There is no supply chain issue but we were too tight on bestselling lines, said Bolland, adding the fashion team headed by clothing supremo Kate Bostock had all my confidence but would nonetheless be strengthened. This turned out to be untrue, as Bostock was fired shortly after. Other personnel changes included the departure of Bostock's number two Andrew Skinner who had been at M&S for 28 years and was responsible for stock management.

Staff who plan the clothing ranges will also work more closely with its marketers: adverts featuring models such as Rosie Huntington-Whiteley caught shoppers' imagination but again M&S misfired by underestimating demand for the products featured.

(Wood, 2012)

The Chartered Institute of Marketing

6 Supplier relationships

There is a variety of different approaches to the management of suppliers and this will be determined by the corporate and procurement strategy, culture of the organisation and resources available.

Enablers of supply chain relationships

- *Common interest* – both parties have a stake in the outcome of the collaboration to ensure ongoing commitment.

- *Openness* – collaboration partners must openly discuss their practices and processes. Sometimes this means sharing information that is traditionally considered proprietary and confidential.

- *Mutual help* – when addressing supply chain problems or opportunities, look for cross company solutions.

- *Clear expectations* – all parties need to understand what is expected of them and the others in the relationship.

- *Leadership* – without a champion, collaboration will never be accomplished.

- *Co-operation, not punishment* – focus on jointly solving problems, not looking for someone to blame.

Financial benefits of established supplier relationships

- Reduced inventory
- Improved customer service
- More efficient use of human resources
- Better delivery through reduced cycle times.

Non-financial benefits of established supply chain relationships

- Faster speed to market of new products;
- Stronger focus on core competences
- Enhanced public image
- Greater trust and interdependence
- Increased sharing of information, ideas and technology
- Stronger emphasis on the supply chain as a whole
- Improved shareholder value
- Competitive advantage over other supply chains.

6.1 Network governance

Another of the emerging themes is the question of network governance.

> ▶ **Key term**
>
> **Network governance**
>
> As a concept, network governance encourages increased efficiency for organisations existing in highly turbulent environments, by co-ordinating internal teams with external partners (such as those in a supply chain) and encouraging permanent communication at all the various management levels.

Any given firm in a supply chain has its own relationships and connections with multiple other players: multiple suppliers and customers, industry contacts, partners/collaborators and advisers – any or all of whom may themselves be connected with each other.

Figure 7.5   Network relationships

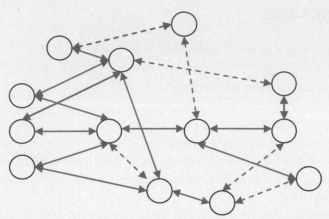

The network metaphor is arguably a more realistic model for mapping and analysing business relationships.

It raises the possibility of a **wider range of connections and collaborations** in the future (eg knowledge sharing, alliances and co-promotions) which may offer mutual advantages – and help to add value for the customer.

- It also recognises the potential of what has been called the '**extended enterprise**': extending the capability of a firm by tapping into the resources and competences of other network contributors (for example, by outsourcing activities like call centres to partners better equipped to undertake them). Some of this extended enterprise, these days, may well be 'virtual': that is, connected purely by information and communication technology links, such as the internet.

Long-term, mutually-beneficial relationships with a customer, competitor or other stakeholder may be developed using a number of approaches now and in the future.

Table 7.1   Development of mutually-beneficial business relationships

Relationship	Comments
Partnerships	Close, collaborative, mutually beneficial long-term relationships, usually with other members of the business system or **supply chain**: eg suppliers or service providers, distributors, retailers and (in B2B markets) customers. Partnership relations focus on **aligning the objectives** of both parties, and allowing both to **share in the value gains** created by the collaboration. The relationship between a client and a long-term advertising agency, business consultancy or major supplier will often be classed as partnerships, for example.
Strategic alliances	Formally structured relationships, in which two companies legally contract to co-operate in limited, specified ways (eg collaborative promotions or product cross-selling) to achieve specific commercial objectives that are of benefit to both parties. One example is the various promotional alliances between credit card companies and airlines, to offer joint loyalty incentives.
Joint ventures	Formal arrangements whereby two independent companies establish a new company, which they jointly own and manage. Their other businesses remain separate from this new, shared venture. (Where more than two companies enter the arrangement, it is called a '**consortium**'.) Joint ventures are often used to overcome barriers to entry into international markets: Western companies operating in Eastern Europe and China, for example, have often been required to form joint ventures with local partners. One provides technical and managerial expertise and investment, while the other supplies access to labour and local markets.
Networks	Looser, dynamic, more informal affiliations of autonomous and broadly equal organisations, which exchange information and pursue ongoing (typically long-term) relationships for mutual benefit. Rather than direct contractual or financial obligations, the relationships are held together by collaboration, communication, trust and mutual advantage.

The Chartered Institute of Marketing

Relationship	Comments
Virtual organisations	A special form of network, where companies (or units of a single company) collaborate, co-ordinate their activities and share data using **information communications technology (ICT)** as their main – or only – point of contact. Relationships may also be formed in **virtual communities** (customer-to-customer or C2C networks), such as online clubs, YouTube or FaceBook, for example, which support user networking and content sharing.
E-relationships	Relationships, networks and interaction based on information and communication technology (ICT): e-mail, websites, e-commerce, e-procurement, e-learning, e-publishing, internet banking, virtual team-working, virtual communities and so on.
Customisation	Relationship ties developed through the adaptation of processes, products, services and messages to the specific requirements of an individual customer or other party: a form of 'one-to-one' marketing. Customisation may be a way of adding **unique value** through a relationship: Dell Computers, for example, allows individual customers to configure their own hardware and software requirements. It may also represent **integration and mutual dependency** (eg a supplier developing equipment or systems specifically for a major customer), which ties the parties together.
Internal customer relationships	Relationships between functions, units and levels in an organisation. Organisations comprise internal supply chains, communication networks and markets. Each link in the value chain towards the end-consumer can be seen as the 'customer' of the one before it: service must be delivered, and value added, particularly in cross-functional relationships, in order to co-ordinate the activities of the firm towards customer value.

THE REAL WORLD

The US divisions of Honda, Hyundai, Nissan and Subaru have agreed to collaborate to support environmental innovation in their supply chains.

The latest manufacturers to sign up to trade association Suppliers Partnership for the Environment (SP), their suppliers will now share ideas with other SP members about new technologies, processes and strategies in order to help the environment by reducing the carbon footprint of the automotive supply chain.

SP's chairman Randy Leslie, vice president and general manager at Johnson Controls, Automotive Experience, said: 'SP is an innovative partnership of automobile manufacturers and suppliers working together to advance environmental sustainability through the automotive supply chain. Our new member companies are committed to reducing their environmental footprint and supporting the environmental innovation of their suppliers and will be an excellent addition to our partnership.'

(Albert, 2012)

6.2 Collaborative supplier partnerships

In a collaborative approach, the buyer seeks to develop longer-term relationships with a smaller number of preferred suppliers. The strategic view is that both organisations can benefit from seeking ways of adding value in the supply chain, to the ultimate benefit of the end consumer. Relationship management is based on trust, mutual obligation and benefit (rather than compliance with contract terms) and information sharing. The supplier participates with the buyer in looking for improvements and innovations: they jointly set targets for improvements in cost and quality, and meet regularly to discuss progress towards achieving these targets. Information is shared more or less freely (in areas of shared activity) in both directions, in order to support joint problem-solving and development.

Collaboration can be seen on a spectrum. At the tactical end, suppliers may be invited to participate in new product development projects, quality drives or cost-reduction programmes, say. At the high-trust, high-integration end of the spectrum are:

- **Outsourcing relationships**: a supplier carries out part of the firm's activities (eg production, data processing, logistics or telesales) on its behalf, under contract
- **Strategic alliances**: contractual collaboration in particular areas (eg co-branding or joint entry into a new international market, eg Star Alliance in the airline industry)
- **Partnership relationships**: buyers and suppliers agree to collaborate closely over the long term, sharing information and ideas for development.

The **benefits of collaborative supplier relationships** can be summarised as follows.

Table 7.2   Benefits of collaborative supplier relationships

Benefits to the supplier	Benefits to the buyer
There will be established points of contact, enabling the development of trust	Purchasing attention is focused on developing deeper relationships with fewer suppliers
Better information about the buyer and its needs enables the supplier to manage the buyer's expectations and offer better service	Better information, supplier commitment and collaborative improvement-seeking should result in better service and quality gains
Better information (and/or systems integration) allows forward planning	A smaller supplier base and systems integration lead to process efficiencies and reduced sourcing costs
Joint improvement, development and value gains will be shared by the supplier	The buyer may get preferential treatment (eg in the case of supply shortages or emergency orders) arising from goodwill
The supplier is likely to get more business, as preferred supplier	The buyer should be able to develop a high degree of trust and confidence in the supplier

Collaborative strategies are currently fashionable, but it is important to note that a collaborative approach is not necessarily the 'best' approach to supply chain relations in all circumstances. Co-operative or partnership relations take time and effort to develop, and may not be worth the investment for the purchase of routine items – especially since the buyer will also be missing out on opportunities to drive price down by adversarial bargaining.

There are also drawbacks, risks and obstacles in getting close or 'cosy' with suppliers, or in being 'locked in' to long-term supply contracts. There is the risk of being locked into a relationship with the 'wrong' partners (incompatible – or unethical, which brings additional reputational risk from being associated with them). There is risk in exchanging information, possibly losing control over confidential data and intellectual property. Over-dependence on a small group of suppliers may make the buyer vulnerable to supply risk if they fail or suffer disruption. Long-term supply partners may get complacent and cease to give excellent service or prices. High switching costs may be a constraint, if better alternative suppliers emerge in the market.

ACTIVITY 7.4

Appraise your own organisation's relationships with its suppliers. Are they adversarial, collaborative – or somewhere in-between?

What suppliers are used by the marketing function – and what type of relationships does it have with them?

What are the features and tools of collaborative supplier relationships, as practised in your organisation?

The Chartered Institute of Marketing

7 Sustainable SCM

With the growth of sustainability related regulatory initiatives adopted in the US and Europe, companies must now begin to incorporate regulatory requirements in their approach to managing ethical, social and environmental risks in the supply chain.

This raises the stakes for companies that operate global supply chains and will necessitate a new, more strategic approach to managing these risks as a truly integrated part of the supply chain strategy. Unethical sourcing practices can inflict major damage in terms of corporate reputation.

THE REAL WORLD

A decade ago, Timberland was among many apparel companies dogged by accusations that some of its products were manufactured by children. Since then, the company has emerged as a leader in social responsibility and transparency. Extensive quarterly sustainability reports and factory audits are among the steps Timberland has taken towards progress on responsible sourcing and factory conditions.

Going beyond improvements in the quality of life of factory workers, Timberland now demonstrates what companies can do to provide a better quality of life for children whose parents manufacture its products. From childcare to clean water projects, companies looking to mitigate their impact on working families and their children can learn some lessons from Timberland.

One side effect of long and tangled supply chains is that children are separated from their parents in long stretches of both time and distance. In China alone, a minimum of 50 million children are left behind, as their parents leave rural areas to work in factories. Besides the emotional impact of living far from their parents, such children often lack the supervision and family structure necessary for the best possible upbringing.

To that end, Timberland partners with organisations including the All-China Women's Federation to provide companionship and education programmes for factory workers' children. Timberland employees spent their own vacation time organising a summer camp for 700 left behind children. According to Colleen Von Haden, Timberland's senior manager of code of conduct, the first camp in 2009 was so successful that it is now an annual event.

As wages and working conditions improve in China, Timberland's factory workers are beginning to demand a better level of work-life balance, something that was once seen as a western luxury. The stress of their children living far away is an overwhelming burden for women, so Timberland collaborates with Verité, an NGO that provides social audits and training, to develop strategies to help workers cope with both shop floor and home stress.

Programmes focused on workers and their children thrive in other countries where Timberland sources its apparel. In India, one factory in Chennai provides day care for of its workers' children. Women appreciate the benefit of leaving their children in a safe environment, while they work their shift at the factory, and enjoy the opportunity to visit their children when they are on a break. Another factory in the Dominican Republic led a project to build a school for both workers' children and others living in the community.

The communities in which some of Timberland's factory workers and their children live lack basic amenities including safe and clean water. While building schools and providing day care are noble, neither are of much benefit if clean drinking water is unavailable and health risks are significant. One of the many water projects that Timberland funded is near a factory in Ambur, India, in a community where residents have long suffered from waterborne illnesses. Located near the factory and a school, a water tower, completed last year, guarantees that local children stay healthy and alleviates families of the expense of payment for water that has been transported over long distances.

One hundred years after strikes in the New England mill town of Lawrence, which gave rise to the organised chant: We want bread, and roses too, demand for a better quality of life now resonates in factories around the world. For workers at garment factories, their roses are opportunities for their children to blossom into productive citizens who will have a more comfortable life than they did. As your workforce matures, Von Haden says, you have to be accommodating to keep those employed in your factories. Timberland's action on this front is one example of how multinational businesses can do a better job of not only protecting their workers in the farthest reaches of their supply chain, but also doing more for their children so they can grow and thrive.

8 Technology and SCM

The growth of e-auctions has been one of the most prominent digital developments in the profession. From groundbreaking efficiency 15 years or so ago, today they are commonplace but their use is still growing. Research conducted by CIPS in partnership with the University of the West of England found that their use has ballooned ten-fold every year since inception in the mid-1990s, thanks to ease of use, applicability across a wide range of purchasing categories and, of course, their ability to deliver potential cost savings.

However, the benefits for suppliers to compete in e-auctions has been less clear. While the buyer is able to post their requirement for a product or service, the suppliers are only able to see the decreasing bids for the tender; the names of the other bidders are invisible to them. This imbalance of power led CIPS and the University of the West of England to hypothesise in their research entitled-Adapt, an independent assessment into the development of auctions as a purchasing tool that the continued ascendance of e-auctions would have an adverse effect on supplier relationship management.

The findings of the I-Adapt research revealed that the majority of buyers surveyed (86%) chose to start using e-auctions as a way of improving the price of their product/service, while 94% evaluated the success of an e-auction as based on obtaining the best market price.

This focus on price inherent in e-auctions led many to conclude that this would be at the expense of factors crucial to successful SRM, such as quality, reliability, account management and overall dependability of suppliers. This would ultimately result in the loss of long-term supplier relationships, a reduced number of suppliers and a decline in overall effectiveness.

Yet, against the original hypothesis of the I-Adapt research, the increase in the buyers' desire for cost reduction did not result in an equal decrease in factors crucial for successful SRM. The research found that 90% of buyers were actively developing supplier relationships, and when asked to rate different aspects of supplier performance – flexibility, quality of product/service, reliability, dependability, and customer support – when using e-auctions they reported that on average they had experienced significant improvements for each of these aspects.

From a supplier's perspective too, e-auctions appear to have their benefits. Vendors surveyed in the I-Adapt research praised the technology for reduced negotiation process time, as well as allowing them to see and react to their competitors' prices. Furthermore, 60% of auctions were won by the incumbent supplier, suggesting that while it did encourage existing suppliers to be more competitive, it was not just a tool to achieve this and does lead to business being won by new participants.

CIPS and the University of the West of England attributed this strengthening of supplier relationships to various aspects of e-auctions. Key among them is the fact that e-auctions tend to come at the end of an exhaustive purchasing process, meaning that buyers chose only to invite suppliers that have passed strict evaluation processes.

CIPS and the University of the West of England have decided to revisit this research later this year by asking CIPS members who have experience of e-auctions to take part in a short survey. This will only take a few minutes to answer and will allow the research team to compare current practice and experience with that they identified in the original survey.

ACTIVITY 7.5

Investigate how technology will continue to impact on SCM in your industry sector — will new models emerge that will change the current way of working?

The Chartered
Institute of Marketing

CHAPTER ROUNDUP

- Explaining why SCM is integral to marketing by reference to the six markets model
- Definitions of contrasting approaches to SCM provided.
- Concepts of Lean and Agile were explained.
- Porter's value chain and how this can contribute to competitiveness.
- Procurement Portfolio tools such as Kraljic's portfolio purchasing model were explained.
- The range and importance of supplier relationships was explained.
- Key emerging themes: sustainability in the supply chain and the impact of technology were discussed with examples.

FURTHER READING

Chopra, S. (2005) Seven-Eleven Japan Co., Harvard Business Publishing (Kellogg School of Management).

Cox, A. *et al* (2004) *Business relationships for competitive advantage: Managing alignment and misalignment in buyer and supplier transactions.* Palgrave Macmillan, 2004.

Ernst & Young (2011) Driving improved supply chain results: Adapting to a changing global marketplace.

Lyons Information Systems. GradeCard. GSK: Reducing costs by managing supplier effectiveness. http://www.lyonsinfo.com/_resources/casestudy_spm_gsk.pdf

Lala, A (2012) Supply chain case study: Canon Middle East. Arabiansupplychain.com, http://www.arabiansupplychain.com/article-7817-supply-chain-case-study-canon-middle-east/

The Guardian (2010-2012) Supply chain. http://www.guardian.co.uk/sustainable-business/supply-chain

Albert, A (2011) Japanese supply chain disruption cuts Toyota profits. Supply management, http://www.supplymanagement.com/news/2011/japanese-supply-chain-disruption-cuts-toyota-profits/?locale=en

REFERENCES

Albert A. (2012) US auto firms gear up for supplier collaboration. Supply Management http://www.supplymanagement.com/2012/us-auto-firms-gear-up-for-supplier-collaboration/ [Accessed August 2012].

Anon (2011) Easyjet profits from business travel. BBC, http://www.bbc.co.uk/news/business-15732969 [Accessed 30 August 2012].

Hines, P. *et al* (2004) Learning to evolve; A review of contemporary lean thinking. *International Journal of Operational and Production Management*, Vol24(10), pp994–1011.

CIPS Intelligence (2009-2012) Supply Chain Management – CIPs positions on practice http://cipsintelligence.cips.org/opencontent/supply-chain-management [Accessed 25 October 2012].

http://www.cips.org/Documents/About%20CIPS/1-Relate.pdf

Kaye, L (2012) How Timberland is building a better life for factory workers' children, The Guardian, http://www.guardian.co.uk/sustainable-business/timberland-better-life-factory-workers-children [Accessed 21 August 2012].

Lysons, K. and Farrington (2005) *Purchasing and Supply Chain Management*, Pearson.

Payne *et al* (2005) A stakeholder approach to relationship marketing strategy: The development and use of the "six markets" model. *European Journal of Marketing*, Vol39(7/8).

Peck, H., Payne *et al*. (1999) *Relationship marketing*. Oxford, Butterworth Heinemann.

Porter, M.E. (2004) *Competitive advantage*. New York, Free Press.

Weele, A.(2010) *Purchasing and Supply Chain Management*. Hampshire, Cengage Learning.

Womack, P. and Jones, D. (2003) *Lean thinking: Banish waste and create Wealth in your corporation*, Free Press.

Wood, Z (2012) MES admits womenswear stock shortages hit sales. The Guardian, http://www.guardian.co.uk/business/2012/apr/17/marks-spencer-womenswear-stock-shortages [Accessed 20 August 2012].

ACTIVITY DEBRIEFS

Activity 7.1

Discussion points

1   Are there any potential risks associated with the 100% of the supply chain network being 100% outsourced in India?

2   Appraise the supplier tiering approach in the supply chain.

3   Are KPI's and SLA's a useful way to develop supplier relationships?

4   Evaluate the 'pull supply' concept as used in the McDonald's supply chain.

Activity 7.2

Discussion points

Evaluate how the primary activities contribute to value – are there any ways in which your organisation can improve this?

Evaluate how the support activities contribute to value – are there any ways in which your organisation can improve this.

Do you think Porter's value chain is a relevant model for your industry? Are there better alternatives?

Has application of the value chain analysis in your industry resulted in new business models to increase competitive advantage?

Activity 7.3

Discussion points

From your analysis are there any potential areas of risk? Suggest how these can be reduced.

Evaluate your organisation's procurement strategy.

The Chartered Institute of Marketing

How useful are purchasing portfolio models in determining procurement strategy?

Select one of the macro environmental factors and evaluate the five-year impacts.

Activity 7.4

Discussion points

Assess the types of supplier relationships in your organisation.

Are these different or does your organisation implement a universal approach?

If your organisation engages in a range of supplier relationships, what are the criteria in which these are decided?

Explain how your organisation encourages collaboration with suppliers.

Evaluate the techniques your organisation uses.

As an industry are there any innovative supplier collaborations in place? Discuss these collaborations.

Activity 7.5

Discussion points

Identify the emerging technologies in your own industry.

Do any of these technologies relate specifically to the supply chain such as robotics in the car industry?

Do the technologies relate to the upstream or downstream elements of the supply chain?

Evaluate the long-term implications of these emerging technologies on your industry.

The Chartered
Institute of Marketing

CHAPTER 8

Strategic thinking

Introduction

Responding strategically to changes in the environment means taking a long-term approach to an organisation's marketing. Whether this is the position the organisation attempts to gain in its market, or its development of capabilities, building and maintaining a competitive advantage is the ultimate goal. Those organisations that have been able to respond to, and anticipate, the changes in their environment are often able to sustain a market-leading position over decades. Therefore, a strategic response has to be more than simply reconfiguring the marketing mix or learning about digital media, it needs to have the potential to give the organisation a sustained competitive advantage. This chapter considers a number of competing and complementary frameworks that can help marketers define a set of choices and decide which future direction is the most appropriate.

Topic list

2.2	Develop contemporary strategic marketing and business responses to a prioritised emerging theme:
	■ Marketing's 'new ground'
	■ Contemporary business strategies

1 Competitive advantage

One of the fundamental tasks facing marketers is to identify the basis on which their organisation competes with other players in their industry (and increasingly beyond). Theorists like Michael Porter (1980) have simplified this into two generic sets of competitive advantage:

■ Cost – an organisation that can produce goods or services at a lower cost than its rivals (while still making a return) can, be said to have a cost advantage. Firms such as Ryanair, Aldi and IKEA are well-known examples of low cost operators.

■ Uniqueness – an organisation that offers goods or services that are differentiated from their rivals in a way that customers value, could gain an advantage by offering something unique. In some cases, the differentiation can be valued sufficiently to create a virtual monopoly. Brands such as Apple, Gucci and Ferrari base their strategy on this form of advantage.

Combined with these two forms of competitive advantage Porter also states that organisations need to define their target market. A strategy aimed at a number of segments has a broad competitive scope and one aimed at a single or very limited number of segments would be a narrow or focused strategy.

1.1 Stuck in the middle, or hybrid strategy?

> ▶ **Key term**
>
> **Hybrid strategy** – is a strategy that combines both low cost and differentiated approaches – also known as best cost or cost innovation, examples might include offering a bespoke or individually tailored product or service at a mass market price, or successfully opening up previously niche products to a broad market.

The one position that was considered untenable for many years was a combination of cost leadership and differentiation. However, recent research has highlighted a growing number of companies, especially those from emerging markets, that are successfully combining strategies.

The success of hybrid strategies challenges the orthodox view, which is that not having a clear value proposition (based on either low cost or uniqueness) can be confusing to the customer and also sets up inherent contradictions within the organisation in terms of goals, structure, systems and culture etc.

However, in recent articles, Peter Williamson (2009, 2010) has demonstrated that there is an increasing number of companies who are overcoming these issues and challenging existing players in seemingly stable industries and markets.

The Chartered
Institute of Marketing

THE REAL WORLD

Haier, a Chinese domestic appliance manufacturer has gained a 60% share of the US market for wine storage refrigerators by focusing its channel activities through Sam's Club, a subsidiary of Wal-Mart. Wine fridges had been a niche market aimed at wine buffs with units costing several thousand dollars. Haier's entry has shaken up the established players, with SubZero/Wolf one of those that has recently reduced its output and workforce, closing its plant in Madison, Wisconsin, in 2012, with the loss of 100 jobs.

(Adapted from Williamson, 2010 and Newman, 2012)

ACTIVITY 8.1

Read the article Cost innovation: preparing for a 'value-for-money' revolution by Peter Williamson in *Long Range Planning*. Vol43, pp343-353 and answer the following questions:

1   What changes in the environment currently favour cost innovators?
2   Which traditional strategies are most at risk from cost innovators?
3   How can organisations compete with cost innovators?

Figure 8.1   Generic strategies

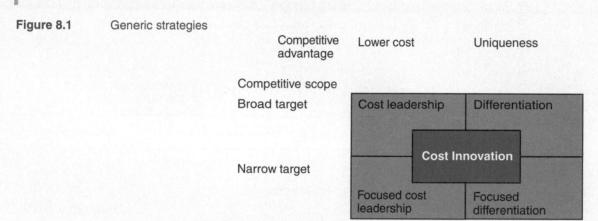

(Adapted from Porter, 1985 and Williamson, 2010)

1.2 Problems with generic strategies

▶ **Key term**

Generic strategies

'Generic Strategies are prescriptions about what the content of a firm's strategy should be. Some offer a very limited choice of options, while others proffer a list of practices that are purported to lead to superior performance' (Bowman, 2008).

Acknowledging that differentiation and cost leadership can be successfully combined overcomes one of the main criticisms of Porter's generic strategies theory. However, there are other issues with applying this concept successfully in the real world. Cliff Bowman (2008) has suggested that one of the main issues with generic strategies is that they are focused on a company view of the industry rather than the customer's perception. As we have seen in Chapter 6, it is customers who will define competitors and substitutes within a market. Bowman's view is that the competitive scope element of the Porter's framework is potentially redundant since, for example, once firms make a choice to be a cost leader, they are limiting their market to a set of segments that are likely to be price sensitive, which means the product or service is unlikely to have broad appeal. This also raises the question of whether firms adopting a cost leadership position are competing with firms who are differentiated, since each is potentially serving a different segment of the market.

1.3 The Strategic Clock

Bowman's solution was to develop a framework based on customer perceptions of use value and price (as opposed to cost, which is largely invisible to the customer). The Strategic Clock gives managers a range of options to choose from in terms of the price/value combination, from low price, low value offerings, which might be categorised as 'No Frills' to high price, high value goods and would be focused on a limited niche or small number of segments with a highly differentiated proposition. According to Bowman the best position for a firm to occupy is the hybrid strategy, which combines low price and differentiation, but this is also the most difficult to gain and sustain. Other combinations are only appropriate in certain circumstances. For example, offering a product with low perceived value to the customer at a high price is likely to lead to failure unless the organisation is in a monopoly situation and the customer has no choice and there are no close substitutes available.

Figure 8.2   The Strategic Clock

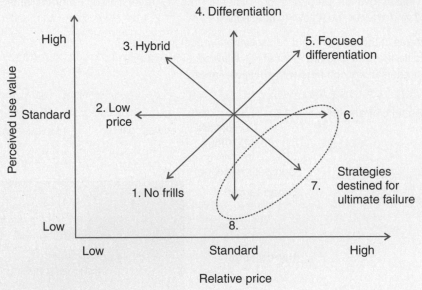

Bowman, (1988)

The Strategic Clock can also be a useful tool for understanding where an organisation should or can compete. Most generic strategy models are focused on business level operations and to apply them to an entire organisation can often produce a piece of artificial or flawed analysis. For example, Marriott, Hilton and Accor all operate in the global hotel industry, but they do not occupy a single position on either Porter's matrix or the Strategic Clock. Each firm has a range of brands aimed at different segments in the market.

ACTIVITY 8.2

Go to one of the following websites and look at the range of brands controlled by the hotel company. Plot the brands on the Strategic Clock. What does this tell you about the firm's strategy?

http://www.marriott.com/default.mi
http://www3.hilton.com/en/index.html
http://www.accor.com/en.html

1.4 Refining competitive scope and source of advantage

By offering managers a limited set of choices, generic strategies have become a standard tool for busy executives seeking quick answers to what are often complex business problems. Even the Strategic Clock is limited to customers' perception of value and price as explicit dimensions. In order to reflect the sort of strategies that are actually being followed in the real world it is necessary to understand what underpins

The Chartered Institute of Marketing

differentiated and low cost or price positions. Porter (1985) lists a series of factors that can drive uniqueness and support a differentiated position, these range from product features to superior R&D, high-quality inputs to the production process and employee skills and training. A cost-leadership position is similarly supported with factors such as low cost inputs, economies of scale and the use of incentive systems to reduce costs.

Mintzberg (1998) attempted to categorise the main factors used to support a differentiated strategy. In his view, price is just another form of differentiation. The main forms of differentiation he identified were:

- **Price** – firms differentiate by charging a lower price than their competitors for equivalent or close substitutes.

- **Image** – use of branding, marketing communications, packaging etc, to create a unique image for a product or service that is actually the same as rivals' offerings.

- **Design** – product features, look and functionality will all be very different from the dominant design in the industry – this is where firms can produce a disruptively innovative product or service.

- **Support** – this strategy is followed by firms who are adding value through after-sales service or other additional support such as credit or extended warranties.

- **Quality** – product features will be enhanced in comparison with standard industry offerings, for example, the product may be more durable, reliable or perform better than those produced by rivals.

- **Undifferentiated** – in contrast to most other writers on generic strategies who stress uniqueness as a key element of competitive advantage, Mintzberg acknowledges that being a copy-cat, or not differentiating, is a viable strategy in some markets.

It is also possible to refine the competitive scope element of Porter's framework. Some products and services clearly lend themselves to an unsegmented approach, but these are becoming rarer. Even those products that aimed at a broad range of segments such as Coca-cola, have developed product extensions with specific target markets in mind, such as Diet Coke and Coke Zero. The hotel groups highlighted in Activity 8.2 appeal to a broad range of target markets but have taken a segmented approach to competing. Accor, for example, has a no-frills motel chain, Hotel F1 and an economy brand, Ibis, both of which appeal to more price sensitive parts of their market. They also own the Sofitel brand, which is aimed at travellers seeking a luxury hotel experience. The brand's hotels are individually designed by leading architects and trade on Accor's French roots, with gastronomic events.

Mintzberg's (1998) conception of generic strategy also included niche strategies where firms focused on one, or a small number, of target markets. However, there is also increasing evidence that niche markets can become a single individual organisation and so customisation is also a choice open to organisations. In the past, this may have been limited to high-end luxury items such as *haute couture*, but the internet is allowing many more customers to request customised products and services and for organisations to deliver them at an affordable price.

| THE REAL WORLD |

Men's clothing store Les Nouveaux Ateliers, based in Paris, believe they are the first firm to use 3D imaging techniques to create bespoke suits at mass market prices. The company was set up in February 2011 by Francois Chambaud, who believed there was a potentially untapped market for tailored suits at affordable prices. The firm uses a 3D body scanner to take up to 200 measurements in a fraction of the time it takes in a traditional, bespoke tailors.

Clients are able to choose the pattern, fabric, style of cut, buttons and all other details. These are fed into a computer programme which sends a pattern to the firm's Shanghai workshop, where the suits and shirts are manufactured. The whole process takes three weeks as opposed to the three months it normally takes for a made-to-measure suit.

(Adapted from Charlton, 2012)

▶ **Assessment tip**

Using one of the generic strategy frameworks to develop a set of choices has an advantage in that it means there are a set number of options. However, this can also constrain a manager's thinking. Uniqueness can take many forms and these can be combined to produce a much wider set of options – one or more of which might be a much better fit for your industry.

When making a strategic recommendation it is important to get beyond suggesting a differentiated or low cost/price approach. Good answers explain how organisations can differentiate themselves from rivals or achieve a lower cost or price.

2 Resources and competencies

▶ **Key terms**

Resources and **competencies** are the assets and capabilities held by an organisation and cover intangible assets such as reputation and brands as well as tangible assets such as capital, property and labour, and knowledge and skills.

A combination of the two elements is necessary to gain competitive advantage over rivals. To sustain advantage, some of the resources and competencies must be genuine strengths, uncommon amongst competitors and difficult or expensive for them to duplicate. This can be illustrated as follows: when you drive a car, the vehicle, the petrol, knowledge of the Highway Code and how to drive are all resources that you draw on when you practice the skill of driving. The ability to drive is a competence. In a race, having a faster car or being better at driving than the other competitors can give you an advantage. However, having a faster car with an expensive custom-built engine and the driving skill, developed over many years, to handle the power could mean that you lead the race from start to finish.

Whatever position an organisation chooses to take in its industry or market, it is important that it possesses or has access to the resources and competencies that underpin its chosen form of competitive advantage.

A firm's assets and its ability to exploit them fully, lie at the heart of many successful firms. Hamel and Prahalad (1990) wrote about core competencies of the corporation in the 1980s and a number of theorists have built on the work of Edith Penrose (1959) to develop the resource-based view of the firm. This puts forward the view that different firms have different resources and competencies and that where an organisation is able to gain and sustain competitive advantage it does so because it is more skilled than its competitors.

2.1 The VRIN framework

Jay Barney (1991) developed a framework for determining whether resources and competencies are likely to lead to competitive advantage. Organisations possess many resources and competencies, some are needed just to enter or maintain a presence in a particular market or industry. These would not necessarily be seen as strengths. Other resources and competencies will help a firm compete successfully and may, if they are a key strength, lead to sustainable competitive advantage for the organisation. To be a key strength each resource or competence would have to meet four criteria:

- Is the resource valuable? – in other words is the attribute a strength that helps the organisation to neutralise threats or exploit opportunities.

- Is it rare? – is the resource only possessed by a few organisations in the industry? For example, in the past only the largest publishers had strong relationships with their distributors, this made it very difficult for small presses to sell large volumes of books, except in exceptional circumstances. The internet and e-books threatens to change all this, although large publishers still have greater bargaining power with the new channels, such as Amazon.

- Is it difficult or expensive for rivals or new entrants to imitate? This might be due to historical reasons: a firm that was able to buy real-estate before a boom in property prices would have an advantage over a new entrant, for example. Another reason could be that the link between the firm's attributes and its position of competitive advantage is not fully understood and, therefore, difficult to imitate, or because the resources and competencies are complex and interdependent. For example, many companies have R&D departments and new product development processes (NPD), but few have truly innovative

The Chartered Institute of Marketing

cultures. Disney's acquisition of Pixar was intended to transplant the latter's creative culture and reinvigorate innovation at the older firm.

- Is it difficult or expensive to substitute? That is: could a smart organisation find a way of achieving the same ends with a different set of resources? A talented senior management team or CEO might be seen as a key strength for some organisations – think about Steve Jobs and Apple, or Richard Branson and Virgin – but it is rare for a single individual or group of senior managers to be irreplaceable. Even Apple's performance appears to be continuing its upward trajectory, despite the death of Jobs in 2011.

2.2 Combining resource-based theory with generic strategies

Although the resource-based view is often portrayed as at odds with the market-based view, which underpins much of Porter's work (1980, 1985) on generic strategies, it is possible to combine both ideas to ensure that the organisation makes more effective choices. Barney and Hesterly (2010) advocate applying the above criteria to the driving factors supporting each type of competitive advantage. So, for example, if a firm differentiates from its competitors on the basis of product features alone, using the VRIN framework will help to evaluate the extent to which this is a sustainable marketing strategy. In general, the harder a strategy is to imitate the more likely it is to give the organisation a sustained competitive advantage.

This can be useful when considering how to respond to changes in the environment. In general, an organisation considering a cost leadership strategy is better to focus on sources of advantage that are difficult or costly to imitate. This might mean developing technical skills rather than technology *per se* and economies of learning rather than economies of scale. The same is true of firms adopting a differentiated position. Product features are often the easiest element of an offer to imitate, so taking out patents, having a mix of products or offering customisation are ways in which advantage can be strengthened. Internal links between different parts of the organisation (such as is found in truly market-oriented firms), building a strong reputation with customers and other stakeholders and providing an exceptional level of service and support are likely to prove much more costly for rivals to duplicate and, therefore, will give the organisation a longer period of competitive advantage.

3 New sources of competitive advantage

So far, we have considered fairly established sources of competitive advantage. With the rapidly changing environment faced by some organisations it can be easy to imagine that these are becoming less important for organisations. However, there are still many examples of organisations that exploit these sources of advantage, as we have seen above. Economists such as Schumpeter have been documenting the impact of disruptive change in markets since the 1930s.

3.1 Adaptive advantages

Rather than dismissing existing theory, Michael Deimler and Martin Reeves, two senior partners with Boston Consulting Group have developed a framework which allows managers to build on these existing ideas. Their **adaptive advantage** is something organisations can develop through effective management of their resources and competencies, allowing them also to fine-tune their position in the industry as the environment presents new threats and opportunities. It could be argued that this approach can also work even in the hypercompetitive environments we covered in Chapter 5. The adaptive advantage suggests that there is a dynamic element to both taking a position and developing resources and competencies. Figure 8.3 below demonstrates how being adaptable can support a range of new sources of competitive advantage:

Figure 8.3   Adaptive advantage

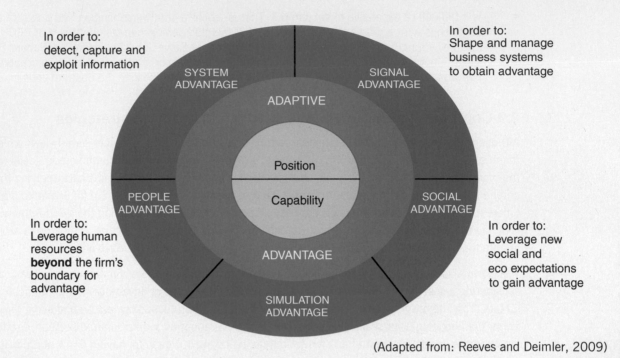

In order to:
detect, capture and
exploit information

In order to:
Shape and manage
business systems
to obtain advantage

In order to:
Leverage human
resources
beyond the firm's
boundary for
advantage

In order to:
Leverage new
social and
eco expectations
to gain advantage

SYSTEM ADVANTAGE
SIGNAL ADVANTAGE
ADAPTIVE
Position
Capability
PEOPLE ADVANTAGE
SOCIAL ADVANTAGE
ADVANTAGE
SIMULATION ADVANTAGE

(Adapted from: Reeves and Deimler, 2009)

ACTIVITY 8.3

Read the article *New bases of competitive advantage* by Reeves and Deimler (2009) on the Boston Consulting Group website.

Find examples of organisations that illustrate the new bases of competitive advantage and assess how each one's strategy enhances customer value (for example, Reeves and Deimler (2009) cite Apple as an organisation that uses systems advantage to compete. Apple's customers benefit through having seamless access to a wide range of services via sophisticated products which can be used on their own or in a fully integrated manner. This is supported by Apple's network of component suppliers, telecom industry partners and software app developers:

	Example	Value to customers
Adaptive		
Signal advantage		
Systems advantage		
Social advantage		
Simulation advantage		
People advantage		

3.2 Strategic responses in hypercompetitive/high velocity environments

As we saw in Chapter 6, some commentators argue that traditional strategic responses may not be successful in rapidly changing environments, where the speed and extent of disruption is significant (D'Aveni, 1995). Markets such as ICT and biotechnology have been cited (Wirtz *et al* 2007) as examples of this type of environment. However, there is research which suggests that generic strategies are still being successfully used in high velocity environments. Wirtz, Mathieu and Schilke (2007) found that German firms operating in high velocity markets were successfully using a range of traditional and new strategies to cope with the rapidly

The Chartered Institute of Marketing

changing environment. These included differentiation based on product features and customisation, image differentiation and a focus on niche markets. There were also firms who were successful through focusing on their skills and resources, like those that proactively sought out new opportunities, or were able to reconfigure their organisation by making use of new knowledge. Other firms benefited from co-operating with other players in their environment (as the value net model in Chapter 6 can support) or were able to leverage their skills into new markets and industries.

4 Business model innovation

▶ **Key term**

Business model – is a summary of what value proposition an organisation is offering, to whom it is being offered, and how the organisation will deliver this at a profit (or produce an acceptable return).

Gaining a clear understanding of the existing options open to firms in obtaining and sustaining a competitive advantage can be like learning to play a musical instrument. The theories and concepts we have covered above are a bit like the scales and standard tunes that a musician must learn to master their instrument. However, there are occasions when improvisation and creativity come to the fore, such as in jazz solos or composing new forms of music. In some environments, change is so rapid and radical that only a completely untried form of strategy may be needed. This will often be underpinned with a new form of business model. The internet has already produced a number of new ways of doing business – for example, infomediaries, who collect detailed information about buyers in exchange for a valued product or service, or affiliates who share the revenue with e-tailers by providing click-throughs (Rappa, 2000).

4.1 Business model templates

There are numerous generic templates for business models each with the same or similar basic components – as illustrated in Figure 8.4 below:

Figure 8.4   Generic business model framework

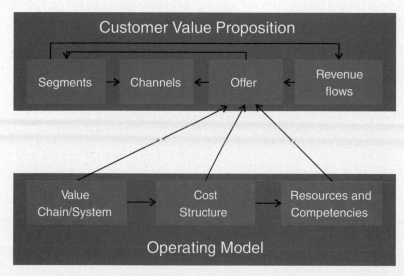

(Adapted from BCG Research, 2009 and Osterwalder & Pigneur, 2010)

In order to innovate, firms need to consider each element of the business model and decide what changes would give them a competitive advantage. The business model can help to draw together a number of disparate strategic elements and focus them on a single framework.

4.2 Business models

There is a wide range of existing business models, many of which have transformed the way business is done in their particular sector. A few examples are discussed below.

- The razor and blades model pioneered by King Gillette is one which is still in common use. Giving away or selling the razor cheaply can lock customers in to buying the disposable blades, which is where the profit is made, as the revenue stream is far greater than the cost of producing the blades, plus the initial cost of giving away the razor. This is still common with mobile telecom contracts, where the handsets are given away or sold at a lower price than their value in order to secure a 12- or 18-month contract for airtime.

- Many web-based companies use a combination of Freemium and Advertiser-Pays models to generate income. Social networking sites like LinkedIn allow users to upgrade by paying a premium rather than the basic service, whose users have to tolerate occasional adverts. The Advertiser-Pays model has been used for many years by free local newspapers, many trade magazines and commercial radio stations.

- Utility style business models – or pay-as-you-go – have been the stock method for water, electricity and telecoms companies. More recently, these have transferred to online music sites such as Spotify.

Business model innovation is a popular topic and there is a huge range of internet resources – some of the best are listed in Further Reading below. Combining business models or taking a common model from one sector to another are often ways in which firms can gain a competitive advantage. Sir Stelios Haji-Ioannou's technique of setting up 'no-frills' operations is one example of this. From the airline business, his Easy brand has moved into car rental, hotels and most recently the low-cost end of the gym market.

THE REAL WORLD

Dutch carpet manufacturer Desso, has developed a closed-loop business model to take advantage of the growing demand for sustainable flooring products in Europe.

The firm operates two cycles in their Cradle-to-Cradle strategy. One cycle is technical and starts with the choice of raw materials. These are specified to be non-toxic, easy to disassemble and recycle. Production is based on renewable energy sources and every effort is made to reduce the carbon footprint the firm creates in its in-bound and out-bound logistics. Desso supplies a variety of segments, from schools and airlines to cruise ships and domestic homes. The firm's Cradle-to-Cradle concept is part of their brand values and is a significant element of their customer value proposition. Once the flooring materials have been consumed, the relationship with Desso's customers does not end as it might with a traditional carpet manufacturer. The company then collects the worn out carpet and breaks it down to its component parts. Where possible these are reused in the production of further carpets. Where they cannot be reused, they enter the second, biological cycle and are composted.

However, Desso's unique perspective in the whole process is to regard their products as nutrients. The composted waste is used in growing new raw materials, which their suppliers turn into the materials used by the Dutch firm to make the next generation of carpets. By 2010, the firm took back carpets from its key partners. By 2020 they plan to increase this to 50% of their customer base. In May 2012, Desso won the Guardian's Sustainable Business Award. The move to a new business model has also proved to be good for revenue generation. Desso has increased its share of the carpet tile market in Europe by 8% from 2007–11 and have also increased its incremental earnings from 1% to 9.2%, despite the fact that over the same period the European market saw a drop of 30%.

Desso (2012)

The Chartered Institute of Marketing

5 The assessment

When you are recommending the strategic marketing response it is important to go beyond the basic description of the strategy. Firstly you should relate your choice of strategy to the previous content of the paper, which will provide part of your justification, but you should also go into further detail about how the strategy would work in practice.

The text below is a section from an A grade paper and while it uses a classic generic strategy from Porter, it combines this with a more contemporary set of ideas around building customer relationships. This might be seen as contradictory, given that cost leadership is the source of competitive advantage chosen, but the paper argues convincingly why the two concepts can be combined.

The section below could have been improved by using Williamson's cost innovation ideas – the text hints at this, but the candidate obviously wasn't familiar with the article – which is relatively recent (2010). However, this section would have achieved an even better mark if this had been included.

There is clear evaluation of the strategies in terms of risk and the recommendations are linked back to the previous content of the assignment which established the price sensitivity exhibited by customers, due to their fixed budgets.

2.3 How to Respond.

2.3.1 Strategies

I propose a strategy with two elements:-

- Focussed cost Leadership
- Customer relationship

Looking at the emerging theme it becomes clear why so many healthcare suppliers are finding it difficult to define strategies to drive innovation. Based upon consumer behaviour looking for the cheapest, focussed cost leadership (Porter 1980) seems the only real strategy. However customer relationship strategies can deliver competitive advantage by leveraging the outputs of a relationship to deliver joint goals, one approach is to utilise the "4 principles of wikinomics" Tapscott and Williams (2008) as a model to deliver an open and sharing customer relationship to build long standing trust. This approach can aid technology development and identify customer targeted innovations that deliver real value. Johnson and Scholes (1989) model; can also be applied to develop relationship marketing with internal developments to deliver benefits in the form of customer advocates; customers who reference how innovations have been developed in partnership to deliver real value.

2.3.2 Cost leadership risks

The risks associated with cost leadership, present as short term goals that lead to organisational cuts, so lean that it only meets current commitments with little or no capacity for growth or innovation. Cost leadership can be interpreted in a negative manner and effect attitudes as it relates to losses; jobs or benefits, impacting morale and diverting resources from the strategic goals.

2.3.3 Relationship management risks

Ill defined goals, communicated in a poor manner will result in poor outcomes. The relationship is commercial, one party wants value for money; the other to implement and deliver technological innovations. A poor selection of partners may deliver nothing. Innovation is vital for moving forward Henry Ford famously said "If I asked customers what they wanted they would have said a faster horse", there is a risk that the wrong customer could ask for just that.

A combination of strong leadership, clear and open communication and strong analytical skills will be required to mitigate the risks identified above. These will need to be the skills of the modern marketer

2.3.4 Strategic Outcomes

Focussed innovations are intended to deliver low risk and higher value technological innovations for healthcare providers as they are developed for real needs. Relationship marketing may enable healthcare suppliers to perform joint value chain analysis (Porter 1985) to identify new solutions and market spaces not considered in which innovative technologies could deliver competitive advantage. The cost benefit is technology innovation based on real value and needs. Since socialised healthcare operates within fixed budgets, if a solution is too expensive; it will genuinely be economically unviable. The U.K. is looking to save £20 billion in the NHS (www.improvementsnhs.uk 2012). The way forward for a sustainable and innovative healthcare market is via working relationships. A strategy that employs a combination of relationship marketing and cost leadership will enable organisations to develop innovations that deliver real value to healthcare providers, present lower risk, driving adoption and acceptance.

The Chartered
Institute of Marketing

- The basis on which an organisation competes can take a variety of forms, but competing strategically is a long-term activity

- Generic positions, such as those described by Porter, give managers a limited choice-set for determining how their organisations will gain a competitive advantage

- Porter states that uniqueness and low cost are the basis of most forms of competitive advantage, with firms also choosing a broad or a narrow scope for their target markets.

- More recently, a combination of strategies (known as hybrid, best cost or cost innovation) has been shown to be successful by researchers such as Bowman and Williamson

- Some generic strategy approaches have been criticised as too simplistic and for not taking account of customer perceptions. Both Mintzberg and Bowman have developed different approaches to address these issues.

- Firms can also compete by developing or possessing unique resources and competencies. Barney's VRIN framework, which evaluates the value, rarity, inimitability and non-substitutability of resources and competencies, can be used to assess their potential for competitive advantage.

- In fast changing environments BCG consultants, Deimler and Reeves have found that firms gain an advantage by their ability to adapt in different ways, through simulation, systems, people, social and signal forms of advantage.

- Business model innovation is a further way firms can respond to a rapidly changing environment.

FURTHER READING

Generic forms of competitive advantage are well covered in the references below – but it is also worth looking at:

Hendry (1990) The problem with Porter's generic strategies. *European Management Journal*, Vol8(4), pp443–450.

Lindgardt, Z. *et al* (2009) *Business model innovation: When the game gets tough, change the game*. Boston Consulting Group.

Osterwalder, A. and Pigneur, Y. (2010) *Business model generation: A handbook for visionaries, game changers, and challengers*. London, Wiley.
And the associated website presentation:
http://www.slideshare.net/Alex.Osterwalder/business-model-innovation-matter

Reeves, M. and Deimler, M.S. (2009) New bases of competitive advantage. *BCG Perspectives*, Boston Consulting Group.

There is a wealth of business model innovation resources, but they are very variable in quality. Useful sources include:

Rappa, M. (2000) Business Models on the web. Digitalenterprise.org,
http://digitalenterprise.org/models/models.html [Accessed 20 August 2012].

Sharp, B. and Dawes, J. (2001) What is differentiation and how does it work? *Journal of Marketing Management*, Vol17(7/8), pp739–59.

Barney, J. (1991) Firm Resources and Sustained Competitive Advantage. *Journal of Management,* Vol17, no. 1, pp99–120.

Barney, J. and Hesterly, W. (2010) *Strategic management and competitive advantage*. Upper Saddle River, NJ, Prentice Hall.

Beavis, L. (2012) Recycling to infinity and beyond. The Guardian, http://www.guardian.co.uk/sustainable-business/best-practice-exchange/desso-recycling-infinity-and-beyond [Accessed 25 July 2012].

Bowman C. (2008) Generic strategies: A substitute for thinking? 360° *The Ashridge Journal*, Spring, pp6–11.

Bowman, C. (1988) *Strategy in practice*. Harlow, Prentice-Hall.

Bowman, C. and Faulkner, D. (1997) *Competitive and corporate strategy*. London, Irwin.

Charlton, E. (2012) *Body scanner takes tailoring to the masses*. Agence France Presse, http://www.abs-cbnnews.com/lifestyle/07/04/12/body-scanner-takes-tailoring-masses [Accessed 25 July 2012].

D'Aveni, R. (1995) Coping with hypercomptetition: utilizing the new 7S framework. *Academy of Management Executive,* Vol9(3), pp45–57.

Desso (2012a) Corporate brochure. http://www.desso.com/DessoDocuments/BusinessCarpets/Brochures/DESSO%20Corporate%20Brochure%20EN%20LR.pdf [Accessed 25 July 2012].

Desso (2012b) Cradle to cradle. http://www.desso.com/Desso/EN/EN-Cradle_to_Cradle/EN-Cradle_to_Cradle-Cradle_to_Cradleampltsupampgtampltsupampgt.html [Accessed May 29, 2012].

Lindgardt, Z. (2009) *Business model innovation: when the game gets tough, change the game*. Boston Consulting Group.

Mintzberg, H. (1998) Generic strategies: toward a comprehensive framework. *In* Lamb, R. and Shivastava, P. (eds.) *Advances in strategic management*, JAI Press.

Newman, J. (2012) Sub-Zero to close Madison plant; 100 will lose jobs. Wisconsin State Journal. 1 February, http://host.madison.com/wsj/business/article_8b2858d8-4c5f-11e1-8600-001871e3ce6c.html [Accessed 25 July 2012].

Osterwalder, A. and Pigneur, Y. (2010) *Business model generation: A handbook for visionaries, game changers, and challengers*. London, Wiley.

Penrose, E. (1959) *The theory of the growth of the firm*. London, Wiley.

Porter, M. (1980) *Competitive Strategy*. New York, Free Press.

Porter, M. (1985) *Competitive advantage*. New York, The Free Press.

Prahalad, C. and Hamel, G. (1990) The core competence of the organisation. *Harvard Business Review*, Vol68(3), pp79–91.

Rappa, M. (2000) Business models on the web. Digitalenterprise.org http://digitalenterprise.org/models/models.html [Accessed 20 August 2012].

Reeves, M. and Bernhardt, A. (2011) Systems advantage. *BCG Perspectives*, Boston Consulting Group.

Reeves, M. and Deimler, M. (2011) Adaptability: the new competitive advantage. *Harvard Business Review,* Jul/Aug 2011, pp134–141.

The Chartered Institute of Marketing

Reeves, M. and Deimler, M.S. (2009) New bases of competitive advantage. *BCG Perspectives*, Boston Consulting Group.

Williamson, P. and Zeng, M. (2009) Value-for-money strategies for recessionary times. *Harvard Business Review*, Vol87(3), pp66–74.

Williamson, Peter, J. (2010) Cost Innovation: Preparing for a 'value-for-money' revolution. *Long Range Planning*, Vol43, pp343–353.

Wirtz, B. Mathieu, A. and Schilke, O. (2007) Strategy in high-velocity environments. *Long Range Planning*, Vol40, pp295–313.

ACTIVITY DEBRIEFS

Activity 8.1

1   What changes in the environment currently favour cost innovators?

Globalisation is changing the way business is done and much of the demand for products and services is now being driven by a new middle class in emerging economies such as Brazil, Russia, India, and China (the BRICS).

Outsourcing and offshoring to lower cost economies has done a great deal to lower labour rates globally, as manufacturers constantly seek to move production to low-cost economies.

The growth of global retailers, such as Walmart and Carrefour, has resulted in a downward pressure on prices and this is passed down the supply chain.

2   Which traditional strategies are most at risk from cost innovators?

Organisations focusing on niche markets are vulnerable to cost innovators taking niche products to mass markets and then being able to lower costs – and also prices – as a result of economies of scale

High-price, customised offers are being undermined by cost innovators who can offer bespoke products/services at a standard price

Organisations may rely on the Adoption phase of the innovation curve to offer new technology at a high price to Innovators and Early Adopters. Cost innovators are offering new technology at low cost and adopting a penetration approach

3   How can organisations compete with cost innovators?

Business model innovation

Use subsidiaries set up to compete on cost and differentiated basis

Joint Ventures and/or Mergers and Acquisitions to regain scale advantages

Alliance with cost innovators to learn their tricks

Discussion points: How far do you think cost innovators present a real threat to incumbents in developed countries?

Activity 8.2

Whichever of the three hotel groups you have chosen you should find that the brands they control cover most of the generic strategy positions in either of the two frameworks. For example, Accor have a no-frills brand in their HotelF1, Etap and Ibis Budget brands, low cost is covered by other economy brands such as Ibis. Mercure and Novotel could be seen as taking a hybrid position as they are differentiated but still benefit from economies of scale and a degree of standardisation, whereas Pullman and MGallery are differentiated and luxury brands, aimed at a more exclusive market, such as Sofitel, could be classed as having a focused differentiation strategy. By adopting a multi-brand strategy and covering all the positions available, Accor are able to compete directly with other leading hotel groups, but can also bring their economies of scale and resources and competencies to bear on markets and segments that might otherwise be dominated by niche or focused players.

Activity 8.3

	Example	Value to customers
Adaptive advantage	Virgin Group	By entering new sectors and challenging incumbents to offer greater value
Signal advantage	Google	Ads are better targeted than in media with less information about viewers and less complete analysis – so customers have less wastage
Systems advantage	Apple	Customers have seamless access to a wide range of products and services
Social advantage	Toyota (Prius)	Lower motoring costs and a greener product – so a feeling of doing good
Simulation advantage	Proctor and Gamble	Products and services that are better tailored to their actual needs – so can be more customised. A greater involvement in the design of the products and services they consume – (co-creation)
People advantage	Red Hat Linux	Some elements of co-creation – but the value is more likely to be seen in the quality of the end product because of the diversity of those having an input – less likelihood of groupthink etc.

Discussion points: Do you think that these new bases of competitive advantage have only started to be used recently? Are they as novel as the consultants would have us believe? Could they be viewed as particular competencies or do they add another layer to the resource-based view? Are they simply new forms of differentiation?

CHAPTER 9

Changing the scope of the organisation and its operations

Introduction

This chapter focuses on strategic responses that relate to changes in where an organisation competes. As we saw at the end of the previous chapter, one way a firm can gain competitive advantage is by changing its business model. This covers the choice of product offers, the choice of markets served, the resources the firms needs and the activities it will undertake. We will now look in more detail at how some of these choices are made and the tools and frameworks managers can use to generate a range of options for changing the scope of the organisation and its operations.

Topic list

A unified framework	1
Strategies for limited growth and innovation	2
Strategies for substantial growth	3
Justifying a strategic response	4
Exemplar paper	5

2.2	Develop contemporary strategic marketing and business responses to a prioritised emerging theme:
	▪ Marketing's 'new ground'
	▪ Contemporary business strategies

1 A unified framework

In Chapter 1 we briefly covered one of the best known frameworks for generating options for growth strategies, Ansoff's matrix. The 'scope' choices open to managers are much wider than this and range from strategies which are about reduction and retrenchment, through those that will deliver limited growth, to activities that can bring about radical changes to the shape of the industry or market in which the firm operates and to the firm itself. There are also a variety of ways in which firms can change the scope of their operations and influence. Changes can be driven from within the firm through organic growth, or via strategic alliances, as we have seen in Chapter 7, mergers and acquisitions are also still a common method used to grow the organisation and respond to changes in the marketplace.

Figure 9.1   Strategic options for changing the scope of the organisation

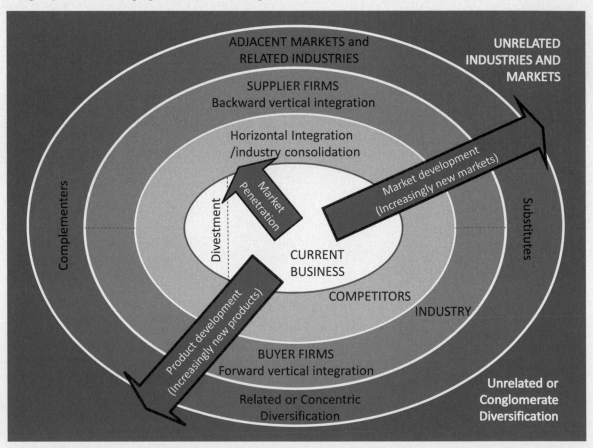

(Adapted from: Ansoff, 1957; De Wit and Meyer, 2010; Barney and Hesterley, 2010; Thompson and Martin, 2010; Rumelt, 1982)

The Chartered Institute of Marketing

1.1 Managing the existing portfolio of products in existing markets – divestment, industry consolidation and market penetration

When resources are limited, concentration of resources is often a better recipe for success than spreading everything too thinly and trying to grow in too many directions. If the most appropriate strategic marketing response to changes in the environment is to 'stick to the knitting' (Peters and Waterman, 1982), then managers have a number of choices that they need to consider:

- **They may decide to do nothing**: an emerging theme may have a profound impact on an industry but marketers may consider that their brands, value proposition and the state of the market is such that they do not have to make any changes. In the current climate – and especially in firms listed on the stock market – this is unlikely to be an option embraced by shareholders and senior managers without very strong evidence.

- **They might choose to rationalise the existing portfolio** of products and brands to focus on those that will generate the greatest returns, or to bring better coherence to the firm's operations. Organic, emergent strategy processes can lead to a firm developing a portfolio which does not have a strong strategic logic. Changes in the external environment can often be the trigger for managers to look more closely at the brands and products they control. Divestment of parts of the business is an option which can help the firm to focus on parts of its portfolio that will generate better returns and respond more effectively to the changes in the environment.

- Outsourcing might also be another option, as focusing on core competences and buying in other processes in the value chain is another way in which a firm can rationalize its operations. We examine this further option when we consider vertical integration below.

- As we saw in Chapter 6, in some phases of the industry life cycle, a viable strategy is to buy competitors. Horizontal integration or industry consolidation can be an effective way of growing the business in a growth or mature life cycle stage or of increasing returns by reducing overcapacity in a declining industry. However, this is not without its risks – especially if it makes the firm too powerful or creates a near monopoly structure and attracts the attention of government agencies.

- Market penetration is another option for firms that want to focus on their existing product portfolio within their current markets. Growth is achieved by increasing market share or growing the market as a whole by, for example, encouraging existing customers to buy more volume or more frequently (or both). The growth rate for this option is likely to be slow and in some sectors it may be difficult to achieve where there are entrenched rivals. However, it is less risky than some of the other options outlined below. The firm will already have many of the resources and competences it needs to compete in the market and possess a good knowledge of the products it is selling and who are its customers. There is some evidence that in certain markets, such as digital music, market penetration is being aided by 'long tail' economic behaviour as unlimited choice is actually encouraging consumers to buy more (Anderson, 2006).

THE REAL WORLD

Breaking up the business

Sometimes the best response to changes in the environment is to focus the business on specific markets and sectors – rather than growing the organisation, there might be a consolidation or reduction in size, which can result in better returns in the long run. According to *The Economist* (March 26, 2011, p.77) this is often used by conglomerates with operations in a number of industries to improve their stock price.

The economic downturn has meant that firms such as Pfizer, Philip Morris International, and Motorola have found it more difficult to interest buyers in parts of their business they wish to sell. Private equity firms, in particular, do not have the same access to low-cost loans that they did pre-2007. As well as attracting investors, breaking up a business into separate companies can also mean that the customer value proposition for each organisation is clearer.

In December 2010, Accor split its hotel operations from its business services division (re-named Edenred) and also sold a number of related operations such as casinos and restaurants. The new hotel company has been able to concentrate on developing its brands worldwide and the overall performance of the company has improved significantly.

(The Economist, 2011; Accor 2011)

▶ **Key term**

Portfolio analysis

This is used at a corporate level to assess the performance of a group of brands, products or business units. Executives can gain an understanding of the current position of the portfolio as a whole in terms of the balance of products. It may be possible or even desirable to support some weaker brands, but there must be sufficient strong products to provide the necessary profits to do this.

Managers can also use portfolio analysis to determine the strength of individual brands or products relative to the rest of their portfolio and their competitors. Finally, portfolio analysis can be used to understand which markets are attractive and the extent to which there is a fit between the firm's brands and the markets they serve.

1.1.1 Portfolio matrices

Using a portfolio matrix can help marketers to determine which product areas to focus on, however, the older, more basic models do not allow for sufficient environmental knowledge to be incorporated. The Boston Consultancy Group (BCG) share/growth matrix simply looks at market growth versus relative market share, which act as proxies for business strength and market attractiveness. Other portfolio models allow for far greater input but require more work to ensure the right factors have been included and weighted in the most appropriate manner. Again the skill of the analyst is an important factor.

1.1.2 Boston Consulting Group growth share matrix

Developed by BCG in the 1970s this framework is designed to analyse the balance of products within an organisation's portfolio. In order to classify each product the growth rate of its market is plotted against its relative market share compared with the leader in the market. The products or brands are then categorised into four groups:

Figure 9.2 Boston Consulting Group growth share matrix

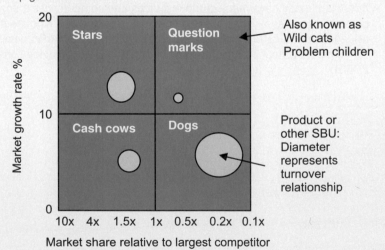

Market share relative to largest competitor

- **Stars** – these are products or brands in high growth markets with a high relative market share. However, they do not usually produce high returns because being in a high growth market they need substantial investment, despite the fact that they will benefit from their market share.

- **Cash cows** – are in lower growth markets – probably in the maturity phase of the life cycle, so do not need the same level of investment as other brands. Their high relative market share means that they do produce good returns and tend to subsidise the rest of the portfolio

The Chartered
Institute of Marketing

- **Question marks** – generally use cash rather than generating profit, but they are in high growth markets and with the right level of investment can improve their relative market share to become Stars.

- **Dogs** – are products in low growth markets and with a low relative market share. They produce little or no return but do not require substantial investment. The recommendation for products in this quadrant is to divest them.

The BCG matrix is one of the more simplistic of the portfolio tools and exhibits many of the main failings of these types of tools because it does not allow for the complexities found in most real-world markets and it provides unrealistic recommendations. For example, divesting Dogs may not be possible if they are used as a loss leader or help with capacity utilisation. Note that the x-axis is a logarithmic scale.

1.1.3 GE Multi-factor portfolio matrix

The failings of the BCG matrix prompted the development of other tools to manage portfolios of products, brands and business units. Most follow a similar 3 x 3 grid and allow for several factors to be included in an assessment of industry/market attractiveness and business strength. The multi-factor matrix adopted by General Electric is covered below, but other matrices in this style include Shell's directional policy matrix.

Figure 9.3   Multi-factor portfolio matrix

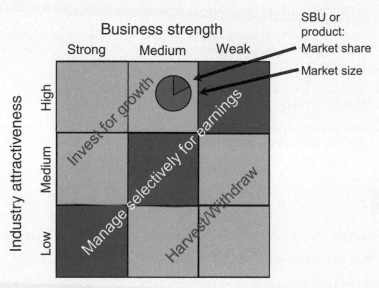

The attractiveness of the market or industry can be measured using a combination of factors including:

- Market size
- Growth rate
- Degree of competition
- Pace of technological change
- Legislative opportunities
- Profit opportunities
- Barriers to entry and exit

Business strength factors can include:

- Market share
- Product quality
- Brand reputation
- Distribution network
- Production capability
- Technology capability
- Company infrastructure

Analysts can add in other relevant factors, so the framework has a good deal of flexibility and the rating for each element can be weighted to account for its significance in the overall assessment of market attractiveness or business strength

1.1.4 The benefits and drawbacks of portfolio analysis

Portfolio analysis has a number of strengths including:

- Helping managers think more strategically about organisation and its environment. By providing a list of factors to be taken into account and producing a clear picture of the firm's portfolio of brands it can provide a more logical basis on which to make decisions

- Improving the quality of plans – collecting the data and information required to complete portfolio analysis means that managers develop a greater knowledge of both the company's key resources and competences and the state of the markets they serve.

- Helping to eliminate weaker businesses – which can be a drain on the organisation and may be only retained for political reasons.

However the tools and techniques have also been criticised for:

- Offering misleading (priority) representation of strategic options: the invest/divest choices do not consider other ideas such as re-positioning or seeking new markets.

- Ignoring the potential and benefits of niching – 'long-tail' economic theory (Anderson, 2006) suggests that niche markets collectively are worth far more than top selling brands – which makes market penetration a much more valuable option than previously.

- Requiring considerable data and time to complete and the outputs may be obsolete very quickly in fast moving markets.

- Only covering the current portfolio of products: in many markets, innovation is a key factor in keeping a portfolio fresh. Most of the frameworks don't have a 'develop new products or brands' imperative in their strategic options.

ACTIVITY 9.1

Using a search engine of your choice, look up sites that critique and support Chris Anderson's long-tail theory.

What businesses are likely to benefit most if this theory is correct?

What are some of the opposing theories and concepts?

---

2 Strategies for limited growth and innovation

2.1 Developing new products

Product development strategy is aimed at providing new products or services to existing markets. As you can see from the unified framework above, this can range from providing new products or line extensions within the firm's current market or industry, to delivering new products which can allow a firm to diversify into related markets or industries. Apple's production of the iPod nano could be seen as a line extension, but the development of the iTunes service is more a case of product diversification.

The Chartered Institute of Marketing

THE REAL WORLD

Serial Innovation

UK cosmetics firm Lush was founded in 1994 on the principal of dovoloping new products on a regular and rapid basis. The company produces over 100 new products every year. Initially manufacturing bath products such as soaps and shampoos, the firm moved into make-up with its Emotional Brilliance range launched in mid-2012. Other innovations include developing palm-oil-free cosmetics and ground-breaking social media marketing campaigns on YouTube. The strategy has led to rapid growth with sales exceeding £250million in over 40 countries in 2011.

(Marko, 2012; Conley, 2005; Fast Track, 2011)

2.2 Developing new markets

Market development can also take a variety of forms. This strategic response is about delivering existing products to new markets and can be aimed at new geographies or new segments. This option may also involve a degree of product development, such as changes to packaging or portion sizes in a new international market.

2.3 Blue ocean strategy

▸ **Key term**

'**Blue oceans** denote all the industries not in existence today – the unknown market space, untainted by competition. In blue oceans, demand is created rather than fought over.' (Kim and Mauborgne, 2004).

In 2005, INSEAD Professors, W. Chan Kim and Renee Mauborgne, wrote a book covering what they termed *Blue Ocean Strategy*. 'Blue Oceans' are uncontested market space, as opposed to 'Red Oceans' which are overcrowded and have many competitors. Firms can create 'Blue Oceans' by developing their products or services to fill gaps in the marketplace.

Many commentators regard Kim and Mauborgne's *Blue Ocean Strategy* as an extension of generic strategy frameworks since one of the key features of a *Blue Ocean Strategy* is that it combines low cost with differentiation.

However, as it considers how a product or service should be changed to avoid competing directly in 'Red Oceans' it can be seen as a form of product development. The concepts used in 'Blue Ocean' strategies also cover market development, by reconstructing market boundaries and reaching beyond existing demand to attract non-customers. So, it can be seen as a way of combining product and market development: but, crucially, it is about creating new industries and markets, ones that do not currently exist.

In order to develop a blue ocean strategy, firms must first understand the key factors that companies compete on and what customers value. By plotting these on a 'canvas' it is possible to develop an alternative offer. Kim and Mauborgne suggest that organisations need to consider four actions to achieve this, outlined in Figure 9.4 below.

Figure 9.4   Blue ocean strategy

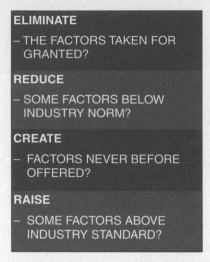

ELIMINATE

– THE FACTORS TAKEN FOR GRANTED?

REDUCE

– SOME FACTORS BELOW INDUSTRY NORM?

CREATE

– FACTORS NEVER BEFORE OFFERED?

RAISE

– SOME FACTORS ABOVE INDUSTRY STANDARD?

(Adapted from Chan Kim, W. and Mauborgne, R. 2005)

To decide which factors to eliminate, reduce, create or raise there are a number of paths which managers can follow, these include consideration of:

- Alternative industries
- Strategic groups within industries
- The chain of buyers
- Complementary product/service offerings
- Functional or emotional appeal to buyers
- Time

The ideas generating from researching some, or all of these paths, can help managers to develop a different approach to their market and reconstruct its boundaries to create uncontested space.

It is also crucial to research and target non-customers to grow the new market. These fall into three groups:

- Those who use current products or services but are not satisfied with their experience and are still looking for alternatives

- Those who don't use the current market offerings because they cannot afford them, or don't find them acceptable

- Those that have little or no knowledge of the market or industry and have never been targeted by firms currently in the market.

ACTIVITY 9.2

Read the October 2004 *Harvard Business Review* article on *Blue Ocean Strategy* and answer the following questions:

1   According to Kim and Mauborgne, what long held strategy concepts does 'Blue Ocean' thinking challenge?

2   Why is a *Blue Ocean Strategy* often difficult for other firms to copy?

The Chartered
Institute of Marketing

3 Strategies for substantial growth

3.1 Vertical integration

3.1.1 Backward vertical integration

Backward vertical integration means acquiring supplier companies, or extending the firm's existing operations further back down the supply chain. This might be a desirable strategy to ensure continuity of supply in volatile markets. Confectionery manufacturer Ferrero has recently entered into a strategic alliance with farmers in South Africa. The firm shipped 450,000 hazelnut trees from South America to Africa in 2008, which the farmers grow on their behalf. This has enabled Ferrero to manage and predict the costs of one of its key raw materials.

3.1.2 Forward vertical integration

Forward vertical integration means moving closer to the end-user of a product or service by moving forward up the distribution chain or acquiring buyer firms. Moving from manufacturing into retail would be an example of this type of strategy and can help firms forge better links with their ultimate consumers, which can provide them with more data for product development etc. The example of the dairy industry in Chapter 6 illustrates how powerful processers and retailers can be. This is often a difficult strategy to achieve without substantial financial resources, although removing the need for intermediaries can be an effective alternative.

3.1.3 Disintermediation

Disintermediation could be seen as a type of forward vertical integration. This has become common in industries and markets which have been affected by the growth of the internet. The music business has seen bands such as the Arctic Monkeys and Groove Armada bypass the record companies, agents, CD manufacturers, wholesalers and retailers by allowing their fans to download their music directly from their own website. Peer-to-peer lending sites such as Zopa and Funding Circle are removing banks from lending by bringing investors and those wanting loans together. However, this sort of strategy is not new. Insurance company, Direct Line used a similar approach using call centres and telecoms technology to remove the need for insurance brokers. In this case the internet has led to a degree of re-intermediation with the growth of price comparison websites such as Compare the Market.com, Go Compare and Confused.com.

3.1.4 Outsourcing

While incorporating all the elements of the value chain within the organisation creates advantages, a vertically integrated firm can also be at a disadvantage when it comes to competing with rivals from low cost economies. For many organisations the solution has been to outsource less critical elements of their operations to economies with lower input costs. Firms in the apparel sector have shifted production from the US and Europe to countries such as China, India and Sri Lanka and more recently to Vietnam and Indonesia. However, there are risks to outsourcing parts of the value chain as this can hollow-out the firm's skills and expertise in areas that may be very difficult to re-build. Outsourcing critical areas of operation that underpin an organisation's competitive advantage can leave a firm vulnerable to its suppliers.

3.2 Related or concentric diversification

When a firm moves into new markets with new products, it is following a strategy of **diversification**. If the markets and/or products are linked in some way to the core business then this is termed related or **concentric diversification**.

The links between the new and existing businesses may be strong: such as a firm moving from selling alcoholic beverages into selling snacks. Some of the technology used to produce the two – food and drink products – may be the same: the distribution channels used will be similar, for example, bars and off-licences or liquor stores. Other related diversification may be less closely linked – such as only sharing suppliers.

THE REAL WORLD

How much diversification is healthy?

When Cisco's CEO, John Chambers, announced in 2009 that the firm would be pursuing growth in 30 'market adjacencies' there were many commentators that questioned the wisdom of the move. While some market development was seen as beneficial, the scale of Cisco's strategy and the fact that the moves into new markets took it further from its core products of routers and switches might stretch the firm to breaking point. The logic behind the moves was through the use of related technology. Most of the new business areas Cisco moved into were connected to networks and so had the potential to drive further demand for its core products. Set-top boxes, video-conferencing products and other devices which connect to the internet would all mean more data flowing through the network and the need for larger and more sophisticated routers.

While pursuing growth in a range of new markets with new products has potentially strengthened Cisco's position in the long term, in 2011 it shed 6,500 jobs after sales failed to meet expectations and closed some of its business units such as the Flip video camera. In July 2012, it announced a further 1,300 redundancies, which some analysts have suggested is due to the firm's lack of focus on its core markets, as a result of its aggressive growth strategy. This has allowed competitors such as HP to attack its previously dominant position in the router and switches business.

(The Economist, 2009; Caruso, 2011; Burt, 2012)

3.3 Unrelated or conglomerate diversification

This is often seen as the most risky form of growth strategy and there is strong evidence that diversifying into areas which are not closely linked or have few features in common with the organisation's core business do not produce good returns. This sort of diversification is known as unrelated or conglomerate diversification. Highly diversified firms are often seen as a risky investment and will be marked down by analysts, who apply a conglomerate discount to their share price. However, there are successful examples of firms following this type of strategy, General Electric and Berkshire Hathaway generate substantial returns for their owners from a very broad set of businesses. GE has aviation, finance, real estate and oil and gas business units in its portfolio.

ACTIVITY 9.3

Visit the websites of the following firms. What sort of strategy are they pursuing, in terms of changes to the scope of their operations? Virgin; Google; Siemens; Disney; Proctor and Gamble; BP.

The Chartered Institute of Marketing

4 Justifying a strategic response

4.1 Is the strategic response a good fit with the current environment?

Managers should be able to justify a strategy by showing how It will enable thc firm to address the issues generated by changes in the environment. This will involve demonstrating how it will help to neutralise threats and exploit opportunities.

4.2 Does the strategic response give the firm a competitive advantage?

As we saw in the last chapter, a detailed explanation of how a strategy will give the organisation an advantage over its competitors is a necessity. If a differentiation strategy is recommended, for example, then the bases of differentiation should be clearly covered.

4.3 Do the firm's key resources and core competences support the strategy?

An effective strategic response needs to be more than just a wish-list. For example, international market development may be an answer to a firm with a saturated domestic market, but without capital and managers skilled in international commerce, the success of the venture is not guaranteed.

4.4 Is the strategic response consistent with the company's mission/vision and supported by key stakeholders?

A strategy is unlikely to succeed if the firm's managers, owners, key customers and/or suppliers do not agree with it. Implementation can be as critical as formulation

---

▶ **Assessment tip**

When you recommend a strategic response it is important that you are clear about why you are suggesting that particular strategy. Justification for your choice needs to be sufficiently detailed to convince the Examiner you have really thought about the options and linked your recommendation back to the analysis earlier in your paper.

---

5 Exemplar paper

Making use of adapted or more advanced versions of strategic choice frameworks is a good way to tailor your recommendations to the context and also to show that you are able to take a critical approach to applying theory. As mentioned in Chapter 8 it is also important to justify your choice of strategic response by linking back to the previous analysis in your assignment. Finally, some explanation of how the strategy could be implemented is also likely to score well in this section of the paper.

The extract below is from an A grade paper and demonstrates many of these features.

The section starts by referring back to the previous analysis in a concise summary that sets the scene very effectively. The candidate then uses an extended version of the Ansoff matrix, which demonstrates that they have gone beyond the basic theory and taken a critical approach. Finally, the candidate synthesises ideas about social marketing into the recommendations, using these as a vehicle to explain how the product development strategy might work in practice. This gives the recommendations a very contemporary feel and adds to their credibility.

Developing a strategic response – Product Development

At present, the industry is suffering from decline (Appleyard, 2011) which will result in aggressive competitive behaviour (Kotler, 2003).

The market is undifferentiated, (Kotler *et al*, 2006) and the barriers to entry are significantly low due to current levels of decline and the investment in resources required (Kotler, 2003).

The shift in transport mode will redefine the structure, size, competitive behaviour and financial models adopted, this will create demands for modified and new products and services.

Therefore, organisations are recommended to adopt product development within an emerging and evolving market, (Gilligan and Wilson, 2009) as an appropriate strategic response.

Product development within an emerging and evolving market

To ensure organisations develop the rights products and services it is strongly advised that a marketing audit is completed to obtain a comprehensive overview of organisational strengths against potential market opportunities. Once identified, organisations may then begin to invest and build on their position, (Kotler *et al*, 2006) and align the marketing mix accordingly (Burkwood, 2007).

A targeted and segmented approach is advised, so organisations can achieve product development for their identified market segments through a manageable and low risk strategy, (Kotler *et al*, 2006).

Those organisations that invest and develop into new products and services for the emerging market are securing their position for the future.

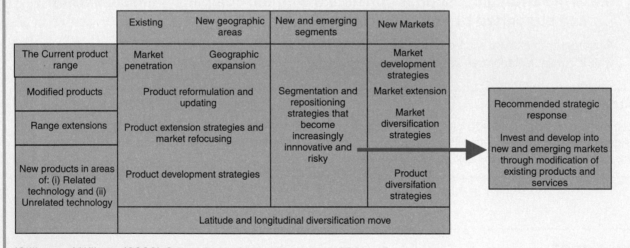

(Gillian and Wilson, (2009) *Strategic Marketing Planning*, p330)

The figure above illustrates an expanded model of Ansoff's original growth matrix (Gillian and Wilson, 2009). Using this model, modified products, range extensions and the development of new products are to be undertaken for new and emerging segments, (Gillian and Wilson, 2009).

Such products and services would include: developments to infrastructure, signage, lighting, surfacing and materials, road markings, traffic calming, security, software, storage, parking facilities, consulting, data and intelligence, market research, training and the possible hire and maintenance of cycles.

Value creation through social marketing

Due to the nature of our emerging theme and the implication of its success on society and the individual, it is recommended that product development is achieved through a social marketing approach.

Through the use of social marketing techniques, new products and services can achieve value propositions and positioning, which correlate with the future needs of the industry (Doyle, 2007). The implementing of principles, processes and products that advance social wellbeing have witnessed increasing growth within recent years, (Gordon, 2011).

Andreasen (1995) defined social marketing as: 'the application of commercial marketing technologies, to the analysis, planning, execution and evaluation of programs designed to influence the voluntary behaviour of target audiences in order to improve personal welfare and that of their society' (2006 cited in Henley, Raffin and Caemmerer, 2011, p697).

The principle of voluntary change in behaviour, improving personal welfare and society (Gordon, 2011) has an obvious synergy with the emerging theme of this paper and through influencing choice and behaviour the industry can support the political agenda and collectively encourage a shift towards sustainable transport, by creating value through the social conscious.

Through product development, organisations may engineer macro-social marketing systems and approaches to ensure investment and commitment for new products and services and achieve relevant positioning and recognition within the market (Kennedy and Parsons, 2012).

The system of macro-social marketing, works as a long-term strategy for social change, and attempts to reduce the effectiveness of offending products and systems, (Kennedy and Parsons, 2012) which would conflict with the success of new products and services.

Micro-social marketing may also be considered for those organisations that directly target the consumer. Micro-social marketing considers the actual marketing mix to encourage behavioural change. If used effectively organisations can encourage early adoption when launching products to market, (Kotler *et al*, 2006) such as new cycling software or maps.

Product development using social marketing approaches

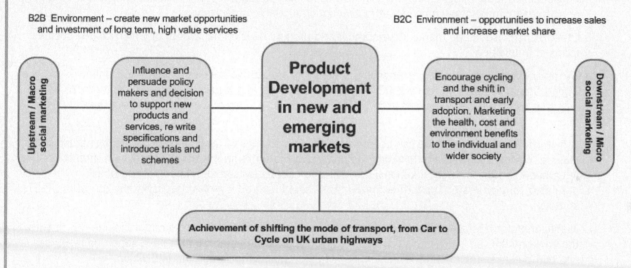

Organisations will have a significant role to play, working with stakeholders in the removal of individual and environmental barriers to secure a sustainable position for new products and services, (Wymer, 2011).

Upstream marketing techniques involves shaping the environment so through persuading and influencing people and processes organisations can create opportunities for products and services to be trialled and introduced (Henley, Raffin and Caemmerer, 2011). Downstream marketing focuses on the individual and their behaviour. Through this technique organisations can channel their products and services directly to the consumer (Henley, Raffin and Caemmerer, 2011).

- Another way to respond strategically to changes in the external environment is to alter the scope of the organisation and its operations. This can include not only options that grow the business, but also ones that result in divesting less relevant or profitable brands or business units.

- Traditionally, firms have used portfolio analysis and tools such as the Boston or GE Multi-Factor matrices to guide their strategic actions. These frameworks help managers decide where to invest and where to divest or withdraw. However, they are heavily criticised and can be seen as oversimplified.

- Growth-focused frameworks include well-known concepts such as Ansoff's product/market growth matrix. This presents a range of options from market penetration, through market and/or product development to diversification. However, these are often too broad but can be refined in combination with other more specific ideas. An integrated framework is presented as a synthesis of these concepts at the beginning of the chapter.

- Some commentators, such as Chris Anderson, now argue that market penetration is an attractive strategy due to the growth of the internet and 'long tail' economics – although this too is a disputed concept.

- As globalisation has fragmented many industries, consolidation through horizontal integration – merging or acquiring competitors can be an attractive option for some organisations.

- Other responses include market development and product development: both of which can be seen as forms of innovation

- By moving into unoccupied market space, some firms are able to gain an advantage by following a *Blue Ocean Strategy*. Kim and Mauborgne's theory recommends that firms change their value proposition in a way that can create new markets or industries for them to occupy and avoid competing head-on with rivals.

- Growth that is more extensive can be achieved through a range of diversification strategies: these can include moving backwards or forwards, up and down the firm's supply/distribution chain through vertical integration strategies. More traditional diversification strategies can be related/concentric or unrelated/conglomerate. The further from a firm's core business it grows the higher the risk of the strategy.

- Justification for a strategic response should be based on clear criteria. These might include: (a) fit with the environment, or, (b) giving a competitive advantage (c) whether the firm has supporting resources and competences (d) the level of coherence with the organisation's mission and vision.

FURTHER READING

There are a number of variations on the traditional Ansoff matrix – the following articles/books present some viable alternatives, which extend the grid to nine options and/or add in contemporary themes or specific contexts:

Barney, J. and Hesterley, W. (2010) *Strategic Management and Competitive Advantage*. Upper Saddle River, NJ, Pearson/Prentice Hall.

Bradley, C. *et al* (2011) Have you tested your strategy lately? *McKinsey Quarterly*. January 2011, pp1–14.

De Wit, B. and Meyer, R. (2010) *Strategy synthesis*. Andover, Cengage/South Western.

Johnson, G. *et al* (2011) *Exploring Strategy*. Harlow, Pearson.

 The Chartered Institute of Marketing

Pleshko, L. and Heiens, R. (2008) The contemporary product-market strategy grid and the link to market orientation and profitability. *Journal of Targeting, Measurement and Analysis for Marketing*. Vol16(2), pp108–114.

Poolton, J. *et al* (2006) Agile marketing for the manufacturing-based SME. *Marketing Intelligence & Planning*. Vol24(7), pp681–693.

Proctor, T. (2000) *Strategic marketing: an introduction*. London, Routledge. Chapter 12.

Rumelt, R. (2000) Note on strategy evaluation, The Anderson School UCLA, http://www.anderson.ucla.edu/faculty/dick.rumelt/Docs/Notes/StratEvaluation1999.pdf [Accessed 20 August 2012].

Thompson, J. and Martin, F. (2010) *Strategic management: awareness and change*. Andover, Cengage/South Western.

REFERENCES

Accor (2011) Accor's strategic vision. http://www.accor.com/en/group/accor-strategic-vision.html [Accessed 1/2/2012].

Anderson, C. (2006) *The long tail*. London, Random House.

Ansoff, H. (1957) Strategies for diversification. *Harvard Business Review*, Vol 25(5), pp113–24.

Barney, J. and Hesterley, W. (2010) *Strategic management and competitive advantage*. Upper Saddle River, NJ, Pearson/Prentice Hall.

Burt, J. (2012) Cisco to cut 1,300 jobs as corporate spending slows amid economic concerns. eWeek.com, http://www.eweek.com/c/a/Enterprise-Networking/Cisco-to-Cut-1300-Jobs-as-Corporate-Spending-Slows-Amid-Economic-Concerns-782164/ [Accessed 20 August 2012].

Caruso, J. (2011) Cisco's moment of truth. Network World, 21 February, http://www.networkworld.com/columnists/2011/022111-editorial.html [Accessed 20 August 2012]

Chan Kim, W. and Mauborgne, R. (2004) Blue Ocean Strategy. *Harvard Business Review*. October, pp76–84.

Chan Kim, W. and Mauborgne, R. (2005) *Blue Ocean Strategy*. Cambridge, MA Harvard Business Review Press.

Conley, L. (2005) Rinse and repeat. Fast Company, http://www.fastcompany.com/53018/rinse-and-repeat [Accessed 25October 2012].

De Wit, B. and Meyer, R. (2010) *Strategy synthesis*. Andover, Cengage/South Western.

Elberse, A. (2008) Should you invest in the long tail? *Harvard Business Review*, Vol86 no. 7/8 pp 88-96

Fast Track (2011) Lush company facts. http://www.fasttrack.co.uk/fasttrack/leagues/dbDetails.asp?siteID=5&compID=2890&yr=2011 [Accessed 20 August 2012].

Frank, R.H. and Cook, P.J. (1996) The winner-take-all society. London, Penguin.

Marko, M. (2012) Lush Cosmetics moves from the bathroom to the beauty table with new emotional brilliance. Vancouver Sun, July 16, http://www.vancouversun.com/life/fashion-beauty/Lush+Cosmetics+moves+from+bathroom+beauty+table+with+Emotional+Brilliance/6942295/story.html [Accessed 20 August 2012]

Peters, T. and Waterman, R. (1982) *In search of excellence: lessons from America's best run companies*. New York, Harper & Row.

Rumelt, R. (1982) Diversification strategy and profitability. *Strategic Management Journal*. Vol3, pp359–369

Tan, T. and Netessine, S. (2009) *Is Tom Cruise threatened? Using Netfix prize data to examine the long tail af electronic commerce*, Working Paper, Wharton.

Thompson, J. and Martin, F. (2010) *Strategic management: awareness and change*. Andover, Cengage/South Western.

Anon (2009), Reshaping Cisco: the world according to Chambers The Economist, http://www.economist.com/node/14303574 [Accessed 20 August 2012].

The Economist (2011) Starbursting, March 26 2011, p77.

ACTIVITY DEBRIEFS

Activity 9.1

It is important to appreciate that most new ideas and theories are contested concepts – no matter how convincingly they are argued or supported. Authors of popular business books are skilled at finding examples that back-up their ideas but that does not mean that their theories are universally applicable or correct. At Postgraduate Diploma level it is important to critically evaluate the concepts you use rather than just accepting they are valid.

In the case of Chris Anderson's long tail theory, there are plenty of sceptics but also many supporters. If you had typed long tail theory criticism into a search engine such as Google, one of the first useful websites you might have hit on, covers the research carried out into Netflix movie sales by two researchers at Wharton School of Business, University of Pennsylvania. Netessine and Tan's (2009) findings challenge Anderson's idea that the niches will outsell the hits. Other criticisms come from Anita Elberse (2008) of Harvard Business School whose findings challenge the assumption that the 20/80 rule had been overturned and that 80% of sales still came from the top selling 20% of most categories.

The long tail theory doesn't just challenge the Pareto principle, but also other economic theory put forward in the mid-1990s by Frank and Cook (1996), who claim that globalisation and mass communications had created a 'winner takes all' environment where the biggest hits would take a disproportionately large share of sales in any category.

The long tail phenomenon appears to be mainly linked to web-based businesses: e-tailers like Amazon, Rhapsody and Netflix are mentioned as supporting the idea. Potentially anything that is virtual – from online games to voucher websites – could benefit from the concept. Small businesses are attracted by the idea and there is some evidence that micro-finance institutions' success has come from exploiting the long tail ideas.

Activity 9.2

According to Kim and Mauborgne, what long held strategy concepts does Blue Ocean thinking challenge?

Branding is one of the key ideas that is challenged – especially in markets where brands do not stand out clearly from each other. However, the article also states that the brands created in a Blue Ocean will create equity that lasts for many years.

Competition – with its roots in military strategy is also criticised in the article.

Having to follow either a differentiated, or low cost strategy, is also challenged in the article. According to Kim and Mauborgne, incorporating both generic options is possible in a 'Blue Ocean'.

Why is a **Blue Ocean Strategy** often difficult for other firms to copy?

The Chartered Institute of Marketing

According to the article, **Blue Ocean strategies** attract a large volume of customers and, therefore, the firm can build substantial economies of scale, making its business model hard to copy by competitors tempted to follow them into the new market.

Changes to a competitor's business model might also be difficult because they will already have established ways of operating and there may well be political resistance to change within the firm. The changes needed to imitate the Blue Ocean strategy might also be at odds with the firm's mission or vision or brand values.

Discussion point: How valid are the assumptions that Kim and Mauborgne make regarding 'Blue Ocean' strategies? The example of the Body Shop creating a 'Blue Ocean' in cosmetics compared with L'Oreal and others has not stopped it being acquired by the French firm. Nintendo has also been held up as an example of a firm following a Blue Ocean strategy, but this has not led to superior profits over a 10 to 15 year period.

Activity 9.3

The best source of information on an organisation's activities is usually in its annual report, which can be found in the investor section of the website. Press releases can also provide key facts (although they need to be treated with caution on occasions) and highlight new developments.

What you will find is that most of these firms are following multiple strategies at different times and responding to market changes in different ways.

Virgin is a classic case of a portfolio manager. One quick way to see this approach in action is to visit the firm's history section on its website at: http://www.virgin.com/history – this takes you from 1968 to 2012.

Over the last 10 to 15 years Virgin has invested in a wide range of sectors and markets: some could be classed as related diversification, such as the launch of Virgin Hotels in 2010 and relates to both the Airline and the Rail elements of its existing businesses, for example. Others, are more conglomerate or unrelated: such as the launch of Virgin Wines and Virgin Money in 2000. The company also follows market development strategies: such as launching Virgin Active in South Africa in 2001, or Virgin Wines in the US in 2010. It has also followed a horizontal integration strategy, such as Virgin Money's purchase of Northern Rock branches in 2011, which could be classed as taking over a competitor. The firm also divests underperforming parts of the portfolio, such as Virgin Charter (closed in 2009) and Virgin Brides (ceased trading in 2007).

Google: you might have struggled to identify Google's approach, using traditional strategy tools and concepts, although in some ways it is similar to Virgin in managing a portfolio of products/services. However, one of the main differences is the speed and breadth of innovation and the involvement of employees at all levels in creating new concepts. This relates back to some of the ideas we covered at the end of the last chapter, under the adaptive advantage model from BCG. Google uses people, systems and simulation as well as signal advantages to adapt to changes in its very fast-moving environment. It diversifies into many different areas – but in an emergent and experimental manner. However, it still invests in certain products (for example Google Earth), manage others selectively and shut down or divest others, such as Knol (on November 22, 2011, Google announced that Knol was to be phased out in favor of Annotum), Froogle (on May 31, 2012 the product was renamed **Google Shopping**), and Orkut (only really popular in Brazil).

Siemens: since Peter Loscher took over as CEO, the German engineering giant has consolidated its position in several markets and divested some of its divisions to concentrate on developing markets and integrated offers that tap into growth areas such as healthcare (growth of an elderly population in many countries is driving this) as well as transport and infrastructure (emerging economies such as China and parts of the Middle East are spending heavily in these areas).

Disney: given its portfolio of products and services – from producing animated films to hotels, theme parks, television networks (ABC) and toys – you might conclude that Disney is a conglomerate, following a strategy of unrelated diversification. There is some evidence of this through the ownership of a real estate company (later divested). However, what links most of its businesses is the characters from the animated films and family movies and the fact that they could all be classed as elements of the entertainment industry. Related

diversification is a better fit – with some horizontal integration – such as the acquisition of rival animation studio Pixar.

Procter and Gamble: has traditionally been seen as following product and market development strategies, with additions to product lines and new versions of products often designed to meet the needs of new international markets. There is a logic to its approach in that almost all its products and acquisitions are related to personal and household products. Many will use similar, or the same, distribution channels and often share suppliers and buyers and even end-customers. For example, the perfumes that feature in household and personal grooming products are likely to be supplied by the same companies. Both will be sold through supermarkets and may appeal to the same segments through television advertising. At its most risky, P&G's strategy might include concentric or related diversification.

BP: has remained in the same industry for its entire history as an energy company. The firm started life as an oil company (Anglo-Iranian) and moved into other forms of energy such as gas and renewables, so there is some evidence of product development as a strategy. The main direction of growth has been through vertical integration, both backward into exploration and forward into areas such as refining, transporting, and retailing. In the past, it has also acquired competitors, such as Burmah (in 2001).

The Chartered
Institute of Marketing

CHAPTER 10

Emerging themes within organisations

Introduction

This chapter takes economic or industry trends and assesses what is happening within businesses or organisations. There are numerous strands and themes which could be considered, but for this chapter we focus on just a few (in detail) to illustrate the way in which implications can be developed and assessed.

Topic list

Marketing's new ground   (1)

New skills for tomorrow's marketers   (2)

Corporate social responsibility (CSR)   (3)

2.3	Propose methods by which marketing professionals can anticipate and adapt to change:
	■ Sources of data and intelligence
	■ Developing intellectual skills and creativity
	■ New forms of networking

1 Marketing's new ground

Throughout this module, the more strategic role for marketing has been implicit. In this chapter, we make that strategic role more explicit.

As market conditions have changed, so there is a need to change business strategy and, therefore, the orientation of business. When demand exceeds supply you have a 'sellers' market and the need for, and role of, marketing is negligible.

■ As demand and supply '**equalise**', so businesses must be more proactive in seeking customers for their products and services. This creates a sales orientation and marketing is used predominantly for sales support. This operational focus is usually built around hitting short-term sales targets and, therefore, filling the sales funnel. Marketing at this stage is really marketing communication.

■ Only when organisations find themselves in '**buyers' markets**', where supply exceeds demand does a customer orientation become critical to success. Marketers end up taking a much more strategic role – helping ensure the organisation develops and delivers products and services that meet/exceed customer needs. The new role of marketing is the '**architect of competitive advantage**'. Marketers have responsibility to use their insight into emerging and changing customer needs to help shape the way the organisations will '**compete**' for those customers.

This is a role that is as much about research and external monitoring as it is about communication and prioritisation.

You can consider marketers to be '**customer experts**' and advocates or as the communication centre for the business, listening as well as informing customers.

Figure 10.1 puts this notion into context.

The Chartered Institute of Marketing

Figure 10.1   Marketing: the communication centre for business

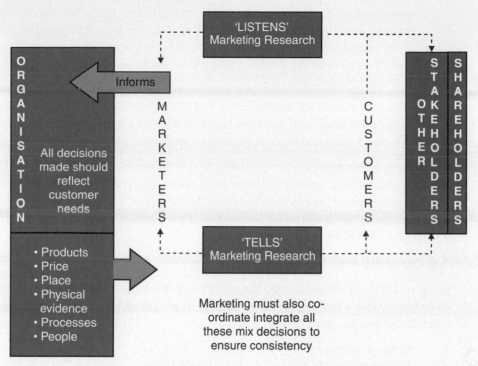

ACTIVITY 10.1

How do you see marketers' role emerging?

Use this diagram as a framework for assessing the new role of marketing in your industry sector.

What do you feel would be the main issues, challenges or responsibilities at points 1-4?

Marketers' role will be:

1_____

2_____

3_____

4_____

1.1 The changing role of marketing

As the orientation and strategy of business has evolved so has the role of marketing within the business.

The emerging themes in this changing role are summarised below:

(a)   **More strategic**, though still with operational responsibilities. You would expect to see marketing matters on the boardroom agenda with discussions about retention levels and acquisition rates, market share, average customer value and share of wallet and the return on marketing investment. These are the 'lead' metrics that are indicators of changing competitive advantage and so are early indicators of strategic wear-out or improving competitive performance. You might expect to see marketing managers in the boardroom to represent this critical agenda.

(b)   **More holistic**: refers to the fact that what we call the marketing mix, the 7Ps, are not all directly controlled by marketers. They may be better described as the business mix. Therefore, marketing must work with professional colleagues and third party suppliers to ensure all aspects of the offer are aligned to deliver customer value. This greater business-wide role requires a more holistic approach.

(c) Marketing's role will be **repositioned** and seen, not just as communications or sales support, but acknowledged as the key value driver for the business. This role will lead to greater respect for marketing and the insight it brings about what customers (and other stakeholders) need and value. There will be increasingly an organisation-wide understanding of why customer-focus matters and how spending on marketing drives long-term shareholder value, building intangible assets through the brand and customer goodwill.

(d) Marketing is evolving steadily from an art characterised by intuitive 'gut-feeling' decision-making, to more of a **science with decisions** based on detailed analysis and increased objectivity. Marketers expect to have to make and argue the business case behind their proposals and recommendations.

(e) Being in the boardroom means being able to **communicate in the financial language of the boardroom**. Marketers must understand shareholder value, return on investment and assess the financial implications of their recommendations because decisions about the mix of customers, products and the marketing mix all affect the bottom line of the business.

1.2 Our role will keep on changing

In Figure 10.1, we are considering the role of marketers in an environment where business success depends on delivering customer satisfaction more effectively than competitors deliver. Essentially, a process of mutually profitable exchange, resulting in:

- Satisfied customers
- The generation of improved business performance

However, we have already investigated some of the emerging themes that are impacting on business strategy and thus on the role of marketers. These are the themes that have broadened the business agenda and include the satisfaction of other stakeholders.

Corporate social responsibility (CSR) broadens the role of marketing still further. The question of the employees and employee brand, community and financial media relations and lobbying industry regulators could all appear on that agenda.

The questions which may need to be considered are: to what extent will marketers control or even take a lead in this broader agenda?

Stakeholder mapping

Three factors must be considered when mapping stakeholder relationships.

1 **Power,** defined as the ability to influence the actions of other stakeholders and to bring about the desired outcomes.

2 The **Importance/urgency** to the stakeholder of the issue.

3 **Legitimacy**, a rightful claim to be involved.

Stakeholder types and groups

This leads to three types of stakeholders and to eight stakeholder groups:

Definitive stakeholders with all three attributes (Power, legitimacy and urgency)

Powerful and legitimate stakeholders who by definition will already be a member of the firm's dominant coalition.

Expectant stakeholders, with two attributes

- **Dominant stakeholders** (Power and legitimacy, but no urgency)

    Those who have both powerful and legitimate claims – hence their influence is assured

The Chartered Institute of Marketing

- **Dangerous stakeholders** (Power and urgency, but no legitimacy)

  Those who have power and urgent claims, but lack legitimacy. May interfere with a situation, disrupt it, resort to coercion and even violence – therefore dangerous.

- **Dependent stakeholders** (Legitimacy and urgency, but no power)

  Those that lack power, but who have urgent, legitimate claims. They rely on others for the power to carry out their will – through the advocacy of other stakeholders

Latent, stakeholders with only one attribute

- **Dormant stakeholders** (Power, no legitimacy and no urgency)

  Those who have the power to impose their will on others but, because they do not have a legitimate relationship or urgent claim, their power remains dormant (eg, some consumers)

- **Demanding stakeholders** (Urgency, no legitimacy and no power)

  Those who **have urgent** claims, but neither power nor legitimacy to enforce them – inconvenient but do not always warrant serious management attention (eg consumer advocates)

- **Discretionary stakeholders** (Legitimacy, no power and no urgency)

  Those who **possess legitimate** claims but have no power to influence the firm nor urgent claims (eg, recipients of corporate charity)

PLUS

Non-stakeholders (No power, no legitimacy and no urgency)

When their **claim is urgent**, managers have clear mandate to give **priority and attention** to that stakeholder's claim (eg, major institutional shareholders, striking workers, protestors).

NB Expectant stakeholder can become a **definitive stakeholder** by acquiring the missing attribute.

Table 10.1 should make this complicated situation crystal clear.

Table 10.1   Stakeholder types and groups

(*) possessing that attribute STAKEHOLDERS	Power	Influence/ Urgency	Legitimacy	Group
1: Definitive	(*)	(*)	(*)	Definitive
2: Dominant	(*)	___	(*)	Expectant
3: Dangerous	(*)	(*)	___	" "
4: Dependent	___	(*)	(*)	" "
5: Dormant	(*)	___	___	Latent
6: Demanding	___	(*)	___	" "
7: Discretionary	___	___	(*)	" "
8: Non-Stakeholders	___	___	___	Non-stakeholder

Mitchell *et al*, (1997) suggest it is possible to identify a typology of eight classes of stakeholders depending on the number of attributes present.

Figure 10.2   Stakeholder classes

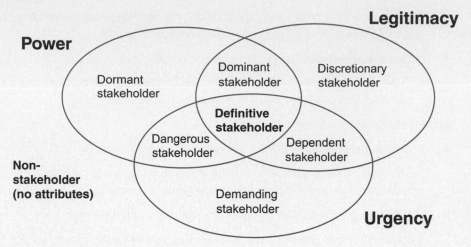

Who else may be involved?

Take a few moments to consider this broader stakeholder agenda. Using Mitchell's stakeholder classes typology identify what groups might be involved in a broader CSR strategy or agenda for your industry.

You can see that an emerging theme for marketers may be the need to work much more collaboratively with these other professional colleagues to ensure CSR initiatives are integrated and the '**brand**' is managed constantly across all stakeholder audiences.

ACTIVITY 10.3

Assessing the current role of marketing in your organisation

Read '**Tomorrow's World**,' one of CIM's **Shape the Agenda** papers, which looks at how marketing has changed over the past 30 years and makes some predictions for its role and structure in the future strategies that encompass environmental sensibility and social awareness. You can assess this article on CIM's website.

Those in B2B companies may still find themselves in a 'sales and marketing' team with responsibility predominantly for sales support. Increased competition and the reality of a buyers' market will be the catalysts that change marketing's role. Wherever you are on that journey, you and your team need to:

- Ensure you have developed your own skills so you can take that more strategic role
- Be able to make the business case to support that new emerging role for marketing

2 New skills for tomorrow's marketers

You will already have seen how these emerging agendas will affect the job roles of marketing professionals. You would certainly expect the job description of ten years ago to look different to a description today.

It is because the role and expectations of marketing are changing that marketing teams need to take proactive steps to ensure they are continually developing their own skills and capabilities in order to rise to these new challenges. The role of continuing professional development (CPD) and encouraging those entering marketing to become professionally qualified are cornerstones for the ongoing learning marketing teams must do.

The following diagram summarises some of the new skills required.

Figure 10.3   New skills requirements for marketers

Your own analysis of the new skills needed will depend on the current role of marketing and the type of sector you operate in. For those working globally the need for language skills may feature.

▶ **Assessment tip**

For the assignment for this module, you will be required to identify and evaluate one or two emerging themes, considering how they will impact on your sector and/or your organisation. In addition, you need to consider and make explicit:

- The implications for marketers and how their role will change
- What they need to do differently in terms of attitudes and behaviours
- What new skills may need to be developed as a result of this '**emerging theme**'.

It is important that you relate the skills section to the emerging theme you have identified and do not just write a generic section that could be applied to any industry.

ACTIVITY 10.4

Diagonal thinking

'Diagonal thinking' is the concept that underpins a new tool designed to aid the recruitment of talent into the creative industries, especially from a more diverse range of people.

It is the culmination of a five-year research project for the IPA, by John Gage and Sarah MacPherson of Agency People, a consultancy specialising in supporting creative businesses. Latterly, sponsored by Creative & Cultural Skills, the research has tested and validated the hypothesis that the most successful individuals working in 'adland' are both linear and lateral thinkers – they think 'diagonally'.

These top brains in commercial creativity are innovative, can explain concepts in both rational and emotional terms, have a broad range of interests and a passion for execution. They can be highly logical, but link ideas hitherto seen as remote from each other; they want to do work that is creative, but also for it to have a practical impact.

Access the following link to see if you are a diagonal thinker http://www.diagonalthinking.co.uk/.

THE REAL WORLD

Sam Phillips, Chief New Business and Marketing Officer, Omnicom Media Group: 'Finding great talent – at all levels – continues to be fundamental to Omnicom Media Group, UK's business success. But, finding this great talent is easier said than done. Even at the entry-level stage be that graduate or school leaver. Despite the weight of available potential employees, it remains as difficult as ever to find people with the right quotients of intellect, emotional intelligence, digital savvy and drive to thrive in our agencies. But on top of looking for all those attributes, these days we're also looking to employ people across a far greater realm of skill-bases than ever before... think data specialists, search gurus, content experts, econometricians... and I could keep going'.

(Phillips, 2012)

ACTIVITY 10.5

Access the Deloitte Report: 'Executing and integrating global mobility and talent programmes'
http://www.deloitte.com/assets/DcomUnitedStates/Local%20Assets/Documents/IMOs/Talent/us_talent_SmarterMoves_062410.pdf
which outlines the capabilities required to develop a global workforce.

The importance of digital skills for marketers

Digital Marketing Organisational Structures and Resourcing (December 2011), a report published by Econsultancy, revealed that, although businesses recognised the importance of digital marketing to their success, they have struggled to develop effective processes and find the resource needed to maximise their digital potential. Only 43% of respondents rated the digital knowledge in their organisation as good or excellent. Although 87% said digital training was a high or medium priority for the digital marketing team, 61% said that digital training remains a low priority for their company in general.

The talent time bomb

Participants in the survey specified that the challenge of finding staff with suitable digital skills was a potential barrier to progress and further identified specific skill areas that are perceived to be the most difficult to recruit. Web analytics and data was at the top of the list, followed by social media, content marketing, SEO, website design and build, and mobile. It is clear that there is already a potential skills shortage in these areas.

The areas where those in the survey predicted the highest growth in demand from their organisation, in terms of resourcing, were remarkably similar to those listed as already the most difficult to recruit: social media, content marketing, web analytics and data, mobile marketing and apps development.

As businesses increasingly adopt strategies that require depth of expertise in these in-demand areas, there can only be one result: a looming talent time bomb. A McKinsey report, released in May 2011 (Big Data: The Next Frontier for Innovation, Competition, and Productivity) identified the global significance of this potential talent time bomb in one specific area: so-called Big Data.

With exponential growth in data, driven by a combination of real-time, growth in data-rich environments, such as social and mobile, increasing focus on owned media, and the internet of things, the capability of analysing large data sets will become 'a key basis of competition, underpinning new waves of productivity growth, innovation, and consumer surplus'.

(Perkin, 2011)

THE REAL WORLD

'2012 is proving to be the year in which the Big Data trend gets noticed. Many more firms will start to analyse huge piles of data to optimise everything, from their supply chains to their customer relationships. A study by the McKinsey Global Institute found that analysing healthcare data could yield $300 billion worth of savings in America alone. Firms will also use data for new business models. Rolls Royce no longer needs to sell all its jet engines: it can charge for their use. By continually assessing their performance, it can predict which engines are more likely to fail, so that customers can schedule their engine changes. For Big Data to become huge there are still some barriers to overcome. The tools to analyse the data are not yet good enough and the people to analyse the data are scarce. By 2018, there will be a talent gap of between 140,000 and 190,000 people.'

(Siegete, 2011)

The Chartered
Institute of Marketing

> **Assessment tip**

Take time at your next team meeting to discuss how well you are prepared to meet the emerging themes facing your organisation. Complete a strengths and weaknesses analysis, prioritising those new skills that you feel will be most important to future performance in your sector. Talk to HR and decide how you can take steps to improve performance in the important areas where you feel there are weaknesses in your skills.

Importance to performance in your sector	Strength		Weakness		
	+10	+5	0	-5	-10
Very important					
Important					
Less important					

2.1 The key strategies for business

How companies compete for customers and succeed in achieving their stakeholders' agenda is changing and will continue to change in response to the themes and trends we have been examining in this module.

Which strategies are most important to you depends largely on the sector you are working in, but being alert and forward-looking will be critical to long-term success.

Figure 10.4   Key strategies for business success

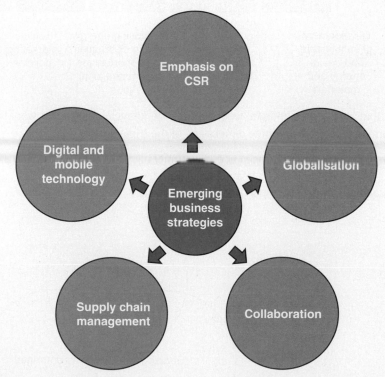

The website http://www.utalkmarketing.com is a training site for the marketing community specialising in digital. They claim 120, 000 users and the site runs a daily briefing that is very useful to all marketers, providing information that will help you to learn about and evaluate emerging themes.

3 Corporate social responsibility (CSR)

CSR has been a recurring theme in this module – not surprisingly when you consider how much is written about the environment, pollution and sustainability.

Even within this area, you can see there are many aspects, themes and dimensions that need to be assessed and considered.

Let us start by looking at CSR and business strategy – how might an organisation audit its current CSR stand or identify further opportunities to strengthen its CSR policies and strategies?

Figure 10.5 has been populated with top-level implications, or options for a CSR approach.

Figure 10.5   Value chain model emphasising options for a CSR approach

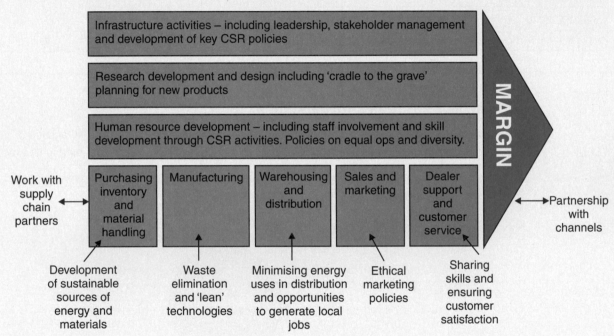

Note that in this case '**margin**' would not just be financial margin but would need to measure improved performance against the three dimensions of the triple bottom line.

Three areas of economic, social and environmental considerations are important to CSR.

Figure 10.6   Integration of CSR's three inseparable components

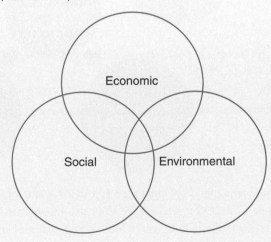

The Chartered
Institute of Marketing

You will find many companies are very explicit about their CSR strategies, so you can find out quite a lot from their websites eg, McDonald's, BP, Innocent.

THE REAL WORLD

Social responsibility at B&Q

'Since 1990, B&Q has taken a positive approach to the challenges that social responsibility presents and have developed solutions that not only address our environmental and social impacts but also add value to our business and its reputation.

B&Q's core values include:

Environment

Every product we sell at B&Q has its own unique life cycle or story. As such, we have a responsibility to ensure that any possible environmental impact is as low as possible during manufacture, use and disposal.

Ethical trading

It is our duty to ensure that everyone involved in B&Q supply chains benefits from trading with us. Our customers want great products at great prices, but not at the expense of the people who make them. We are committed to sourcing products responsibly.

Diversity

At B&Q we are committed to eliminating all forms of discrimination and ensuring an inclusive environment irrespective of age, gender, marital or civil partnership status, colour, ethnic or national origin, culture, religion, religious belief or similar philosophical belief, disability, political affiliation, gender identity, gender reassignment or sexual orientation.

Community

We have a significant influence on the communities in which we operate, and our aim is for all our stores to be welcomed as "good neighbours" in the communities that they serve, including the contribution of skills and funding to selected community projects.'

Visit the B&Q website at www.diy.com, calculate your personal eco-footprint and carbon emissions with its one planet living footprint calculator and look at the customer advice it is providing to help educate its customers about the environment and its resources.

B&Q has been working with award-winning environmental charity BioRegional to develop an extensive range of one planet home® independently accredited products. One planet living® is a lifestyle where we can all enjoy an excellent quality of life while staying within our fair share of the earth's resources. It provides advice on saving energy, water, recycling and growing your own.'

How do your CSR policies and strategies compare? What changes might happen over coming years? Use the value chain approach to help your assessment.

ACTIVITY 10.6

About sustainability

To illustrate the range of converging themes and issues covered within CSR we can take just one aspect – sustainability and analyse just what that covers and means.

Sustainability is a term used frequently in the media and by marketers in their discussions about CSR and the ethics of their organisation. But, what does it include?

Spend a few minutes thinking about sustainability – what topics would you include if you were speaking about the question in the context of your sector and business activities?

> **▶ Assessment tip**
>
> **Tutor comment**
>
> Remember Gary Hamel's advice:
>
> (a)   Think of your own vision of the future
> (b)   Consider what you would need to do to compete in that future
> (c)   Build the capabilities and competences you need to prepare for that future.
>
> This structure may be a useful one to consider when planning your discussion paper for your assignment

> **▶ Assessment tip**
>
> **Tutor comment**
>
> Notice how by focusing on a very specific aspect of change you can be much more specific in your comments and it is likely your discussion paper for your assignment will be much more specific and powerful.

> **▶ Key term**
>
> According to the UK Institute of Business Ethics, **ethical marketing** is *'the application of ethical values to business behaviour ...'*

Ethical marketing

A number of countries have an Institute of Business Ethics (IBE) – you may like to Google IBE and make some comparisons of their agendas and concerns.

Let us look at another example of how business practice may be changing – the emerging theme is of increased ethics and morality in business and marketers have a considerable role to play.

According to Wikipedia:

'Ethical marketing is an honest and factual representation of a product, delivered in a framework of cultural and social values for the consumer. It promotes qualitative benefits to its customers, which other similar companies, products or services fail to recognise. The concern with ethical issues, such as child labour, working conditions, relationships with third world countries and environmental problems, has changed the attitude of the Western World towards a more socially responsible way of thinking. This has influenced companies and their response is to market their products in a more socially responsible way.

In the UK, the Institute of Business Ethics site contains lots of useful material for reviewing and monitoring this aspect of CSR. http://www.ibe.org.uk/.

'The subject matter of business ethics reflects its mixed origins. In crude terms, it can be described as the union of business and society studies with mainstream business studies subjects through the medium of moral philosophy along with environmental issues relevant to business. What results is attention to the ethical aspects of any and all the many different areas of business activity (accounting, marketing, human resource management, and so on), with the activity also examined in terms of the ethical dimension to the economic, legal, political, and environmental context in which it is carried out at both a local and global level. The range of topics this can cover is vast and varied. Moreover, new areas of study are constantly **emerging** in the wake of developments such as globalisation, e-commerce, and accounting scandals such as Enron.

There is a great deal of congruence, with certain broad areas emerging as more or less standard. They divide, roughly speaking, into four very general and inevitably overlapping categories.

(a)   First comes very reflexive and often very theoretical questions to do with the nature of business ethics as a subject and the application of ethical theory to business.

(b)   Then come questions to do with the responsibilities and accountability of businesses and, in particular, large corporations.

(c) Then come what can be called *'functional'* questions to do with particular areas of activity (accounting, marketing, and so on).

(d) Finally, we have what might be called *'global'* questions to do with the rights and wrongs of particular economic systems along with questions concerning international business and the natural environment.'

ACTIVITY 10.7

How ethical are you?

Visit http://www.ethicsandbusiness.org/cases.htm provided by the Centre for Ethics and Business at Loyola Marymount University. Socrates comes to Wall Street: a post-meltdown dialogue on Business, Ethics and Leadership at http://www.ibe.org.uk you will find a number of questionnaires and inventories to help you take stock of your own and your organisation's view on ethical issues. There are also links to other sites and resources associated with ethical issues and dimensions.

Title of questionnaire/inventory	Source	Topic areas
ROT (Rice orientation test)	Chris Rice	Attitudes towards ethical issues
The business ethics questionnaire	Simon Webley	Attitudes towards business ethics
Ethical practices questionnaire	Simon Webley	Identifying the seriousness and importance of certain ethical and unethical practices

Are ethics a big issue?

You may be wondering just how much evidence there is of ethics becoming an important aspect of business strategy and policy. How transparent will organisations need to be?

ACTIVITY 10.8

How activism forced Nike to change its ethical game

With three weeks until the opening ceremony of the Olympic Games, activists are busy cranking out yet another round of anti-sweat shop campaigns and shock-horror exposés. But, do these campaigns really make any difference?

Perhaps surprisingly, the answer is yes.

In the new Olympic special edition of *Ethical Consumer* magazine the spotlight is on Nike and the impact that 20 years of campaigning has had in changing the corporate culture of one of the world's biggest sportswear brands.

It's worth remembering that in the 1990s the global boycott campaign of Nike was so successful that it has now become an object lesson in how giant corporations can be brought to account by ordinary consumers.

'Nike was targeted by campaigners because it was the world's best-selling brand and because it initially denied responsibility for any malpractice taking place in its sub-contractor factories,' explains Rob Harrison, editor of *Ethical Consumer*.

With the campaign scoring a direct hit on Nike's bottom line, the corporation today operates with an openness and transparency that would have been unthinkable 20 years ago. For example on the *Fair Labor Association* website it's possible to read more than 150 reports of Nike factory inspections conducted by independent third parties.

Problems still exist in Nike's supply chain and the company still doesn't make publicly available all supplier factory information, meaning that Nike is unlikely to be recommended as an Ethical Consumer best buy company any time soon.

However, according to Harrison, Nike should be credited with progress: 'For a company which 20 years ago was denying that workers' rights at supplier factories were any of its concern, Nike has come a long way.'

The same can also be said of other leading sportswear brands including Adidas, Puma, Reebok and Timberland.

Just how far the sportswear industry has come was neatly illustrated last summer when Greenpeace launched its Detox Challenge, which targeted global brands including Nike and Adidas with the aim of stopping their suppliers from dumping toxic chemical waste into waterways around the world.

Within a matter of weeks, Nike produced a plan to go toxics-free free by 2020 with similar plans announced in the same record-breaking time by Adidas and Puma with more companies falling in line later on.

Without even breathing the word 'boycott', campaigners were able to steer companies to a place they were happy with.

'It was clear that the lessons of the 90s had been painfully learned,' observes Harrison. 'If there's a case to answer it's better to concede early rather than hoping it will go away.'

So does this all mean that anti-sweatshop campaigners will soon be looking for other jobs? Sadly no, as groups such as *War On Want* and *Playfair 2012* attest. They have been actively targeting Olympic sponsor Adidas for its alleged sweatshop abuses. Anna McMullen from *Labour Behind the Label* explains that the clothing industry is far from being sweat-shop free:

'Poverty levels of pay remain a problem right across the clothing industry. In the Philippines for example, recent *Playfair 2012* research found 50% of workers making Adidas Olympic-branded gear have to rely on loan shark payouts, while in China many workers can only afford to live in cramped dorms far from their families.'

Campaigners including McMullen are now focusing their efforts on the organisers of events such as the Olympics.

'The International Olympic Committee (IoC) has repeatedly refused to take responsibility for ensuring that workers producing goods for the Olympic brand have their rights respected,' says McMullen. 'If campaigners are not to return to square one every time the games come around then the IoC must show leadership on this issue.'

(Simon Birch, 2012)

Questions

1 Assess how Nike has been affected by activism.

2 Forecast the wider implications for the sportswear industry.

3 Identify what new marketing, skills, attitudes and behaviours Nike has had to adopt to incorporate more ethical business practice into their marketing strategy

THE REAL WORLD

The financial arm of the Co-op has this to say about its operations: 'It's no secret that financial services providers are in business to make profits. One way they do this is by taking your money and lending it to someone else at a higher rate of interest. But, what they rarely tell you is who they lend it to.

With other banks and insurers, you have no say in where your money is invested and how these companies behave. For example, your money could be loaned to companies involved in the fur trade, arms dealers who supply oppressive regimes, or multinational companies with poor environmental records – and you wouldn't know a thing about it.

That's where we're different

We have given our customers a say in what we do with their money. In 1992, after a long consultation with our customers, The Co-operative Bank launched its Ethical Policy – a first amongst UK high street banks and still unique today. The Policy ensures that we will always stand up for the issues that our customers feel passionate about. We allow you to have your say on the issues that matter to you, such as human rights, animal welfare, fair trade and the environment. So simply by being our customer, you're helping us change the world, little by little, every day.

Since its launch in 1992, The Co-operative Bank has withheld over £1.2 billion of funding from business activities that its customers have said are unethical. While at the same time, increasing commercial lending sixteen-fold to almost £9 billion.

Extension to Co-operative insurance

Since 2011, The Co-operative Bank's ethical policy has been extended to cover the investments underpinning our home and motor insurance products. As a result, we do not purchase bonds issued by organisations that do not meet the criteria of the Policy.'

For more information read: The Co-operative Group Sustainability Report. http://www.co-operative.coop/sustainabilityreport

The Chartered Institute of Marketing

Marketing and morality

Visit CIM's website and take time to consider one of the *Shape the Agenda* articles '*Marketing and Morality*'. You can see this is a topic of considerable importance in the practice of marketing, and ethical marketing practices cover everything from promotion to pricing strategy.

When you have read the article, look at your own marketing activity – how far along the moral pathway have your business practices travelled?

Draw up a list of recommendations you would make for a Code of Conduct for marketers working in your sector.

3.1 Fairtrade

THE REAL WORLD

One example of ethics at work in the marketing arena is the growth of Fair Trade products.

Visit http://www.fairtrade.org.uk/ for more examples, cases and insights into the changes in this context. You can see consumer interest is growing.

3.1.1 Sales of Fairtrade certified products in the UK

Table 10.2 Estimated UK retail sales by value 2001-2011 (£ million)

	2001	2002	2003	2004	2005	2006	2007	2008	2009	2010	2011
Coffee	18.6	23.1	34.3	49.3	65.8	93	117	137.3	160	179.8	194.3
Tea	5.9	7.2	9.5	12.9	16.6	25.1	30	64.8	70.3	82.6	86.7
Cocoa products**	3.3*	3.9*	7.3*	9.6*	13.2*	16.4*	25.6*	25.6*	44.5*	162	217.1
Sugar products**	4.5	5.7	8.7	14.3	19.5	23.7	50.6	107.7	164.6	384	464.1
Honey products**	3.2	4.9	6.1	3.4	3.5	3.4	2.7	5.2	3.6	6.8	4.1
Bananas	14.6	17.3	24.3	30.6	47.7	65.6	150	184.6	215.5	206.6	208
Flowers	n/a	n/a	n/a	4.3	5.7	14	24	33.4	30	27.6	26.3
Wine	n/a	n/a	n/a	1.5	3.3	5.3	8.2	10	18.1	18.5	20.7
Cotton	n/a	n/a	n/a	n/a	0.2	4.5	34.8	77.9	73.2	51.7	41
Fresh Fruit	n/a	0.1	1	5.9	8.5	17.6	28	32.2	24.3	15.5	12.1
Fruit Juices	0.4	0.8	1.1	2.3	4.6	7.7	13.8	21.1	13.1	15.2	16.5
Other***	n/a	n/a	n/a	6.7	6.4	10.1	8.3	21.8	26.2	23.5	12.1
TOTAL	50.5	63	92.3	140.8	195	286.3	493	712.6	843.4*	1173.8	1319.3
Year-on-Year Growth	53%	25%	47%	53%	38%	47%	72%	45%	18%	39%	12%
Chocolate	5.4	6.2	9.2	13.7	18.4	23.2	35.8	38.3	88.6	346	413.1

(Fairtrade Foundation, 2012)

* *After review, the 2009 and historical cocoa figures have been reviewed and the sales values updated. The figures against these products represent the cocoa part of all products containing cocoa, the honey part of all products containing sugar.

***These figures cover all Fairtrade commodities not covered by other categories. These include vegetables, dried fruit, pulses, rice, quinoa, sesame seeds, nuts and oils, and spices. In the leisure sector even the provision of sports balls are covered by the Fairtrade guarantee.

Chocolate includes figures listed elsewhere in this table (e.g. sugar and cocoa) so are not included in the totals.

'The global economic downturn made 2009 an incredibly tough year for the world's poor seeking a fair deal for their produce... The global economic turndown has been felt worst in developing countries, where an estimated 50 to 90 million more people were thrown into extreme poverty in 2009, according to UN Millennium Development Goal figures. Meanwhile, in the UK, just over seven in ten people told YouGov that they cut back on their personal budgets in some way as a result of the recession, such as eating out less. Yet the UK public has remained staunchly loyal, resulting in another increase in the value of Fairtrade sales, up on 2008 by 12% to an estimated retail value of over £799m, and 71% (who don't already buy everything they can Fairtrade) of people say they are willing to swap one or more products to Fairtrade in the next two weeks, according to the new YouGov poll commissioned by the Foundation.'

THE REAL WORLD

Sales of Fairtrade products in the UK soared by 40% in 2011 to more than £1 billion despite the tough economic climate. The Fairtrade Foundation said the huge rise in sales showed that shoppers in this country are continuing to embrace ethical values.

Launching Fairtrade Fortnight, the foundation said that every day in the UK people consume 9.3 million cups of Fairtrade tea, 6.4 million cups of Fairtrade coffee, 2.3 million Fairtrade chocolate bars, 530,000 cups of Fairtrade drinking chocolate and 3.1 million Fairtrade bananas.

New categories are also growing, with more than one million cosmetic products using Fairtrade ingredients being sold in 2010.

Sales of Fairtrade products in the UK were worth £1.1 billion last year, compared with £836 million in 2009, said the foundation.

Chief executive Harriet Lamb said: 'It is fantastic to break the first billion. Fairtrade is going from strength to strength because the public want it, it makes business sense and, most importantly, because it's working for the millions of farmers, workers and their families who see Fairtrade as their lifeline in these tough times. They will be cheering to know that UK shoppers and businesses still care.'

Major companies have introduced Fairtrade products, which helped the increased sales, including Cadbury's Dairy Milk, all Starbucks espresso-based coffee, Nestlé's four-finger Kit Kat Sainsbury's tea, coffee and sugar, Morrison's roast and ground coffee, Tesco Finest Tea and Tate & Lyle retail sugar.

The growth is set to continue, with the Co-op's announcement of increased Fairtrade goods, Waitrose converting its own label tea and several products in the Duchy Originals range, Topshop launching a new range of Fairtrade cotton denim and Marks & Spencer introducing a new Fairtrade cotton range.

Marketers need to ask themselves how soon will Fairtrade products be expected rather than an opportunity for differentiation.

(Evening Standard, 2011)

3.2 New ways of engaging with customers

CSR and ethics are about how you do business. Other emerging themes at this level involve the ways in which we can engage customers and, in particular, the use of mobile and new media from developing SMS campaigns to networking sites like FaceBook and Myspace or LinkedIn for business contacts.

Today, marketers can use YouTube to promote their products and there are a number of examples of viral campaigns, for example, Dove Evolution, Cadbury's Gorilla advertisement and T Mobile *Life's for Sharing*. See the following link for more details of this http://www.slideshare.net/UnrulyUK/mobile-t-mobilelifes-for-sharing.

Tablet commerce may be the 'new kid on the block' when it comes to online retail, but as a recent Forrester research poll indicates; many online retailers are seeing that half of their mobile commerce transactions come from tablet devices.

The Chartered Institute of Marketing

Moreover, 7.6% of the U.S. population will be tablet users by the end of 2012, according to eMarketer estimates.

(Schmelkin, 2011)

New special interest sites mean that customers are clearly choosing what they want to know about and the style of communication they prefer.

Does this new media give customers more power?

It certainly provides a forum for marketers to find out what customers really want and help co-create products and services. One-way communication is changing to dialogue and that may be challenging for how we do things in the future.

The *Future of M Commerce – Did You Know 4.0?*

Access the following YouTube link for some predictions about M Commerce:
http://www.youtube.com/watch?v=quO-sxqFYcE.

How will these affect your own industry?

CHAPTER ROUNDUP

- From a seller's market with limited role for marketing to a buyer's market where competitive advantage is key to winning and retaining customers and evolving to take account of the broader stakeholder agenda.

- You assessed the current role of marketing in your organisation.

- We examined the range of new skills marketers need in order to meet the demands from a new more strategic role. Today marketers need to be more analytical and professional planners.

- We identified some of the current business strategies being adopted in different sectors.

- We examined both the question of ethics in business and its impact on marketing and how digital marketing is changing how we engage customers. We also focused specifically on CSR – considered the importance of the Triple Bottom Line and the broadening stakeholder agenda.

- We used the Value Chain to assess how CSR could be embedded across the business.

- We looked at one aspect of CSR – sustainability.

- We considered how business ethics in the banking and sportswear sector has impacted on these industries.

FURTHER READING

CIM (2007) *Tomorrow's world*: *re-evaluating the role of marketing*. Cookham, The Chartered Institute of Marketing.

Frandsen and Johansen (2011) Rhetoric, climate change, and corporate identity management. *Management Communication Quarterly* 25: 511.

http://www.goldmansachs.com/search/search.gscgi

E Consultancy (2012) *The State of Digital Marketing in Asia*. http://econsultancy.com/uk/reports/digital-marketing-asia

Chui, M *et al* (2012) *The social economy: unlocking value and productivity through social technologies. McKinsey Global Institute*

REFERENCES

Evening Standard (2011) Fairtrade sales up 40% to top £1bn.
http://www.standard.co.uk/newsheadlines/fairtrade-sales-up-40-to-top-1bn-6571682.html [Accessed 25 October 2012].

Fairtrade Foundation (2012) Facts and figures on Fairtrade.
http://www.fairtrade.org.uk/what_is_fairtrade/facts_and_figures.aspx [Accessed on 7 June 2012].

Fairtrade Foundation (2012) Public loyalty to Fairtrade in 2009's tough economic climate leads to double digit growth as Fairtrade sales reach 800m
http://www.fairtrade.org.uk/press_office/press_releases_and_statements/february_2010 [Accessed 7 June 2010].

Hatton, A. (2000) *The Definitive Guide to Marketing Planning*. Harlow, Prentice Hall.

The Chartered Institute of Marketing

Phillip, S. (2012) Finding great talent is easier said than done. IPA, http://www.ipa.co.uk/news/finding-great-talent-is-easier-said-than-done [Accessed on 7 August 2012].

Schmelkin, A (2011) Make Way for T Commerce. E-commerce Times, m-commerce, http://www.ecommercetimes.com/story/72884.html

Mitchell, R.K. *et al* Toward a Theory of Stakeholder Identification and Salience: Defining the Principle of Who and What really Counts. *Academy of Management Review* 22(4): 853-888

Perkin, N. (2011) *Digital marketing organisational structures and resourcing best practice guide.* Econsultancy, http://econsultancy.com/uk/reports/digital-marketing-organisational-structures-and-resourcing-best-practic [Accessed on 7 August 2012]

Siegele, L. (2011) Welcome to the yotta world. *The Economist, The World in 2012*

The Co-operative Group (2012) Inspiring through co-operation: sustainability report. http://www.co-operative.coop/sustainabilityreport [Accessed on 25 October 2012].

ACTIVITY DEBRIEFS

Activity 10.1

How do you see your role emerging?

Marketers' role will be:

1   To ensure there is an external focus and awareness of what is happening in the marketplace, providing customer insight and a commentary on emerging themes.

2   To ensure that marketing is 'positioned' effectively internally. No matter how good the external focus is, it can only affect business performance if it is listened to, and acted upon. This means a much more strategic role for marketing with a broad appreciation of its role as 'architect of competitive advantage.'

3   Innovation and creativity are needed to help create offers that deliver competitive advantage – marketers need to be a source of innovation and have the skills needed to bring together the 'ingredients' of the offer to ensure integration and consistent positioning.

4   In future, communication with customers is more likely to be a dialogue than a broadcast – how we use new media, social networks and manage permission marketing will be on our agenda for some years to come.

5   Evaluate how your own organisation is responding to these predictions for skills.

Activity 10.2

Who else may be involved?

The answer to this question will vary across organisations and sectors, but your answers could have included:

(a)   HR teams responsible for employee relations and the employee brand.

(b)   Corporate PR teams who may be responsible for broader community communications and media relations. This role may not be managed by marketing but report directly to the MD or chairperson.

(c)   Finance teams can take the lead with shareholder and financial media.

(d)   Some organisations employ a CSR manger or director.

(e)   Smaller companies may find that the owners or senior management teams take direct responsibility for these broader stakeholder issues.

Activity 10.3

Assessing the current role of marketing in your organisation.

No two organisations are the same when it comes to how they view, use and organise the marketing function. Some, for example the public sector, are still relatively new converts to the value of marketing. Others like FMCG firms have a long history of marketing activity.

Activity 10.4

This will depend on your answer to the diagonal thinking exercise.

1   Are you surprised by your results?

2   Do you think this will be a useful analytical tool for the marketing team?

Activity 10.5

1   Summarise the Deloitte findings and evaluate the implications for your sector.

Activity 10.6

Your list will be sector specific but you might have included some or all of the following

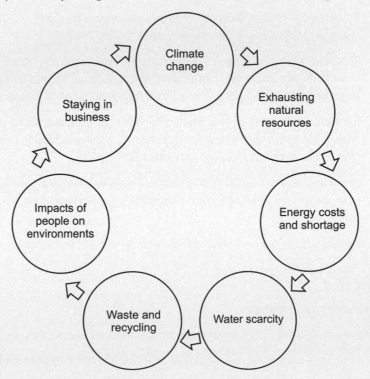

The Chartered Institute of Marketing

Activity 10.7

Discussion points

Your reflection will depend on your own response.

1   What have been the implications of ethics in your industry over the last ten years?

2   What are you predictions for the next ten years?

Activity 10.8

Discussion points

1   Nike has changed its business practices to be more open and transparent as ultimately profit was affected.

2   Corporate reputation can be a valuable asset for an organisation and enhanced by an organisation that follows a CSR agenda and behaves in an ethical way. Valuate the current corporate reputation of Nike.

3   Sportswear brands such as Nike and Adidas are global brands and sponsorship of sporting events such as the Olympics is a key part of their marketing strategy. How can they ensure that they protect their brand equity and corporate reputation?

4   How have the skills, attitudes and behaviours in your own industry changed to incorporate more ethical business practice? Analyse how they will develop.

Activity 10.9

Discussion points

1   Compare your responses with those of other people in your marketing team and seminar group.

2   Are there differences across industries?

3   You might find it useful to research other codes of conduct such as the CIPS Code of Professional Practice.

The Chartered
Institute of Marketing

Index

The Chartered
Institute of Marketing

Index

The Chartered
Institute of Marketing

Notes

The Chartered
Institute of Marketing

The Chartered
Institute of Marketing

The Chartered
Institute of Marketing

The Chartered
Institute of Marketing

The Chartered
Institute of Marketing

The Chartered
Institute of Marketing

Review form

Please help us to ensure that the CIM learning materials we produce remain as accurate and user-friendly as possible. We cannot promise to answer every submission we receive, but we do promise that it will be read and taken into account when we update this Support Text.

Name: _____   Address: _____

_____

1. How have you used this Text?
(Tick one box only)

☐ Self study (book only)

☐ On a course: college_____

☐ Other _____

3. Why did you decide to purchase this Text?
(Tick one box only)

☐ Have used companion Assessment workbook

☐ Have used BPP Texts in the past

☐ Recommendation by friend/colleague

☐ Recommendation by a lecturer at college

☐ Saw advertising in journals

☐ Saw information on BPP website

☐ Other _____

2. During the past six months do you recall seeing/receiving any of the following?
(Tick as many boxes as are relevant)

☐ Our advertisement in *The Marketer*

☐ Our brochure with a letter through the post

☐ Our website www.bpp.com

4. Which (if any) aspects of our advertising do you find useful?
(Tick as many boxes as are relevant)

☐ Prices and publication dates of new editions

☐ Information on product content

☐ Facility to order books off-the-page

☐ None of the above

5. Have you used the companion Assessment Workbook?   Yes ☐   No ☐

6. Have you used the companion Passcards?   Yes ☐   No ☐

7. Your ratings, comments and suggestions would be appreciated on the following areas.

	Very useful	Useful	Not useful
Introductory section (How to use this text, study checklist, etc)	☐	☐	☐
Chapter introductions	☐	☐	☐
Syllabus learning outcomes	☐	☐	☐
Activities	☐	☐	☐
The Real World examples	☐	☐	☐
Quality of explanations	☐	☐	☐
Index	☐	☐	☐
Structure and presentation	☐	☐	☐

	Excellent	Good	Adequate	Poor
Overall opinion of this Text	☐	☐	☐	☐

8. Do you intend to continue using BPP CIM products?   ☐ Yes   ☐ No

On the reverse of this page is space for you to write your comments about our Support Text. We welcome your feedback.

Please return to: CIM Publishing Manager, BPP Learning Media, FREEPOST, London, W12 8BR.

TELL US WHAT YOU THINK

Please note any further comments and suggestions/errors below. For example, was the text accurate, readable, concise, user-friendly and comprehensive?